ORTHODOX CHRISTIANS AND MUSLIMS

Orthodox Christians and Muslims

Edited by

N. M. VAPORIS

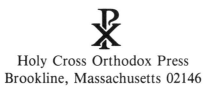

Holy Cross Orthodox Press
Brookline, Massachusetts 02146

We are extremely pleased to acknowledge the generosity of His Eminence Archbishop Iakovos who generously provided the funds for the publication of this volume.

Published by Holy Cross Orthodox Press
50 Goddard Avenue
Brookline, Massachusetts 02146

Cover design by Mary C. Vaporis

Library of Congress Cataloging-in-Publication Data

Orthodox Christians and Muslims

"The studies in this volume first appeared in the Greek Orthodox theological review, volume 31 (1986), numbers 1 and 2"—T.p. verso.
Papers read at a symposium held March 1985 at Hellenic College/Holy Cross Greek Orthodox School of Theology.
Includes bibliographies and index.
1. Islam—Relations—Orthodox Eastern Church—Congresses. 2. Orthodox Christian Church—Relations—Islam—Congresses. I. Vaporis, N. M. (Nomikos Michael), 1926-   . II. Holy Cross Greek Orthodox School of Theology (Hellenic College) III. Greek Orthodox theological review.
BP172.5.O77077   1986   261.2'7   86-15405
ISBN 0-917651-34-0 (pbk.)

Contents

ORTHODOX CHRISTIANS AND MUSLIMS

Editor's Note

THE ORTHODOX CHRISTIAN-MUSLIM SYMPOSIUM

The Greek Orthodox Theological Review enthusiastically welcomes the opportunity to publish the excellent papers read at the historic symposium, held at Hellenic College/Holy Cross Greek Orthodox School of Theology in March 1985. This was indeed an historic meeting when one considers that Orthodox Christians have known and have interacted with Muslims since the seventh century, and that this encounter has taken place on all continents, save possibly Australia. One can only hope that this symposium can be attributed to other reasons than "only in America," for it is obvious that Muslims and Orthodox Christians have much to learn from each other despite their fourteen-centuries-old acquaintanceship.

Moreover, the symposium held in Brookline proved to be so enlightening for all participants—thankfully, even in ways beyond the academic—that one can only hope that it will be followed by many others both here and abroad.

In preparing the papers for publication, I have had the benefit of the generous assistance of Professor Robert Haddad of Smith College whom I wish to thank. Finally, it should be noted that for technical reasons, we have employed a sign that resembles the Greek *circumflex* for the *macron* sign over the transliterated Arabic words.

N. M. Vaporis

Welcome

ARCHBISHOP IAKOVOS

I CORDIALLY SALUTE and welcome each of you to the annual symposium, held each year at our School of Theology and College in honor of one of the greatest ecumenists of our era, Patriarch Athenagoras I.

In the courtyard of the school's chapel stands a statue of Patriarch Athenagoras. The statue has two main features: the impressive figure of the Patriarch holding the "Chalice of Reconciliation"; and the base of the statue which appears cracked, symbolizing the division within Christianity and the people of the earth. As we look at the statue, we are reminded of the Patriarch, with his soul-penetrating eyes, searching the future. In his presence we have a memory and a message that stimulates us in our quest for unity.

I am grateful to the faculty of Holy Cross Greek Orthodox School of Theology for its inspired decision to dedicate this year's "Patriarch Athenagoras Lectureship" to Orthodox Christianity and Islam. These religious traditions lived side by side for so many centuries in what was once the Ottoman Empire, a dominion comprising the lands from Egypt and North Africa to the Bosporos and the Dardenelles. Their common denominator, the faith in one God, in one Supreme Being, in whom we all exist, we move, and we have our being, has enabled Christians and Muslims to develop mutual respect and tolerance for one another and set the example of what we call today "coexistence."

Today, in our ever-changing and ever-challenging world, Christians are seeking unity, while Muslims are witnessing a worldwide resurgence. Within this setting, we are experiencing an urgent need to approach one another, to understand each other, and to see if we

1

can reach a common understanding as to the role religion can play in a terribly turbulent society. Sacred wars and fanaticism resolve nothing. Men and women everywhere are looking for peace, security, and humanitarian coexistence.

I am certain that the notable participants in this symposium will address these and other social issues with an enlightened soul, illuminated by the ageless principles of love and justice—the fundamental values that underlie both of our traditions and their adherents.

Let me hope that this symposium will offer nourishment and hope, not only to theologians and historians, but to the hearts of all those present and those absent.

May the Spirit of God guide you in your deliberations.

Greetings

THOMAS C. LELON

THE SYMPOSIUM ON Orthodox Christianity and Islam is an historic occasion for all of us. It is the first such symposium to be held in the history of our institution; it is, I hope, the beginning of a new era— one of dialogue, as can be seen in the title of the keynote address: "The Importance of Orthodox Christian-Muslim Dialogue," to be given by the Most Reverend Constantine, Metropolitan of Derkon and President of the Patriarchal Synodical Commission on the Dialogue with Islam.

This event is a unique opportunity for us to listen to each other openly and sympathetically, to understand each other precisely, to transcend our own boundaries, and to learn from each other as much from "within" as possible.

For these three days, we will all gather as one community in a spirit of inquiry to engage in the dialogue which covers a wide range of interreligious and intertheological issues. During our dialogue, we must recognize our areas of mutual interest and those differences that truly make a difference.

I wish to thank the Rev. Dr. George Papademetriou, Coordinator and Chairperson of the symposium, and the Hellenic College/Holy Cross Greek Orthodox School of Theology faculty for their efforts in this endeavor.

I extend to you a very warm welcome to Hellenic College/Holy Cross Greek Orthodox School of Theology.

3

Introduction:
Orthodox Christians and Muslims in Dialogue

GEORGE C. PAPADEMETRIOU

ORTHODOX CHRISTIANS AND MUSLIMS have a long history of contacts and encounters in the Byzantine and Ottoman Empires and currently in the Middle East and Turkey. The ignorance of each other's faith and culture has resulted in great misunderstandings and conflicts. As a result of these past misunderstandings, there is need for mutual enlightenment. We need to avoid dangerous misconceptions and unfounded myths of the two great faiths in examining and discussing the fundamentals of each religion. Along with the intellectual examination of the similarities of and differences between the two faiths, we must also confess honestly the great injustices committed to each other.

In the past it was not possible for Orthodox Christians and Muslims to sit together to discuss openly and honestly their respective faiths. Although Orthodox Christians lived alongside Muslims for many centuries, and in many areas still do, they could not interpret Islam objectively. The Byzantines, as we shall hear from the experts, were engaged in polemics, pointing out the weaknesses and contradictions of the Islamic religion and of its founder Muḥammad. Later, during the Ottoman period, it was impossible for the subjected Orthodox to accept a true picture of the religion of the their overlord. Even later, when Greece was independent, Greek scholars did not give the religion of their neighbor, Turkey, an objective presentation.[1]

---

[1]Anastasios Yannoulatos, *Islam: A General Survey* (in Greek) (Athens, 1979), p. 9. See also the Islamic aggressionist policies in Francis E. Peters, "The Early Muslim Empires: Umayyads, Abbasids, Fatimids," *Islam: The Religious and Political Life of a World Community,* ed. Marjorie Kelly (New York, 1984), pp. 73-93.

For their part the Muslims also were unable to interpret objectively the Christian faith even though they had a sketchy knowledge of Jesus through the Qur'ān. Although it is true that the Muslims have a special place in the Qur'ān for Jesus as prophet and have praise for his mother Mary, there is a misunderstanding even in the Qur'ān, that is, "Allah is the Messiah and the Son of Mary." Nowhere do Christians claim that "God is Jesus," only that Jesus Christ is God.[2]

Despite these differences, popular religious expressions of Christian Orthodoxy and Islam, especially asceticism and mysticism, were closely connected. It is interesting to note the commonality of these two religions, of their mystical experience of God's presence.[3] There was also a philosophical sharing. The West owes a debt for the recovery of classical philosophy, especially Aristotelian, to Islamic scholars who received it from the Byzantine heirs of the classical legacy of Greek philosophy.[4] In the Middle Ages, instead of conversations, numerous disputes took place in Islamic centers between Christians and Muslims, including one in which Saint Gregory Palamas was the Orthodox Christian spokesperson at Bursa.[5] It seems the overall picture of the medieval and later contacts were polemical in nature.

In the contemporary American setting we choose to hold a dialogue. A contemporary American scholar states that "'a new dimension is added to the experience of religion—the understanding in love of the religion of one's neighbor. And once this dimension is opened, it becomes clear that a living faith implies the obligation to open one's mind and heart to a sincere perception of the faiths of others.'"[6] In

---

[2]Gerard S. Sloyan, *Jesus in Focus: A Life in its Setting* (Mystic, CN., 1983), pp. 192-93. For a Muslim understanding of Jesus, see the excellent chapter, "The Jesus of the Qur'ān," pp. 188-96. See also *We Believe in One God. The Experience of God in Christianity and Islam,* ed. Annemarie Schimmel and Abdoldjavad Falaturi (New York, 1979).

[3]H. A. R. Gibb, *Mohammedanism: An Historical Survey.* 2nd. ed. (London, 1953), pp. 128-29.

[4]Alfred Guillaume, *The Legacy of Islam* (London, 1968), p. 249. See also Robert M. Haddad, *Syrian Christians in Muslim Societies: An Interpretation* (Princeton, 1970).

[5]Dialexis. *Soter,* 15 (1892) 140-46. George C. Papademetriou, "Judaism and Greek Orthodoxy in Historical Perspective," *The Greek Orthodox Theological Review,* 21 (1976) 105-07.

[6]Jacob B. Agus, "Foreword," *Jewish Monotheism and Christian Trinitarian Doctrine,* Dialogue by Pinchas Lapides and Jürgen Moltmann, trans. Leonard Swidler (Philadelphia, 1981), p. 17.

this "age of dialogue," we must confess our painful past, and begin the road of mutual respect, recognizing our common heritage in the faith in the one God, the God of Abraham, Isaac, and Jacob. This common experience is beyond any other reward. The present symposium brings together for the first time prominent Orthodox Christian and Muslim theologians to discuss similarities and differences as well as to hold a dialogue on theological, historical, and philosophical topics of common interest. The objective of this conference, it seems to me, is to gather committed believers from both religions to offer a scholarly basis for their philosophical and theological positions. It is not limited to any particular period of history or any specific doctrine. It hopes to offer challenges and new direction in the relations of Orthodox Christians and Muslims, and furthermore, to emphasize the existential religious experience of both. That is not to overlook, however, the essential differences, but we do want to stress as a common element the supreme importance of the personal belief-commitment for the future of both religions. The hope is that this symposium will be a testimony to the trust and hope in the one God and his unfathomed purpose for mankind. It is an effort for further understanding and peaceful coexistence in a world which is constantly shrinking.

The late Ecumenical Patriarch Athenagoras lived in his early youth with Muslims and talked about it in his later years as follows:

> The area where I was born had been occupied by the Turks a century before the fall of Constantinople. In my village there were both Turks and Christians, but we lived peacefully together; the Moslems were invited to christenings and in turn the Christians were the guests at circumcision feasts.

> It was a sort of biblical coexistence and we all felt that we were children of Abraham. The Muslims ate mutton and lamb during the festival of Baihram and we Christians ate the Easter lamb....

> The dervishes were very good to me [continues Patriarch Athenagoras]; they were very tolerant toward the Christians and some of them were well known for their intelligence. We had one dervish in my village by the name of Jamil. He often came to visit us at home and dine with us. My mother and sister, in particular, were very fond of him and kept no secrets from him. Jamil knew

their innermost thoughts better than our village priest.[7]

On behalf of the faculty of Holy Cross Greek Orthodox School of Theology and the entire campus community of Hellenic College, I am honored to welcome you to this symposium on Orthodox Christianity and Islam. I hope that your stay here will be pleasant and especially that it will benefit you in expanding your religious knowledge and will enrich your experience in the spirit of understanding in the world religious community.

---

[7]Demetrios Tsakonas, *A Man Sent by God: The Life of Patriarch Athenagoras of Constantinople* (Brookline, 1977), pp. 9-10.

The Importance of Orthodox Christian-Muslim Dialogue

METROPOLITAN CONSTANTINE OF DERKON

FIRST I WOULD LIKE to congratulate the organizing committee of the Holy Cross Greek Orthodox School of Theology, for undertaking the initiative to organize this symposium on a timely topic of great importance: namely the dialogue between Christians and Muslims.

I would also like to express my sincere thanks to Dr. Thomas C. Lelon, President of Hellenic College and Holy Cross Greek Orthodox School of Theology, to the Rev. Dr. Alkiviades Calivas, Dean of Holy Cross Greek Orthodox School of Theology, and to the Rev. Dr. George C. Papademetriou, Chairman of the Faculty Lectureship Committee, for their kindness in inviting me to participate, thus affording me the extraordinary opportunity to address and meet such distinguished theologians and scholars, both Christian and Muslim.

These days, when Christian churches try to come nearer to each other through dialogue, it is not only proper and right, but at the same time necessary to extend this dialogue towards other religions as well, especially the monotheistic ones. The dialogue with Islam, a religion second only to Christianity in number of followers, is naturally of great importance and interest. Moreover, Islam has long ago come out of the narrow boundaries of the Arabic peninsula, surpassing the geographical borders of the Middle East, to find its place in today's world of global character. The vigorous existence of Islam in countries of South Asia, its huge expansion among young nations of the African continent, its perceptible presence in Europe and lately in America, give evidence enough to convince every man of good will to try to get in close contact with the Muslim world. Although there was a time when this world was not known beyond the Middle East and the Mediterranean countries, today it is a worldwide accepted concrete certainty. Especially these days, the last decades of the twentieth century, the world of Islam attracts the interest of the Western world as never before.

Neither Islam nor Christianity are of Western origin; it would not, however, be right to say that they are exclusively Eastern-oriented religions. It may seem strange to the modern world, but Islam appears to adapt itself more or less to modern living conditions, including in itself great treasures of mysticism and metaphysical wisdom, a source of nourishment for longstanding generations of theorists and hermits alike. With broadening dimensions Islam aspires to reconcile man with the surrounding universe, the creature with the Creator.

It is a great pity that, though the two religions have emerged and developed in neighboring countries, they have not as yet come to really know each other. Mutual accusations have been launched in the past, some of which have not been forgotten even today. Muslims have been blamed for fatalism, fanaticism, polygamy, etc.; Christians, for polytheism and distorting the divine Revelation and the commandments of God.

We must confess that many special studies about Islam have been done by Christians, particularly during the last two centuries, thus a literature rich in content and wisdom has come to light. However remarkable these studies might be from the historical, literary, and religious point of view, they have contributed very little to a mutual understanding and rapprochement because they were addressed to specialized academic circles.

We are astonished by the fact that Eastern religions, completely unknown to the West, attracted people's interest, sympathy, and love, while religions from the same root of Abraham remained aloof or even hostile to each other. Nevertheless, the day by day increasing interest in the world of Islam and its important role in worldly affairs, gave impetus to a dialogue between Christians and Muslims.

Muslims and Christians are called today to ask themselves about the different aspects of their common course through a turbulent history of fourteen successive centuries; they are called in the name of God to realize the teachings of this course in order to find out that the paths of their dialogue could oblige them tomorrow to give the best evidence and make it possible for them to live together in an exemplary friendly cooperation in the service of God, mankind, and the world.

If we bear in mind the great variety this dialogue offers, its perspectives, its historical conditions, and the circumstances under which it should flourish and develop, it would be superflous to mention how important it is from the Orthodox Christian point of view. It is true that the need for a dialogue has been pointed out several times in the past without, however, an appreciation of the demands or methods for it. We should avoid any offhand syncretism among religions because this might spoil friendly cooperation and harm prospects for further meetings. A real dialogue depends on the courageous efforts of people who wish to know each other's differences, to understand their common points and values, and to answer sincerely and clearly the call of God in their innermost soul and conscience.

It is quite natural for Christians and Muslims to differ fundamentally whenever they meet to talk, since they belong to different religions and their definitions and evaluations vary. Nonetheless, it is very important to create and develop a spirit of mutual understanding, love, harmony, and respect for each other. The Orthodox Christians especially, who wish to be known for their fidelity to the Gospel, especially cannot be indifferent to such serious research by people who, though foreign to Christian belief, have undertaken the task of honoring God in their own way. Neither of them should concede for the sake of superficial harmony and cooperation or the strong opposition they might possibly face from the other side. They should together search for possible ways to find some mutually agreeable meeting points. Beyond any possible comparisons, it is necessary to look for common values under which Christians and Muslims could be united in their religious practice and their obligations towards God and humanity.

Through this dialogue Orthodox Christians and Muslims are called to know each other better. They are called to examine more deeply their faith and their religious beliefs, to search diligently for God's will, and to try to bring man back to God, who calls everyone, who forgives everyone, and who transforms everyone. Thus when we speak of a dialogue between Orthodox Christians and Muslims, we by no means mean either proselytism of each other's religion or the sowing of questions and doubts about the religion in which someone has been reared. On the contrary, within the bounds of spiritual antagonism, "they will contest in beneficent deeds" (see Qur'ān, 5.48). They must help each other to improve themselves the way God has shown them and to come nearer to him, thus making the world better.

Therefore, Christians and Muslims are called to meet, to know each other better, to make themselves understood, and to work together. Fortunately enough there is a basis for such cooperation: common belief in the one, living and existing God, the benevolent and merciful God who created heaven and earth. Holy Scripture and the Qur'ān agree on many points in attributing God's qualities and characteristics. Though the two sides approach God's mystery in different ways, they have the possibility of searching out the real dimensions of the inexpressible splendor in the language of theology and mysticism.

Abraham and the prophets have an outstanding place in the Qur'ān even if not all the names of the prophets are mentioned. Though the Muslims do not recognize the Godhead of Jesus Christ, they respect and honor him as a prophet and they also venerate his mother, the Virgin Mary, who some of them recognize as "the Seal of Holiness." The Christians are delighted by the fact that the Qur'ān recognizes the grandeur and the virtues of Jesus Christ, and they are conscious of the basic difference separating the two religions: the belief that Jesus Christ is the Son of God according to Christians, and simply a prophet according to Muslims. The Christians are prepared to accept favorably what is mentioned in the Qur'ān about Jesus Christ and to be satisfied by the fact that the holiness of his life and the greatness of his teachings have attracted even Muslims. The Muslims believe in Christ's divine mission. They believe that he is Mary's son, born without any human intervention; however, they disregard his incarnation. Likewise, denying his crucifixion and his resurrection, they accept Christ's ascension into heaven and his Second Coming in the fullness of time.

Other common points between Muslims and Christians are their belief in the Judgment Day, the resurrection of the dead, and the just retribution for everyone according to the life he has led in this world. These are some areas to which the Qur'ān gives much importance.

Moreover, a very interesting common point between the two religions is the doctrine regarding the angels. According to the Qur'ān, the angels are created by light and are continuously under God's command. They are executors of his orders. They intervene between him and man. Among the angels Michael and Gabriel hold a special place. Under God's command Gabriel carried the Qur'ān from heaven and dictated it to Muḥammed. He also brought the message to the Virgin Mary that she would give birth to Jesus Christ. Gabriel is often called "God's Spirit." The angels watch over people's lives; they keep records about their deeds in the Bible which will be opened at the Last

Judgment. Not only do the Muslims believe in the existence of the benevolent angels, but they also strongly believe in the active existence of Satan in everyday life, the fall of which is clearly mentioned in the Qur'ān.

In the Islamic doctrine of man we come across many fundamental biblical principles. Man is God's creature; man has been created in the image of God, his Lord. He is endowed with reason and moral qualities, and he is the best divine creature. God created the beautiful image of Adam from clay and water and infused part of his spirit into him. Afterwards he ordered the angels to worship him. God put man as his representative on earth and gave him the power to conquer nature. He equipped Adam with great intellectual qualities and put him in paradise. Accepting the biblical teaching, the Prophet of Islam claims that man caused his own fall, because he did not obey God's orders and ate the forbidden fruit in paradise. Nevertheless, the original sin is not of great importance for Islam, because straight after his disobedience, Adam was forgiven by God.

Though Islam does not accept original sin, it recognizes its consequences in man's life; in other words, though God forgave Adam, he did not bring him back to his previous position. God forgave Adam, because forgiveness is one of his characteristics; but though man does not bear the original sin, in this world he is under continuous judgment. Man can, however, overcome this judgment by the light of Revelation, without there being any need for God's redeeming action. The believer is delivered from his sin by trusting in the one and only God.

Both religions, each according to its own principles, try to create a better and just society, despite the many insuperable obstacles; such obstacles should not hinder their cooperation for a better world. This is the problem to which Christians and Muslims are called to find positive solutions.

It is true that the Christian communities of Arabia, the Byzantine Empire, and some communities of the European West have done their best to carry on the dialogue with Islam for a long time. Perhaps there is still a long way to go before the desired solution is found. Nevertheless, no one can underestimate the interest shown by the Roman Catholics, especially during the last few years, proofs of which are the decisions taken by the Second Vatican Council. Here it also should be pointed out that the World Council of Churches has always been interested in such a dialogue. By and large, we cannot disregard the efforts by the Christian communities all over the world to try to find any potential way to bridge the differences whenever possible. Of course, we must consider the history and the geographical factors which play a great role as far as the success and extension of this dialogue is concerned.

These days in all the five continents, Christians and Muslims come nearer to each other than ever before. They work together in cultural, social, and economic fields alike. Orthodox, Catholics, and Protestants complement each other when they try to coordinate their approaches and their social and personal experiences in whatever concerns Islam. In their efforts, their aspects might differ. The ones who have understood the grandeur and the content of the divine predominance, the greatness of the paternal generosity, and the importance of obedience in their life will be able to appreciate the meaning of submission in Islam. On the other hand, the others who are very sensitive to the demands of justice and the rights of man and who approach God through the redeeming sacrifice of Jesus Christ will have some difficulty in understanding Islam's problems. In their insistence and devotion to the values of the divine transcendence or in the marvels of the Trinity, the Christians will realize that the dialogue with the Muslims will be easier when it is based on the absoluteness of God, although it could also be based on a mutual commitment to serving human values.

Despite the deep theological differences and dramatic conflicts in the past, Orthodox Christians and Muslims are closer spiritually and geographically because they have common cultural and religious backgrounds, and when two worlds agree and communicate spiritually, their approach is easier. Bearing this in mind, the great significance and importance of the dialogue between Orthodox Christians and Muslims is easily understood.

Orthodox Christians had come into contact with the Muslim world before its expansion to the Iberian peninsula. They rightly claim that they are acquainted with the spirituality and mentality of the Muslim world much better than the Western Christians. This is why they strongly believe that a sensitive approach of Christians and Muslims will be fruitful. It will first be a dialogue among people and later among scholars who will look better and more deeply into the history and content, and above all into the problematic aspects of the two religions. It will be a dialogue among friends with common interests, among simple people who are beyond any fanaticism and bigotry; such a dialogue will pursue the possibilities for a meeting. It will be a sincere dialogue full of love without any political objective.

Both sides should be convinced that it is the same Almighty God who invites them, even if each one of them interprets him from a different perspective. Both should realize that God speaks to his people through world history, even if his manifestation seems different to each of them.

Orthodox Christians and Muslims are invited to collaborate on a plan of values which will lead their common obligation to the welfare of mankind. This way, they will realize that, sharing their common religious experiences, it is possible for both of them to respond to God's will and look more deeply into the wealth of holy values which both Christians and Muslims developed through their history. Having realized God's multilateral activity, through the history of salvation, they should not confine their dialogue to satisfying a narrow circle of intellectuals. When the dialogue is enlarged and based on concrete realities, is enriched by new experiences of religious values, and has overcome the limits of tradition and environment inherited from the past, the two sides will be invited to a continuous transformation. This change will make them give up spiritual stagnation in order to adopt an active and a dynamic spirituality which will be the resumption and reconsideration of values; a sincere and objective inquiry will take place, so that God's influence and word will be manifested upon mankind.

Of course, dialogues differ as far as cause, history, method, purpose, and content are concerned. Some of them are ancient, some recent, and some contemporary. Some of them go on; some cease; some reappear and gain impetus. They are influenced positively or negatively by people, events, and circumstances. Some of them require a long preparation period and others a short time. Their degree of success depends very much on friendly and brotherly relations being constantly cultivated. If there have been differences and hostilities for centuries, or if the partners ignore each other because of their different mentalities, then their behavior must be reconsidered through their sincere relations and fraternal love. Then the dialogue among hearts starts, which becomes the dialogue of love. Today Orthodox Christians and Muslims are invited to inaugurate this type of dialogue, beyond any good or bad implications, beyond any political activities and interferences.

The struggle for the survival of social justice, freedom, and peace—the common interests of mankind—are in reality factors which, while they continue to exist, unite and create a new climate for human relations, making the dialogue more and more fruitful. Another encouraging factor besides the goodwill which has already been expressed by both sides is the foundation of cultural institutions whose purpose will be the encouragement of dialogue, the creation of an atmosphere for breaking down the long-standing barrier which had hindered any possibilities for a dialogue and had caused unwillingness and embarrassment for discussions, however desirable, by both sides.

The study and teachings of the Hellenic-Islamic-Christian philosophy which is the common heritage of the Western and Middle East civilizations will help tremendously in the dialogue between Orthodox Christians and Muslims. This will certainly be realized in the near future, since this field is just starting to be explored as far as Muslim sources are concerned. As it has been mentioned by a wise man, who is a speaker at this symposium, while referring to the Islamic philosophy of the Middle Ages, "there are still many unknown events, many writings forgotten for centuries and not studied since. These writings come to light little by little; they are issued and studied over again." It is providential that the efforts concerning the dialogue take place in a period when science and technology guarantee an unlimited objective where contemporary cultural spirit contributes to the fact that mankind knows itself better, something that did not exist in the past.

The above-mentioned elements should strengthen the hope that the deep wish for the unity of the believers will be realized. At the same time, both Christians and Muslims will be aware of their great obligation and responsibility to support the dialogue steadily with patience and respect. Their common monotheism will help them to understand better that God's will for unity will have the last word.

Eastern Orthodoxy and Islam: An Historical Overview

ROBERT M. HADDAD

> . . . there is none like [Constantinople] in the
> world except Baghdad, the great city of Islam.
> (Benjamin of Tudela, late twelfth century)[1]

> . . . there are two lordships, that of the Saracens and that of the
> Romans, which stand above all lordship on earth, and shine out
> like the two mighty beacons in the firmament. They ought, for
> this very reason alone, to be in contact and brotherhood and not,
> because we differ in our lives and habits and religion, remain
> alien in all ways to each other, and deprive themselves of cor-
> respondence . . . [2]

THESE WORDS, written over a millennium ago by Nicholas I
Mystikos, Patriarch of Constantinople, to the Caliph al-Muktafī
(902-908), could serve as keynote to this symposium. I would, however, supplement the patriarch's call with the words of an Orthodox
son of Antioch, authored but a few years ago:

> Byzantium and Islam in the eighth and ninth centuries (and even
> beyond) seem almost to present the aspect of a single society whose
> two major segments, despite their overt mutual hostility, display
> prominent signs of cultural unity and often confront the discerning
> observer with a parallel religio-political evolution in which similar

---

[1] Marcus N. Adler, *The Itinerary of Benjamin of Tudela* (London, 1907;
reprint N.Y., n.d.), p. 12.

[2] R. J. H. Jenkins and L. G. Westerink (trans.), *Nicholas I, Patriarch of
Constantinople: Letters* (Washington, D.C., 1973), p. 3.

questions are posed and strikingly similar answers given.[3]

In pursuing selectively the theme of mutuality of questions posed and answers given, it would be appropriate to begin with what is for each tradition the central event: God's supreme revelation to man. I need hardly remind the company here gathered that the true Islamic analogue to Christ is not Muḥammad but the Qur'ān, the divine word revealed by God to the Arabian Prophet. Muḥammad's role then is similar to that assigned by Christianity to the Virgin, the human agency through which the divine word was conveyed to man. The distance separating the personal logos of Christianity from the impersonal logos of Islam has appeared to virtually all Christians and Muslims unbridgeable. Yet even in this divergence we do not fail to detect convergence. For the word as person or as book raised a question of critical import: is this logos created or uncreated? And those in the Christian and Muslim mainstreams produced, though not without intense internal strife, precisely the same resounding reply: the logos—the arguments of Arians and Mu'tazila notwithstanding— is *uncreated,* existing from all eternity with God.

Then too the Christian concept of revelation as divinity incarnate and the Islamic concept of revelation as eternal decree carried a similar mandate for society: nothing less than the transformation of the profane into the sacred—and this, in the Christian East, with few of the pessimistic reservations voiced by Augustine and subsequently pervasive, if not dominant, in Latin Christianity. In the East, man had not fallen with a thud. Just as the incarnation, the descent of divinity into flesh—into the material order he had created—makes possible the sanctification of the whole material order, including those merely of flesh, so the *sharī'a,* the divine law of Islam, elaborated largely on the basis of the Qur'ān and the utterances of the Prophet, makes it possible to charge all human action with sacred significance, to transform life into a sacred ceremony. The logos of Islam, like the logos of Christianity, makes possible man's sanctification, that transformation known to Orthodox Christians as *theosis.*

Despite radically different historical beginnings, Orthodox Christianity and Islam (again in contrast to Latin Christendom) developed remarkably similar attitudes toward temporal authority, itself deemed susceptible to the sanctifying process made possible by the logos. True

---

[3]Robert M. Haddad, "Iconoclasts and Mu'tazila: the Politics of Anthropomorphism," *The Greek Orthodox Theological Review,* 27 (1982) 301-02.

it was that the Christian Church existed for over three hundred years under a non-Christian and generally unsympathetic political authority, during which time she developed her own organization, her own modes of internal governance and not a little of her fundamental doctrinal equipment. When, in the late fourth century, the Church officially captured the State (or, some might argue, was captured by the State), two highly developed structures were joined: the Roman state with its law, administration and political universalism to the Christian Church with her distinctive institutional arrangements and her *religious* universalism. To maintain that State and Church became one would be errant nonsense. Still, they *were* joined, particularly in the person of the emperor (one God, therefore one emperor, one empire, one Church) and the line of demarcation between them, between authority temporal and spiritual, while never erased, certainly blurred. That State and Church tended to shade, one into the other, did not simply represent conformity to pre-Christian practice and theory but, also, the Christian conviction that the incarnation dictated the baptism, the sacralization of all society—institutions as well as individuals. (For many, though not all, the incarnation dictated too the sacralization of profane knowledge, and to this central endeavor we shall return.)

In contrast to Christianity, Islam endured but the briefest period without political power. It is surely significant that the Muslim calendar commences not with the onset of the Qur'ānic revelation in the year 610 A.D. but with the emigration of the Prophet from hostile Mecca to welcoming Medina in 622, to Medina where Muḥammad, as religious and political leader, governed the nascent Muslim community as a religio-political entity. Many Muslims since have regarded as normative the unity of the temporal and spiritual spheres. But the notion, still current, that the Islamic community subsequently saw no de facto distinction between temporal and spiritual authority cannot withstand careful scrutiny. Within one hundred years of the Prophet's death in 632, Arab Muslim, not unmixed with Arab Christian, arms had won an empire extending from the Pyrenees in the West to and beyond the gates of India and China in the East. This explosive expansion gave rise to a development of the temporal authority that was inevitably more rapid than the emergence of the theocratic institutions implied by the Qur'ān and the Prophet's community at Medina. The *sharī'a*, the divine law, that would be one of the Muslim's salient means of sacralizing his and his community's life, was not to emerge fully until the mid-ninth century. The more or less complete articulation of dogmatic theology, not to mention mysticism, came still later. Meanwhile the Sunnī caliphs, the successors to the Apostle of God, had to govern and so they did, but hardly on the basis of finely wrought theocratic institutions. Not surprisingly, in Islam as in Byzantium, the historical reality could but dimly reflect the pious norm which was itself, in part, spun out of an idealized view of selected historical facts.

The different evolutions of early Christianity and Islam notwithstanding, emperor and caliph enjoyed similar authority with regard to the military, the administration and even religious patronage— which is to say the appointment of bishops and *qāḍīs*. They also tended, not unnaturally, to view religious unity as a corollary to political unity, and this led them beyond their generally acknowledged mission to preserve the integrity of doctrine into the attempt to *define* doctrine. But almost from the time that Constantine yielded to the flaming vision of the Cross and, more than three hundred years later, when the caliphate was born, there existed in Christianity and Islam a tradition of opposition to "imperial" attempts to control doctrinal definition. One has but to read Eusebios' "Oration on the Thirtieth Anniversary of the Emperor Constantine's Succession" or Abū Yūsuf's epistle to the Caliph Hārūn al-Rashīd (786-809) to sense the only half-buried doubts of the man of religion in contemplating the awesome power of his sovereign—absolute in the temporal realm but possessing also an inexactly defined religious authority. Basically, Eusebios and Abū Yūsuf, in rhetoric similar and similarly charged with anxiety, aim at *persuading* Constantine and Hārūn of their duties as Christian and Muslim ruler respectively. This although Eusebios, in using such phrases as "For he who would bear the title of sovereign . . . " and "This is a sovereign who . . . ,"[4] tends to be more circumspect than Abū Yūsuf with his characteristic "Do not . . . "[5] But then Abū Yūsuf, unlike Eusebios, had been requested by his ruler to provide a "mirror for princes."[6] One wonders too whether the absence of any clearly defined and regularly

---

[4] The text of Eusebios' oration may be found in H. A. Drake, *In Praise of Constantine: A Historical Study and New Translation of Eusebius' Tricennial Orations* (Berkeley, 1976), pp. 83-102; see especially pp. 89-90.

[5] Abū Yūsuf Yaʿqūb, *Kitāb al-Kharāj*, trans. A. Ben Shemesh, Vol. 3 of *Taxation in Islam* (Leiden, 1969), pp. 35-39.

[6] Ibid., p. 35.

upheld law of succession in Byzantium and Sunnī Islam reflected not merely pagan Roman precedent but the religious idealization of the imperial dignity: the ruler's *piety* should loom larger than his paternity.

The critical episodes that determined, once and for all, the Orthodox Christian and Sunnī Muslim rulers' authority in definition of doctrine were the Iconoclastic and Mu'tazilī controversies. Certain emperors, in sponsoring Iconoclasm in the eighth and ninth centuries, and three caliphs of the second quarter of the ninth century, in pronouncing Mu'tazilī doctrine normative, clearly sought to establish the ruler's right to define doctrine on behalf of his community. Both controversies also shared an important doctrinal concern: I mean the legitimacy of an anthropomorphic depiction of divinity. The divinity of Jesus, held the iconoclast, could not be represented in the sheer anthropomorphism of the icon. The divinity of God, asserted the Mu'tazila, could not be represented by a literal rendering of the verbal anthropomorphisms of the Qur'ān. The resolution of these decisive struggles occurred at roughly the same time—in the 840s. And in roundly rejecting the maximalist religious claims of emperor and caliph, Orthodox Christianity and Sunnī Islam established the principle that the earthly arbiter of doctrine and practice can be nothing other than the consensus of believers, a consensus pronounced by those whom the believers acknowledge as their leaders, pronounced also and more subtly by time-sanctified practice and belief. In adherence to the principle that religious authority derives from the consensus of the confessing community, Orthodox Christianity and Sunnī Islam continue to stand as one.[7] Nor am I convinced that the de facto situation differs greatly in Shī'ī Islam despite the special intercessory position accorded the *imāms* descended from the House of the Prophet.

Despite the Church's assertion of her independence of state dictation in matters as basic as definition of doctrine, the emperor continued to bear the title "Pontifex Maximus" (Supreme Magistrate), the same pre-Christian imperial title that would come to be arrogated by the popes in wake of the empire's collapse in the West and the ensuing political fragmentation in the sphere of Latin Christendom. The post-Iconoclastic emperors lost nothing of their theoretic authority over the army, administration or even over religious patronage. The wearer of the purple yet remained the icon of Christ on earth

---

[7] On the affinities between the Iconoclast and Mu'tazilī controversies, see Haddad, *The Greek Orthodox Theological Review*, 27 (1982) 287-305.

just as the considerably humbled post-Mu'tazila caliph continued to reign as the shadow of God on earth. And both rulers would rationalize the gradual erosion of their *effective* political authority in much the same way. As the image of Christ on earth who should have enjoyed, but even within Orthodox Christian territory did not enjoy, universal political sway, the emperor (or the imperial spokesmen) advanced the theory of a "family of princes," all of them subject ultimately to the *basileus* in Constantinople and deriving from him what legitimacy was theirs.[8] It would appear that the eleventh-century Muslim thinker and apologist for the 'Abbāsid caliphate, al-Māwardī, in conceiving the so-called "amīrate by seizure," sought similar justification for the existence of sundry Muslim rulers where there should have been one.[9] In Islam too the usurpers were to be assimilated by resort to legal fictions analagous to those that obtained in kindred Byzantium. Both attempts failed even as the ideal of unitary political authority endured.

In the event, of course, Orthodox Christian political fortunes would pass from the Byzantines of the Second Rome to the Muscovites of the Third. In 867 the Ecumenical Patriarch Photios had, prematurely and with some exaggeration, celebrated the conversion of the Rhos and included their leaders within that "family of princes" forever subject to Christ's icon in Constantinople. Photios announced that the erstwhile savage Russians, now won to Christianity, rested easily under the ecclesiastical authority of a Byzantine bishop as "subjects and friends" of the empire.[10] In 1395 Anthony, Patriarch of Constantinople, wrote to the Grand Duke Basil of Moscow in defense of the tattered Byzantine imperial prerogative:

> It is not a good thing, my son, for you to say "We have a Church but no Emperor." It is not possible for Christians to have a Church without an Emperor, for the same imperial sovereignty and the Church form a single entity and they cannot be

---

[8] Deno J. Geanakoplos, *Byzantium: Church, Society, and Civilization Seen through Contemporary Eyes* (Chicago, 1984), pp. 31-32.

[9] 'Alī ibn Muḥammad al-Māwardī, *Al-Aḥkām al-Sulṭāniyya*, trans. as *Les status governementaux* by E. Fagnan (Alger, 1915), see especially pp. 59-70.

[10] David Knowles with Dimitri Obolensky, *The Middle Ages*, Vol. Two of *The Christian Centuries*, eds. Louis J. Rogier et al. (N.Y., 1968), p. 312.

separated from each other. . . . [11]

The Muscovites were so well persuaded by Anthony's advocacy that we hear the Greek patriarch echoed by the Russian monk Filofei in his justly famous letter to Tsar Basil III assuring his temporal lord that:

> . . . all the realms of the Christian faith have converged into your single realm. You are the only Christian tsar in all the world. . . . Two Romes have fallen, and the third stands, and a fourth there shall not be. Your Christian realm shall not pass under the rule of another.[12]

The two-headed eagle of Byzantium had made its passage north.

Similarly, al-Māwardī, for whom the caliphate "was established to replace the prophetic office (of which the Prophet had been the last representative) in defense of the faith and worldly interests,"[13] formulated his "amīrate by seizure" in the hope of restoring the real authority of the 'Abbāsid caliph, God's shadow in Baghdad. This was to be achieved by tying the vastly eroded effective authority of the caliphate to the military power of the apparently strongest "amīrate by seizure" or sultanate. Al-Māwardī's efforts would accomplish little but the legitimation of non-caliphal authority pending the metamorphosis of the most powerful "amīrate by seizure"—and this would prove to be the Ottoman sultanate—into the new caliphate. And, after all, why not? The Ottoman sultan did the duties of a Sunnī caliph within the boundaries of a considerable empire, just as the Muscovite prince came to perform those of *the* Orthodox Christian emperor. The Ottoman sultan, Sulaymān I (1520-1566), master of an empire stretching from central Europe to the Indian Ocean, took his title "Caliph on Earth" seriously enough to study personally Islamic jurisprudence and to assign the learned the task of bringing secular laws of state into conformity with the *sharī'a*.[14]

---

[11]Quoted in George Ostrogorsky, *History of the Byzantine State*, 2nd ed., trans. Joan Hussey (Oxford, 1968), p. 553.

[12]George Vernadsky (ed.), *A Source Book for Russian History from Early Times to 1917*, Vol. 1 (New Haven, 1972), p. 156.

[13]al-Māwardī, *Al-Aḥkām al-Sulṭāniyya*, p. 5.

[14]Halil Inalcik, *The Ottoman Empire: the Classical Age, 1300-1600*, trans. N. Itzkowitz and C. Imber (N.Y., 1973), p. 182.

Well, the empires are departed and with them, I think, the possibility of any unitary theocratic or quasi-theocratic society. And if I have dwelt upon them at length it is not only because emperor and caliph were central to Orthodox Christian and Muslim history until the modern age but because their disappearance has revealed them as hardly crucial to the survival and indeed the health of either religious community. I am myself no enthusiastic partisan of the wholly secularized nation-state for it is more than likely that universalist faiths were instituted by God in part to restrain the parochial excesses to which ethnicity (real or imagined), language and territoriality are prey. But few Americans—least of all members of the Orthodox Christian minority—can be oblivious of the blessings that secularized polity may confer upon a religiously pluralistic society. The nation-state, moreover, is apt to be our lot for the foreseeable future, and while the task of curbing the wild beast may have much to do with man's vision of transcendent authority, the effort to translate that vision into political structure is unlikely to be more successful now or later than it has been in the past. Perhaps that "Augustinian" pessimism over the earthly city, subdued but by no means absent in Orthodox Christianity and Islam, deserves therein a more honored place.

I remarked earlier in certain parallels between the logos doctrine in Orthodox Christianity and in Islam. Each faith clearly rests upon the bedrock of its revealed word but, just as obviously, each widened the scope of reason as a means of clarifying, even expanding, the truths of revelation. Some comments now about this process, for it seems to me that in ordering priorities between reason and revelation, Orthodox Christianity and Sunnī Islam underwent a comparable evolution in religious thought and sensibility.

At the advent of Islam, Hellenistic philosophy had already made substantial inroads into Eastern Christian theology—I mean here not only Orthodox or Chalcedonian Christianity but also the non-Chalcedonian or semitic Christianity represented by the Monophysites and Nestorians. It is to be emphasized that Islam found its post-Qur'ānic voice, phrased many of its characteristic definitions, in a Middle East which, west of Iran, remained heavily Christian—particularly *semitic* Christian—although yielding gradually and inexorably to the faith of the Arabian Prophet. It is to subtract nothing from the immensity of the intellectual and artistic achievement of the classical age of Islam to insist that Eastern Christendom posed many of the critical questions and provisioned the avid Muslims with much of the material and disciplined discourse necessary to phrase distinctly Islamic answers to those questions. Withal, the early Islamic centuries comprise for Eastern Christians under Islamic rule a twilight zone, less an era of creativity—that could only be the prerogative of the politically dominant community—than an era of transmission. And what was transmitted to Muslims included much of the Hellenistic philosophy already adapted to the uses of patristic theology. The era of transmission would end with semitic Christianity spent but with many of its attitudes and adherents assimilated by Islam, a process of appropriation whose monumental impact on world history has yet to inspire the scholarly attention it merits. My satisfaction in the initiation of serious dialogue between Orthodox Christians and Muslims in the United States is, as you may suspect, diminished somewhat by our failure here to include representatives of semitic Christianity. For not only were the non-Chalcedonians the great transmitters to Islam but it may even be argued that Monophysite and Nestorian Christology, the former by de-emphasizing Christ's human nature and the latter particularly, by diminishing his divine nature, have something of a logical conclusion in Qur'ānic Christology. I exaggerate slightly but a Jesus whose human nature is submerged tends to become simply God and the incarnation recedes into the problematic, while a Jesus whose divinity is compromised tends to become simply man. It may be telling that the preferred Nestorian description, "Jesus, Son of Mary" (rather than "Son of God") is also the favored Qur'ānic designation for Jesus the Prophet. Islam was no mere bystander in the Christological controversies.

Let us be mindful then that Islam's earliest and most intimate contact with Eastern Christianity involved the non-Chalcedonian rather than the Chalcedonian churches. The eve of the Muslim conquests found most of Egypt and Syria Monophysite, and Mesopotamia largely Nestorian. The Arab tribes between Arabia and Byzantine Syria had adopted the Monophysite creed while those between the Peninsula and Iranian-controlled Mesopotamia had embraced Nestorianism. And, as I intimated earlier, evidence exists that some of these Arab Christian tribes joined their Muslim brothers in the conquests. For we are not to forget that many non-Chalcedonians viewed the Muslim advance as deliverance. The following testimony, although not contemporaneous, comes from the Coptic (Egyptian Monophysite) bishop, Sāwīrus ibn al-Muqaffa':

... and [Muḥammad] brought back the worshippers of idols to the knowledge of the One God. . . . And the Lord abandoned the army of the Romans . . . as punishment for their corrupt faith, and because of the anathemas uttered against them, on account of the council of Chalcedon, by the ancient fathers.[15]

The Arab Muslim conquests, like the later Ottoman invasions, were prepared by schism within Christendom. And both Islamic surges answered eloquently the question: "How successful was Christianity in recementing 'Roman' society?"

The Syrian and Mesopotamian adherents of semitic Christianity were, in any event, the main channel for the transmission of Hellenistic philosophy and science to the Muslims. The intrusion of Greek philosophy now raised for Islam, as it had centuries before for Christianity, the problem of the appropriate relationship between revelation and reason or, stated differently, the degree to which profane knowledge could be sacralized. The way to resolution would be long and difficult but certainly by the thirteenth century Islam, like Orthodox Christianity, had reduced natural reason to near total subservience to revelation as an instrument for knowing God, an outcome signaled by the rise of Sufism and Hesychasm to pre-eminence in the theological and devotional life of Sunnī Islam and Orthodox Christianity respectively. Even a mere historian is aware that rational and mystical theology are not mutually exclusive so long as the former does not claim for itself comprehension of the whole truth independently of revelation and its complements, grace and illumination. But, however unfortunately, the struggle appeared to many of the central actors to have involved such a claim by the practitioners of rational theology. The most outspoken upholders of revelation, all too often sustained by a rather arid *kalām* in Sunnī Islam, and in Orthodox Christianity by what Father John Meyendorff has termed "the theology of repetition,"[16] succeeded all too well in driving philosophy and, in its train, the sciences to the margin of intellectual concern. I am not asserting that philosophy and science simply died in

---

[15]Sāwīrus ibn al-Muqaffaʻ, *History of the Patriarchs of the Coptic Church of Alexandria,* Arabic text ed. and trans. B. Evetts, *Patrologia Orientalis,* T. I (Paris, 1907), pp. 492-93.

[16]John Meyendorff, *A Study of Gregory Palamas,* trans. George Lawrence (Crestwood, N.Y., 1964), p. 238.

the East before the thirteenth century. These disciplines continued for a while to sway certain individuals in Orthodox Christianity and Sunnī Islam and endured, however modestly, in Shī'ī education into early modern times. In late thirteenth-century Byzantium, George Akropolites calculated and predicted the time of an eclipse of the sun,[17] while the great Sunnī cosmologist, ibn al-Shāṭir (d. 1375/76),[18] flourished in the fourteenth century. Not long before the fall of Constantinople, private schools in the city continued to dispense Aristotle[19] while Sunnī Muslims of the period seem not to have been wholly bereft of the Doctor of Doctors.[20] The fact remains however that the sciences and their mistress, philosophy, found little place in the curriculum of the religious academies.[21] And if we must name the salient figures in Orthodox Christian and Sunnī theology from the late medieval into the modern period, they would surely be Gregory Palamas (d. 1359) and al-Ghazālī (d. 1111) respectively, not, by way of contrast, Gregory's contemporary and antagonist, Barlaam the Calabrian, or al-Ghazālī's nemesis, ibn Rushd (d. 1198). Latin Christianity, on the other hand, while boasting its mystical theologians and practitioners, would have to indicate Thomas Aquinas (d. 1274) as her characteristic theologian. And the Angelic Doctor would come to dominate the curriculum in the Western lands, among those "Franks" whom Orthodox Christians and Muslims would persist in deeming barbarous long after good sense might have suggested a more respectful attitude. Of the intellectual turn taken by Latin Christendom, ibn Khaldūn (d. 1406) was aware. "We hear now," he wrote in the late fourteenth century,

---

[17]Geanakoplos, *Byzantium*, p. 437.

[18]See Victor Roberts, "The Solar and Lunar Theory of Ibn ash-Shāṭir: A Pre-Copernican Model," *Isis*, 48 (1957) 428-32; E. S. Kennedy, "The Planetary Theory of Ibn al-Shāṭir," *Isis*, 50 (1959) 227-35.

[19]Geanakoplos, *Byzantium*, p. 408.

[20]"Philosophy, prohibited from being taught in public, was taught privately . . . " [George Makdisi, "Interaction between Islam and the West," *Medieval Education in Islam and the West*, eds. George Makdisi et al. (Paris, 1977), p. 297].

[21]On the situation in Sunnī Islam, see ibid., pp. 296-97. Long before the fall of the Second Rome, the profane instruction available at the Imperial University had been kept distinct from the studies provided future clerics at the Patriarchal School (Meyendorff, *A Study of Gregory Palamas*, p. 29).

that the philosophical sciences are greatly cultivated in [Western Europe] and along the adjacent northern shore of the country of the [Latin] Christians. They are said to be studied there again and to be taught in numerous classes. Existing systems of expositions of them are said to be comprehensive and the people who know them numerous and the students of them very many.[22]

In ibn Khaldūn's own disregard of the philosophical sciences, we may detect the representative position of Sunnī Islam.

It should be known that the (opinion) the (philosophers) hold is wrong in all respects. . . . The problems of physics are of no importance for us in our religious affairs or our livelihoods. Therefore, we must leave them alone.[23]

Meanwhile in Byzantium, ibn Khaldūn's contemporary, Demetrios Kydones (d. 1397/98), felt compelled to defend his interest in Aquinas and in the Latin theologian's use of Aristotle.[24]

It may be true that a more knowing Orthodox Christianity and Islam, whose long experience of Greek philosophy perhaps induced immunity to its excesses, saw more clearly than freshly exposed Latin Christianity the danger to revelation implicit in a thoroughgoing Aristotelian victory. The syllogism as an absolute, a natural law wholly apprehensible to man's reason, would, in the hands of the nominalists, encourage the desacralization of knowledge and precisely that separation between faith and reason that Aquinas had labored to avoid. It may be argued, however, that if Thomas inadvertently established a foundation for the subsequent bifurcation of knowledge into distinct realms, sacred and profane, so, working from the opposite pole and also inadvertently, did al-Ghazālī and Palamas in insisting that logic and the sciences could add little to the knowledge of God imparted by revelation and illumination and are of themselves inadequate for imparting knowledge of beings and the created order. Knowledge of the Artisan is little to be furthered by knowledge of his art, and the tools for study of that art fell to rust and decay. In sum,

---

[22]Ibn Khaldūn, *The Muqaddimah*, trans. Franz Rosenthal, Vol. 3 (N.Y., 1958), pp. 117-18.
[23]Ibid., pp. 250-52.
[24]Geanakoplos, *Byzantium*, p. 378.

responsibility for the desacralization of knowledge cannot simply be laid at the Latin Christian door. While Latin Christianity plunged headlong into scholasticism, thence into a progressively desacralized understanding of nature and finally into a desacralized control over nature, the East, Christian and Muslim, contented itself with a syllabus that tended to deny the unity and sacred character of all knowledge, if only by relegating wide areas thereof to curricular oblivion. If the victory of natural reason over revelation was too pronounced in Latin Christendom, it must be insisted that the triumph of revelation over natural reason in the East was no less pronounced and certainly more thorough than either Palamas or al-Ghazālī intended. Palamas held, after all, that:

> . . . if one says that philosophy, insofar as it is natural, is a gift of God, then one says true, without contradiction and without incurring the accusation that falls on those who abuse philosophy and pervert it to an unnatural end.[25]

There is echo here of al-Ghazālī's argument, delivered some two hundred years earlier, that while nothing in logic, mathematics and the physical sciences "entails denial or affirmation of religious matters," the study of them may engender evil consequences.[26] Orthodox Christianity and Islam stand heirs to a less one-sided epistemology than that commonly attributed to Palamas and al-Ghazālī and some revival of it may be in order. It is clear in any case that if resacralization of knowledge is a problem, it should concern Orthodox Christians and Muslims no less than Latin Christians.

For an historian, at least, certain related issues continue to nag. The era the West terms "medieval" witnessed a contest among Latin Christendom, Orthodox or Greek Christendom and Islam—all three societies born of the Roman imperial collapse, all three claiming explicitly or implicitly to be the new Rome, the new Athens, the new Jerusalem, the authentic heir to Roman political universalism, Hellenistic high culture and the promise of the Hebrew prophets.

---

[25]Gregory Palamas, *The Triads,* ed. John Meyendorff, trans. Nicholas Gendle (N.Y., 1983), p. 27; see also pp. 119-20, n. 27.

[26]al-Ghazālī, *Freedom and Fulfillment: An Annotated Translation of al-Ghazālī's al-Munqidh min al-Ḍalāl and Other Relevant Works of al-Ghazālī* by Richard J. McCarthy (Boston, 1980), pp. 73-76.

A dispassionate observer, say from China, contemplating this tripartite medieval world early in the second Christian millennium, would likely have declined to predict a Latin Christian victory. In the arts of civilization, the Orthodox Christian and Islamic worlds would have struck our hypothetical observer as so much richer and more powerful than the lately beleaguered agrarian world of Latin Christendom that he could scarcely have predicted the death of Byzantium in the fifteenth century and the erosion of Islamic intellectual vitality well before the great recession of Islamic political power initiated around the mid-seventeenth century. One wonders: did Latin Christendom emerge from the medieval contest, poised for seizure of global hegemony, because of its greater fidelity to Athens?

I do not wish to expose myself to charges of crass historicism—least of all from my immemorial friend, Seyyed Hossein Nasr—when I observe that the crucial decisions concerning Aristotle, reason and revelation were made in a Byzantine and Muslim world sorely beset by nomadic expansion—specifically that of the Turkomens—and in a Latin Christendom which, by contrast, found itself for the first time in centuries free of external threat. Is the conviction that reason leads us to God as surely as revelation, as surely as the mystic's illumination, apt to have greatest appeal in a society made optimistic by mundane circumstance? Is there not also a striking complementarity between the metaphorical canonization of Aristotle by the Latin Church and the West's assumption of global leadership in technology, a leadership that Western Europe and her trans-Atlantic offspring have yet to relinquish? Again, is there a point at which mundane threat ceases to spur creative innovation and encourages rather a disintegrative insularity in the mechanic as well as intellectual arts and the conviction that the great voyages have already been made?

As for mysticism, its evolution in Islam was marked by a phenomenon unparalleled in Christianity: the emergence, beginning in the late twelfth century, of brotherhoods (*ṭarīqas*) each founded by a specific master of the Ṣūfī way and spreading throughout the Islamic world. The lodges of a particular *ṭarīqa* governed the devotional life of their adherents, deepening the awareness of God's immanence and accessibility, complementing the *sharī'a* in shaping life as a sacred ceremony. The *ṭarīqas,* which in the Ottoman period came to embrace perhaps three-quarters of the adult male population, also functioned, especially when affiliated with guilds, as socio-economic units, the story of whose comprehensive influence on Islamic society has yet to be written. Hesychasm, by contrast, remained largely a monastic discipline, although a number of its devotional devices—notably of course the *Jesus Prayer*—pervaded and to some extent continue to pervade the Orthodox Christian faithful with something like the force of the *dhikr,* the mention or remembrance of God, among the Ṣūfīs. The sacred ceremony in which the Orthodox Christian was and should still be immersed and which, to my mind, most nearly approximates the Muslim duality of *sharīʿa* and *ṭarīqa,* is the liturgical cycle, the sacramental transmutation of the days and years into an unending celebration of Christ's sacrifice and of those models of sanctity whom the believer seeks to emulate, those men and women whose *theosis* is fact.

The tenor of my preceding remarks notwithstanding, I am acutely aware that the history of the encounter between Orthodox Christianity and Islam has been largely one of hostility, overt and covert, during which Islam, more often than not, prevailed. Presentations other than mine will expose some of the warts, and none of us needs reminding that mutual hostility scarcely belongs to an unremembered past. Nor, in my emphasis upon Orthodox Christianity and Islam as kindred religious cultures, do I mistake kinship for identity. The supersessionist claim of Islam, resting upon the logos as book, is matched by Christianity's inability to accord perfect legitimacy to any revelation beyond that of the incarnate logos, and inevitably the rest may be silence. I trust not, for, as I have sought to indicate in however abbreviated a fashion, Orthodox Christianity and Islam mirror one another in so many ways that full appreciation of one is served by thoughtful and sympathetic attention to the other. Obviously I am not pleading for that tolerance born simply of secular indifference. While such has had its uses, it is for believers of either hue finally insufficient. On the other hand, as an Orthodox Christian who has been an earnest student of Islamic history for thirty years, I cannot minimize the difficulty of understanding, much less standing in the sacred space of another. I am able to testify, however, that the effort to do so has yielded reward beyond anything this play of words can tell. And we have Muslims participating in this conference (and I know at least two of them) who have probed Orthodox Christianity with the minds and hearts of informed Muslim believers and come away not unsatisfied. Permit me to wonder whether Muslims and Orthodox Christians under officially atheistic governments are prone to see one another as the salient enemy.

Let the last word, as the first, go to Patriarch Nicholas Mystikos as he addresses now the *amīr* of Crete:

Since he [Patriarch Photios (858-67, 877-86)] was a man of God and learned with regard to human and divine matters, he realized that, though a dividing wall of worship separated us, yet the attributes of human wisdom, intelligence, dependability of conduct, love for mankind, and every other attribute that adorns and elevates human nature with its presence, ignites, in those persons who care for that which is good, friendship toward those imbued with the qualities they have.[27]

------

[27]Geanakoplos, *Byzantium,* p. 340.

Muslim and Byzantine Christian Relations:
Letter of Paul of Antioch and Ibn Taymīyah's Response

MUZAMMIL H. SIDDIQI

MUSLIM AND BYZANTINE CHRISTIAN RELATIONS are generally viewed as little more than continual warfare. It is true that for centuries they fought each other, but beside confrontations between armies on battlefields there were also debates, polemics, cultural exchanges, and commercial relations. History of these exchanges is little explored and studied. Some of these exchanges were very significant and are of great importance for understanding the history of dialogue between Muslims and Christians in general and in particular between the Muslim and the Byzantine Christian community. Both communities were living very close to each other and dialogue for them was not mere academic exercise but something of existential importance. In this paper I would like to discuss the dialogical exchange that took place between two Muslim and Christian theologians of the twelfth and thirteenth centuries. This paper is part of a thesis that I have presented to the Harvard University Center for the Study of World Religions and is being readied for publication soon. In my thesis I have discussed at length the social and historical context of this exchange. Here I shall concentrate only on the theological issues discussed in the works of these two writers.

First is the work of Paul of Antioch who prepared it in the form of a letter to Muslims. He entitled his work as *Risāla ilā ba'ḍ aṣdiqā'hi al-Muslimīn* (Letter to Some of His Muslim Friends). Paul was a Melkite theologian who lived in the twelfth century. He was born in Antioch, spent his early life as a monk and was later appointed as the bishop of Sidon. There are about twenty-four small treatises attributed to him. Paul Khoury, who edited and translated into French this *Letter to Muslims*, has accepted only five as authentic writings of Paul of Antioch.[1]

Paul's works were primarily apologetic and written in clear and didactic style. He often referred to reason as the criterion and touchstone of all religious truth[2] and made use of rational arguments in explaining his position. The apologies of Paul are markedly sober and irenic. Khoury says:

> L'oeuvre de Paul de Sidon semble trancher sur l'ensemble de la litterature apologetique chretienne de langue arabe, si ce n'est pour l'originalite ou la profondeur des idees, du moins par l'attitude comprehensive qu'elle revele et le ton irenique qu'y prend de discours.[3]

The most famous work of Paul of Antioch was however his letter to some of his Muslim friends. This letter was widely circulated among the Christians of the Near East. As is so with the famous apology of al-Kindī,[4] this letter too was copied and re-copied.

The letter is interesting and important for several reasons. First of all it was written in an atmosphere of irenic confrontation with Islam. The author was not only defending his own faith but was also expressing some of his feelings about Islam and the mission of Muḥammad. These feelings were quite different from those of earlier Byzantine[5] or other Arab-Christian authors.[6] Paul did not accuse the Prophet of being an imposter or liar or warrior who waged wars and

---

[1] These are: a short treatise on reason, a treatise explaining why many nations along with the Jews accepted the Christian religion voluntarily, a letter to some of his Muslim friends, a treatise on Christian sects and another treatise explaining briefly the doctrines of Union and Unity; Paul Khoury, *Paul d'Antioch eveque melke'ts de Sidon* (Beirut, n.d.), pp. 1-101, French translation on pp. 123-202.

[2] Ibid. pp. 15, 24, 41, etc.

[3] Ibid. p. 6.

[4] See William Muir, *The Apology of al-Kindy* (London, 1882).

[5] One may refer here to an important study of these works by Adel Theodore Khoury, *Les theologiens byzantin et l'Islam* (Louvain, 1969).

[6] See Daniel J. Sahas, *John of Damascus on Islam* (Leiden, 1972) and James T. Addison, *The Christian Approach to the Moslem* (New York, 1942).

Prophet of being an imposter or liar or warrior who waged wars and used the sword, accusations made by a number of earlier Christian writers. He recognized that Muḥammad had a religious mission. However, this mission, he argued, was not universal and hence did not include Christians who had already received a superior message, namely the law of Christ. Muḥammad was sent, he said, to the ignorant Arabs who were living in darkness and who had never received a prophet before him. This can be proved, Paul claimed, from the Qur'ān itself; he cited several verses to support his arguments.

Let us analyze the letter in some detail. The author starts with a statement that he made a journey to the Byzantine territories, Constantinople, the land of the Amalfi, some Frankish province, and Rome. Because of his high office as bishop of Antioch he was able to meet some of the chiefs, elders, dignitaries, and scholars of these countries. At the request of one of his Muslim friends who asked him about the journey and about the views[7] of these people concerning Muḥammad, the author undertook to write this letter. All the arguments for Christianity or against Islam are thus put in the mouths of the people of those lands, and the author represents himself only as their spokesman and a reporter. Whether this was exactly the case or Paul used this style as a literary device remains open to conjecture.[8]

The dialogue begins with a discussion of Muḥammad and his book, al-Qur'ān. Paul argues that Islam is not a universal religion and that the message of Muḥammad was addressed to the pagan Arabs only. He quotes[9] the Qur'ānic verses concerning its Arabic origin (Sura 12.2) and Muḥammad's having been sent among the Gentiles and among those who did not receive any messenger before (62.2; 28.46; 36.6). These Paul considers as proofs from the Qur'ān itself for his arguments.

---

[7] Reference should be made here to some excellent works discussing the Western views of Islam in the Middle Ages. See Norman Daniel, *Islam and the West: the Making of an Image* (Edinburgh, 1960); R. W. Southern, *Western Views of Islam in the Middle Ages* (Cambridge, MA, 1962).

[8] Ibn Taymīyah, probably, accepted as true Paul's account of his journey. Thus he always narrates Paul's arguments as "they said (*qālū*)" or "the reporter from them said (*qāla al-nāqil 'anhum*).

[9] Although the letter abounds in the Qur'ānic quotations, a good number of them are quoted inexactly. See par. 6, verse 1 (Sura 12.2), par. 8, verse 2 (Sura 3.42), par. 10, verse 1 (Sura 3.55), etc. These errors might have occurred due to the negligence of later scribes since we do not find Ibn Taymīyah or others referring to this rather serious error in the letter of Paul.

The second theme of the letter is Christ in the Qur'ān. Paul says that since the Qur'ān has honored Christ and his mother, has mentioned the miracles performed by Jesus Christ and his virgin birth, and has praised the Gospels and the followers of Christ, this proves that the Prophet of Islam had no intention of converting Christians to his faith.

Following this discussion the author takes basic Christian doctrines such as the Trinity, the Incarnation, and the union and explains that there is no basic contradiction between these doctrines and the Islamic affirmation of *tawḥīd* (oneness of God). Paul's discussion of these doctrines is not very much different from the works of the Arab-Christian theologians of this period. The Trinity is explained in terms of "the essential attributes" (*al-ṣifāt al-jawhariyya*) or "names" (*al-asmā'*) and illustrated with the traditional analogy of the sun, its light, and its rays.

The union of the divine Word with humanity in the person of Christ is described with the familiar analogy of the fire and ironsheet. What distinguishes Paul's work is that here too he quotes the Qur'ān to prove his doctrines,[10] and argues that the Christian doctrines of the Trinity and the Incarnation are similar to the doctrines of attributes (*ṣifāt*) in Islamic theology and should be considered with the same caution and care as the apparently anthropomorphic verses in the Qur'ān.

The intrinsic quality of this work as well as the external conditions and situation in which it was produced are noteworthy. It is no wonder, then, that three Muslim theologians gave attention to this work and not only read it but also found it worth answering and commenting upon.

Muslim writers who answered this letter were: Shihāb al-Dīn Aḥmad b. Idrīs al-Qarāfī (d. 684 A.H./1285 A.D.) who was a Mālikī Jurist and lived in Egypt.[11] Shams al-Dīn Muḥammad b. Abī Ṭālib al-Anṣārī (d. 727 A.H./1327 A.D.) who was known as a Ṣūfī and

---

[10]For example he refers to Sura 2.255. Three names, he says, are used here: *Allāh, al-Ḥayy,* and *al-Qayyūm.* Also he refers to *Bismillāh* where he says only three attributes are mentioned, namely *Allāh, al-Raḥmān,* and *al-Raḥīm*; see Paul Khoury, *Les theologiens byzantin et l'Islam,* pp. 70-71.

[11]*Al-Ajwibat al-Fākhirah 'an al-As'ilah al-Fājirah* on the margin of 'Abd al-Raḥman Bashizadeh, *Kitāb al-Farq bayn al-Makhlūq wa al-Khāliq* (Egypt, n.d.).

was a native of Damascus.[12] And Taqī al-Dīn Aḥmad b. Taymīyah (d. 728 A.H./1328 A.D.) who was a Ḥanbalī theologian, a prolific and influential writer and spent most of his life in Damascus and Egypt. The answer of Ibn Taymīyah is the most substantial and interesting. His work is now available in four volumes consisting of about 1500 pages altogether.[13] Ibn Taymīyah's wrote his whole book as a long continuous answer to Paul. He identified six arguments in Paul's letter:

1. The claim that Muḥammad was sent only to ignorant Arabs and his alleged proofs from the Qur'ān and reason.
2. The claim that the Qur'ān praises Christ, Christian scriptures, and followers of Christ and this means that Christians are not invited to Islam.
3. The claim that the prophecies of the Torah, psalms, and Gospels confirm Christian doctrines of the Trinity, hypostases (*aqānīm*), Incarnation, etc.
4. The claim that these Christian doctrines can be proved by reason as well as scripture.
5. The claim that words like hypostases (*aqānīm*) are similar to attributes (*ṣifāt*) and names (*asmā'*) of God in Islam.
6. The claim that Jesus came with perfect teachings and anything after perfection is redundant and thus unnecessary and unacceptable.

Ibn Taymīyah begins the book with a long preface; after praising God and asking blessings upon his Prophet Muḥammad, he speaks about the universal message of Muḥammad, the comprehensive nature of the Qur'ān, and the unity of all prophetic religions. He also mentions some special characteristics of the religion of Muḥammad and his community. Muḥammad, he emphasizes, was the final among God's prophets, who were sent to all peoples and who preached the same message of Islam although there were differences among the religious codes (*sharī'a*) that each gave to their people. Islam is a middle way both in matters of doctrine as well as religious law and morality. Islam is not as lax as the Christian religion nor as rigid as Judaism. The *Ahl al-Sunnah* from amongst the Muslims are, furthermore, on the middle path in comparison to other sects within Islam.[14]

---

[12]*Jawāb Risālat Ahl Jazīrat Qubrus,* Ms. Utrecht: Cod. Mss. Oriental 40.

[13]*Al-Jawāb al-Ṣahīḥ liman Baddala Dīn al-Masīḥ* (Cairo, 1964).

[14]*Al-Jawāb,* 1, pp. 1-9.

Ibn Taymīyah then mentions the occasion of the writing of *al-Jawāb*: how he received a copy of a letter written by Paul of Antioch which put together many arguments against Islam that are often repeated by Christian scholars. He explains that it is also widely circulated and that many old copies of it are available, and then he summarizes the letter in six points.

To answer these points, he first quotes the exact words of Paul and then offers his own comments. He will show, he says, that Christians have no correct rational or scriptural foundation for their beliefs. The Gospels as well as other scriptures contradict their doctrines.[15] He then goes on to treat each of the six points as follows:

Universality of Muḥammad[16]

The question as to whether the message of Prophet Muḥammad is for the whole mankind or for Arabs only occupies Ibn Taymīyah for a long time. He devotes almost 200 pages of his book to answering this question. Paul's argument had been that the message was meant for Arabs only, because the divine Word, al-Qur'ān, was given to Muḥammad in Arabic and also because the Qur'ān itself claimed that Muḥammad was sent among the Arabs (Sura 2.151; 3.164).

Ibn Taymīyah in his answer first makes an epistemological observation. He says that the question of the truth of any claimant to prophethood should precde the question of the universality or non-universality of his mission. Therefore the first question to be settled is whether or not Muḥammad was a true prophet. If one accepts that he was truthful in his claim to prophethood then one must also believe in all his statements. The authentic words of Muḥammad, his own deeds and the deeds of his companions and caliphs prove that Muḥammad's mission included the whole of mankind: Jews, Christians, and Gentiles. Ibn Taymīyah then narrates historical examples of the Prophet's contacts with Jews and Christians and his preaching to them.[17] He

---

[15]Ibid. pp. 19-26.

[16]Ibid. pp. 26-229.

[17]He mentions the Christian delegation that the Prophet received in the year 10 of Hijrah in Madinah from Najran. Also the Negus of Abyssinia accepted Islam. Waraqahb Nawfal recognized his prophethood, and a group of Christians came to him after the migration to Abyssinia and accepted Islam. The Prophet also sent letters to kings and rulers, among them Heraklios of Byzantium and the Muqauqas of Egypt, who were Christians; see *Al-Jawāb*, 1, pp. 65-101.

quotes other Qur'ānic verses that speak about the universality of his mission (Sura 7.158), 34.28). Ibn Taymīyah then discusses in detail the verses of the Qur'ān that are mentioned by Paul and argues, giving supporting evidence from the life of the Prophet himself, that there is no contradiction between Muḥammad's mission to Arabs and his mission to mankind at large.

Finally he tries to answer those from among the Christians who do not regard Muḥammad as the prophet of God and deny his mission even to Arabs. It is rationally impossible he says to accept Moses and Jesus as prophets of God and not to accept Muḥammad as his prophet. Whatever evidence there is to prove the truth of any prophet is enough to prove the truth of Muḥammad's prophethood and the doubts that one may raise against him could be equally strongly raised against the prophethood of any other prophet.[18]

Concerning the argument that because the Qur'ān is in Arabic it must be for the Arabs only, Ibn Taymīyah says that all religious books were revealed in some particular language. Translation is, however, allowed for the sake of those who do not understand the Arabic language.[19] Because of the Qur'ān the Arabic language has become a universal language. As the disciples of Jesus went with the gift of many languages to other nations, so were the messengers of the Prophet Muḥammad. He sent them with his letters to kings and rulers, and each one of them spoke the language of the people to whom he was sent.[20] To those who might claim that the Gospels were translated by apostles who were infallible,[21] while the Qur'ān

---

[18]Ibid. pp. 166-88.

[19]Ibid. p. 190. This is rather noteworthy and shows that in spite of his belief in the inimitability (*i'jāz*) of the Qur'ān and the superiority of its language, he did not forbid the translation of the Qur'ān. See a good study on this subject but without reference to Ibn Taymīyah's views, A. L. Tibawi, "Is the Qur'ān Translatable?" *Muslim World* 52 (1962) 4-16.

[20]Ibid. 1, p. 193.

[21]This claim is not made by Paul of Antioch but it was probably a popular argument since it was common belief among Christians at this time that the Apostles of Jesus made translations of the Gospels in all languages of the earth. About Ibn 'Assāl, D. R. McDonald writes, "He seems to have had no doubt in his mind that the Coptic was an original text; Coptic, Greek, and Syriac were all on one footing. They all emanated apparently from the Apostles," "Ibn al-'Assāl's Arabic Version of the Gospels," in D. Eduardo Saaverdo, ed., *Festschrigh D. Francisco Codera* (Zaragoza, 1904), p. 375.

was translated by common and infallible people, he answers that first of all the disciples of Jesus did not translate the Gospels into all languages of the earth. There exists, for example, no Arabic translation of the Gospels prepared by any one of the apostles. Further, the work of translation does not require infallible people and, moreover, the disciples of Jesus were not infallible.

Paul had argued that since the prophets had already come before Muḥammad and given them (the Christians) the Torah and the Gospels in their own language, it was not necessary for Christians to follow Muḥammad. Ibn Taymīyah answers that the advent of one prophet does not negate the advent of another. Among the Israelites a number of prophets used to come. Also not all Christians have received their scriptures in their own languages. Furthermore there are many innovations and alterations in their holy books. He himself has found, he says, many discrepancies and differences among various versions of the Bible in Arabic.

Paul had remarked that it was against the justice of God to command people to follow someone whose language they do not understand. Ibn Taymīyah replies that Paul of Antioch himself knows Arabic and understands the Qur'ān. Since there are many who are learning the Arabic language today in order to read books on other technical subjects, why can they not learn Arabic in order to read the Qur'ān as well?

The Qur'ān and the Christian Religion[22]

Answering Paul's argument that since the Qur'ān praises the Christian religion it means that Christians are not addressed by Islam and need not be converted to Islam. Ibn Taymīyah answers that the Qur'ān has certainly praised Christ, his mother, and his true followers, and in this sense Muslims follow the middle path between Jews and Christians. They neither reject Christ as Jews do nor do they deify him as do the Christians. He mentions the story of the birth of Jesus as it occurs in Sura 19 and gives a brief interpretation of some verses explaining the meaning of such words as *rūḥ* (spirit) and *ibn* (son).

But going back to Paul's argument, he says Christ also praised the Torah, even more than Prophet Muḥammad praised the Gospels, but Christians believed that Jews still had to follow Christ and would not say that since he had praised their scripture they were no longer

---

[22]*Al-Jawāb*, 1, p. 229-2, p. 90.

required to believe in him. Similarly, Christians cannot base their argument in this matter upon Muḥammad's praise of the Gospels.[23]

Here he also discusses the important question of the salvation of those who do not accept the Prophet. Will they be punished in Hell? He elaborates his answer to this question in the light of the Qur'ān and criticizes some earlier Muslim theologians who, he believes, held incorrect views. His general position is that no one will be punished unless, after knowing the truth, one resists it in obstinacy (*'inād*).[24]

Ibn Taymīyah believes that Christians are in error and Prophet Muḥammad did not praise them in their errors. Explaining the reasons for Christian errors, he says that they followed ambigious and difficult statements that came to them from their prophets and did not adhere to clear and straightforward teachings. Certain extraordinary things they saw and believed to be miracles (*āyāt*) though in reality they were just demonic tricks. Moreover certain false reports reached them which they believed to be true. Ibn Taymīyah believes that the stories of the resurrection of Jesus and his appearance to disciples were of this later sort. It was the devil, he says, who appeared to them and claimed that he was Christ. "This type of thing," he says, "happens in our own days. In Tadmur some people saw a giant flying in the air who appeared to them several times in different costumes and told them, 'I am Jesus, son of Mary' and asked them to do things which Jesus would never ask them to do." Such stories, he says, are frequently mentioned in countries where people practice polytheism (*shirk*) such as India. There are some people who claim that they have seen their shaykh appear to them and he has helped them. Such a report also reached Ibn Taymīyah about himself. Someone came to him and told him that he had been in trouble and sought Ibn Taymīyah's help in a distant place, whereupon Ibn Taymīyah appeared to him and helped him. Ibn Taymīyah says, "When he related this to me I told him that I did not help you but it must have been a devil who appeared to you in my image to lead you astray because you committed *shirk* when you sought the help of someone other than God."[25] Ibn Taymīyah agrees that to see someone in a dream is possible, but says that to see someone in the

---

[23]Ibid. 1, p. 275.

[24]Ibid. pp. 309-13.

[25]Ibid. pp. 319-20.

of wakefulness while he is dead or actually absent is impossible because a body cannot be in two places at the same time.

Ibn Taymīyah turns then to Christian scriptures and says that the Gospels were not written by Jesus, something that Christians themselves admit. The *taḥrīf* (alteration or change) took place mainly in the interpretation; as the different councils met they gradually altered the meanings. Thus Christian doctrines are not based upon the Gospels but upon incorrect interpretation. The present Gospels, however, do not represent the Gospel that was the word of God revealed to Jesus Christ, although they do contain some parts of it.[26]

On Christian Doctrines[27]

In this section, Ibn Taymīyah critically examines several Christian doctrines and criticizes the rational methodology of Paul of Antioch. Paul, in his defense of the terms such as Father, Son, and Holy Spirit, had explained that Christians had used these "names" only to say that God was substance (*shay'*), living (*ḥayy*) and rational (*nāṭiq*). Ibn Taymīyah argues that instead of beginning with rational justification for the Trinity, Paul should have presented the scriptural proofs. It is not that Christians want to say that God is substance, living, and rational, and so they say that he is Father, Son, and Holy Spirit, but rather they claim that their scriptures have used these "names" for God. They, however, differ among themselves in the interpretation of these names.

Ibn Taymīyah does not believe that Christian doctrines can be proved from the Bible. He emphasizes that one must examine three things before accepting anything on the authority of the prophets (or scriptures). If transmitters are known, then one must determine the authenticity of the transmission (*isnād*). If the statement is translated from one language to another, as in the case of the Gospels, then one must confirm the soundness of the translation. Finally, in interpretation one must make sure whether they (the prophets) really intended the meaning that one is giving to their words.[28]

Ibn Taymīyah demands that these three premises should be established. He himself, however, without discussing the first two points of transmission and translation, goes directly into the problem of

[26]Ibid. p. 368.
[27]Ibid. 2, p. 90-3, p. 137.
[28]Ibid. 2, p. 122.

interpretation. Thus such words as *uqnūm* (hypostasis) and *tathlīth* (trinity), etc. are rejected because they do not occur in the Gospels and their interpretation is not justified. Words that indicate *ḥulūl* (indwelling) are found in the Gospels, but they can also be interpreted in different ways. Ibn Taymīyah discusses at length the meaning of the word *ḥulūl* and also mentions its different usages among the Sūfīs. The doctrine of the two natures of Christ is then discussed at length and Ibn Taymīyah takes note of differences among the three main sects of Christianity, namely, the Melkites, Jacobites, and Nestorians. In order to criticize these sects he makes extensive use of the letter of Ḥasan b. Ayyūb, a Christian convert to Islam who had criticized the theological positions of the three main sects of Christianity, saying that ecumenical church councils had contributed to the alteration of the religion of Christ. Ibn Taymīyah quotes almost the whole letter of Ḥasan b. Ayyūb.

In his references to Christian history, he relies upon the work of the Melkite historian Eutychius Sa'īd b. al-Biṭrīq. It is interesting to note that in his arguments against the Jacobites and Nestorians, he uses Ibn al-Biṭrīq's criticism of these two sects. Similarly in his criticism of the Melkites, he uses some non-Melkite sources such as Ḥasan b. Ayyūb, who was probably a Nestorian before his conversion to Islam.

The Trinity and the Attributes[29]

The question of the similarities and differences between the Muslim doctrines of divine attributes and the Christian doctrine of the divine Trinity is discussed at some length. Ibn Taymīyah reiterates his position that the doctrine of the Trinity is not based upon the Gospels. He says that there is no quarrel with a person who accepts what is brought by the prophets. The words like *uqnūm* and *tathlīth* are not found in the vocabulary of Jesus. Divine attributes are the same in the Qur'ān and the Bible.

Ibn Taymīyah believes that the biblical concept of God is similar to that of the Qur'ān because the source of both of them is God.[30] Discussing the baptismal formula in Matthew (28.19), he says that it cannot mean what it is taken to mean in Christian theology. The word "son" is never used in the Bible for a non-created being and

---

[29]Ibid. 3, pp. 137-228.
[30]Ibid. p. 146.

"spirit" (*rūḥ*) does not mean "life" (*ḥayāt*).

Discussing in detail the meaning of each word, "Father," "Son," and "Holy Spirit," he says that knowledge of the prophets' language and understanding of their words in the light of their own meaning is obligatory. Doing otherwise will lead to alteration (*taḥrīf*). The same mistake was committed by the monists (*ittihādiyūn*) from amongst the Ṣūfīs, such as Ibn 'Arabī and his followers.

Explaining the Muslim position on the names of God (*asmā' Allāh*), he says that Muslims speak in two ways. Some use only those names that are mentioned in the Qur'ān, while others say that whatever name is linguistically correct and the meaning of which is acceptable in *Sharī'a* can be used. Ibn Taymīyah's own position is that the names and attributes that are not mentioned in the Qur'ān are allowed to be used in speaking about God; but in praying to him only the Qur'ānic names and attributes should be employed.

The Nature of Islam, Judaism, and Christianity[31]

Paul of Antioch, in speaking about Judaism and Christianity, said that the teachings of Moses were based upon justice ('*adl*) but the teachings of Jesus were based upon charity[32] (*faḍl*) and there is nothing greater than charity which might be expected from the teachings of Muḥammad. Ibn Taymīyah accepts Paul's general characterization of Mosaic laws as well as Jesus' ethical teachings, but says that even in the laws of Moses there were exhortations to perform charitable acts. Islam, however, is the perfect religion because it combines both: it commands whatever is just ('*adl*) and recommends (*mandūb*) whatever is charitable (*faḍl*). Here he also makes some comparisons among the teachings of the three religions. About Christians he says that they are not following the Gospels but the canons of their elders.

Finally, Ibn Taymīyah takes up the question of prophecies about Muḥammad in other scriptures and his miracles. He says that Christians have a well-known objection to Islam. They claim that the Prophet Muḥammad's advent was never foretold in previous scriptures while there are many prophecies about the advent of Christ. Christians

---

[31]Ibid. pp. 229-74.

[32]The word "charity" is used here more in the Latin sense of *caritas*. Apparently Paul could have used the word "*hubb*" also but he preferred "*faḍl*," probably to rhyme with " '*adl*."

make this charge on the assumption that unless a person is foretold by other prophets, he cannot be considered a true prophet. It is not necessary for a prophet to be foretold by others. Many prophets before Muḥammad were not foretold, such Abraham, Noah, and most of the prophets who came among the Children of Israel. However, the prophecies concerning Muḥammad do exist in the Torah and the Gospels. To prove this he produces a sizeable collection of these quotations from the Old and New Testament.[33] The rest of the work is then devoted to the discussion of the miracles of Muḥammad and the proofs of his prophethood.

Ibn Taymīyah is often called by historians a very strong-headed person and a harsh critic of his opponents, but in *al-Jawāb*[34] he comes out very irenic and gentle, nonetheless persuasive, insightful and intelligent. Ibn Taymīyah sees both the Islamic and Christian traditions as stemming from the same source and hence susceptible to similar interpretations. Christians, he argues, have forsaken the prophetic source and foundation of their faith and adulterated the teachings of Jesus by introducing many alien elements which are either contrary to his teachings or inconsistent with them. In his critical examination of the Christian tradition, he tries further to identify the true message of Jesus Christ and in this he invariably reaches the conclusion that the message of Jesus was the same as the message of Muḥammad. He ends his long response with the Hadith:

Abu Harairah reports from the Prophet that he said, "We, the community of Prophets, have one religion" (*innā ma'āshir al-anbiyā' dīnūnā waḥid*).

It is not incorrect to say that Christian Islamic debates and dialogues generally revolve around these subjects. Sometimes the parties are gentle and irenic and sometimes harsh. It is the nature of these two traditions; both have scriptural claims, both have universal missions, both have similarities and differences. Dialogue requires understanding of both. I appreciate this opportunity to present these approaches so that we may learn from them and improve upon them.

---

[33]*Al-Jawāb*, 3, p. 281-4, p. 21.

[34]*Al-Jawāb*, 4, p. 323.

What an Infidel Saw that a Faithful Did Not: Gregory Dekapolites (d. 842) and Islam

DANIEL J. SAHAS

IN HIS PRESENTATION Professor Haddad spoke about the cultural unity of Islam and Eastern Orthodox Christianity, as well as of the mutuality of questions and answers given by men of faith in the two religious traditions. Professor Nasr spoke eloquently about the spiritual affinity of the two traditions as these are manifested in the Ṣūfī and the monastic traditions respectively. To these two spheres of "dialogue" I want to add the worship and liturgical experience, which the Christian East sees as a vital and dynamic forum in which men of faith can meet in a unique encounter; an experience which they can cultivate as a unique dimension and component of a true inter-faith dialogue.

The particular text I have in mind seems also to combine and reinforce the elements which Professors Haddad and Nasr have presented to us.

In Migne's *Patrologia Greaca* there is a rather brief "Historical Sermon" attributed to Saint Gregory of Dekapolis, under the long title: "'A Historical Sermon by Gregory Dekapolites; Very Profitable and Most Pleasing in Many Ways, About a Vision Which a Sarracen Once Had, and Who, As a Result of This, Believed and Became Martyr for Our Lord Jesus Christ."[1] Ferdinandus Cavallera has indexed this sermon under the patristic and Byzantine polemic literature against Islam.[2] However, modern scholars of the Byzantine anti-Islamic

---

[1] PG 100.1201-12.
[2] Ibid. 162.129.

literature have bypassed it.[3] Strictly speaking, this is an hagiological
text which describes the conversion of a Muslim prince to Christianity,
indeed to monastic life, and his subsequent death as a martyr of the
Christian faith. The Muslim convert after his conversion to Christianity and his entrance into the monastic order assumed the name
Pachomios, a common name among monks in the Christian East, after
the founder of the cenobitic monasticism.

An introductory invocation ("Father, give your blessing") and
a supplicatory ending ("With the prayers of the most blessed martyr
and of the all-pure Mother of God Mary who is ever-virgin, and of
all the saints, for the remission of our sins. Amen.") betray a text
which has survived as a lection, usually read during meals in the re-
fectories of cenobitic monasteries in the Orthodox world.

However, beyond the exact purpose and character of the narrative and even if this was not the intention of its writer, the story has succeeded in providing us with insights and information about Muslim-
Christian relations in the eight/ninth century.

The author of this sermon, as the title indicates, is Gregory Dekapolites. Information about Gregory we obtain mainly from a *Life* composed by Ignatios (b. ca. 780), "deacon and sacristan of the Great
Church of God," that is, of the see of Constantinople, who became
later a professor of rhetoric and poetry at the patriarchal school of
Hagia Sophia, and from 845, bishop of Nicaea.[4] Ignatios lived
during the second phase of the Iconoclastic controversy (787-843);

---

[3]Adel-Théodore Khoury, for example, following H.-G. Beck (*Kirche und
theologische Literatur im byzantinischen Reich* [Munich, 1959], p. 579) suggests simply that "Le récit attribué au Decapolite, outre qu'il appartient
au genre hagiographique et donc ne fait pas partie des textes qui nous in-
téressent directement ici, doit être daté du XIVe siècle environ" *Les théo-
logiens byzantins et l'Islam. Textes et auteurs (VIIIe-XIIIe S.)* (Louvain,
1969) p. 46. While the text is definitely hagiological, it is not, because of
this, irrelevant to Muslim-Christian relations. The assumption also that it
dates from the fourteenth century can easily be questioned, on the basis
of a number of internal indications, as the subsequent analysis of the text
will show.

[4]F. Dvornik, *La vie de saint Grégoire le Decapolite et les Slaves Macédo-
niens au IXe siècle* (Travaux publiés par l'Institut d' études slaves No. 5,
Paris, 1926); Greek text of the *Life*, pp. 45-75. Dvornik has edited the *Life*
from eight manuscripts, three of them of the twelfth, one of the thirteenth,
two of the fourteenth, one of the sixteenth and one of the seventeenth
century!

other iconophile personalities,[5] his own teacher Tarasios, patriarch of Constantinople from 784 to 806[6] and Nikephoros, patriarch of Constantinople from 806 to 815.[7] Ignatios' choice to write the *Lives* of these three men betrays his sympathy towards the moderate iconophiles, rather than the more "intransigent" monks of the monastery of Studios in Constantinople. The latter advocated a total segregation between Church and State, and opposed hesychastically inclined monks such as Gregory.[8]

Gregory was born in Irenopolis, one of the ten cities (*deka poleis*) which composed the complex of Dekapolis of Isauria in Interior Syria and Jordan.[9] Thence his surname Dekapolites. He was born between 780-790[10] and possibly later.[11] The only firm date of his life is that of his death on 20 November 842.[12] Early in his life Gregory left home for the ascetic and contemplative life of the monastery. After a number of years, spent either in monasteries or in solitude as a hermit, he felt the need to embark on a missionary expedition, defending the iconophiles and the veneration of icons, and healing people. His long travels took him to Ephesos, Prokonessos, Ainos, Christopolis (Kavala), Thessalonike, Corinth, Region, Neapolis, Rome, Syracuse,

---

[5]I. E. Karagiannopoulos, *Πηγαὶ τῆς Βυζαντινῆς Ἱστορίας*, 4th ed. (Thessalonike, 1978), pp. 228-29.

[6]I. A. Heikel, ed. *Ignatii diaconi Vita Tarasii archiepiscopi Constantinopolitani.* Acta Societatis Scientiarum Fennicae, 17 (Helsingfors, 1891); also, PG 98.1385-1424.

[7]Carolus de Boor, *Nicephori opuscula historica* (Leipzig, 1889); PG 100.41-160.

[8]Cf. Dvornik, *La Vie*, p. 17ff.

[9]The other nine cities were Germanicopolis, Titiopolis, Dometiopolis, Zenopolis, Neapolis, Claudiopolis, Caesarea, Lauzados and Dalisandis. Constantine Porphyrogenitos, *De thematibus libri duo* (ed. I. Bekker, Bonn, 1840), 1, p. 36.

[10]H. G. (Henri Grégoire) in his review of Dvornik's *La vie*, in *Byzantion* 7 (1932) 642.

[11]The *Life* states that Gregory died "at a mature age as far as the spiritual and perfect exercise is concerned." Dvornik, *La vie*, p. 72, 1.10-11. This wording may imply that he died at a relatively young physical age. Indeed, according to the *Life*, Gregory died after a serious and painful disease. Ibid. p. 70, 1.12-16.

[12]This specific date is stated in the Life of Joseph the hymnographer [H. G. in *Byzantion* 7 (1932) 643], and corroborated by the evidence in Gregory's *Life.* Dvornik, *La vie*, p. 72; 1.9

Ontranto, Thessalonike again, and Constantinople. Gregory's public life coincides with the reign of Emperor Theophilos (829-842) during which time Iconoclasm was raging again.

The *Life* of Gregory Dekapolites is an hagiological account, embellished with numerous miraculous acts, something which reflects mainly the interests of its author, Ignatios. Nevertheless, it constitutes a source of information on the state of Iconoclasm during its second phase (787-843), and on the Slavs in the area of Thessalonike. Some Byzantine-Arab relations are mentioned only marginally. Actually the *Life* mentions only one incident involving Muslim Arabs: Gregory, as he was leaving Otranto, Italy, encountered a unit of Saracen soldiers. When one of them raised his hand to kill Gregory with a spear, the soldier's hand instantly became stiff. Gregory healed his offender by touching the former's afflicted hand.[13] Yet, the entire *Sermon* attributed to Gregory—possibly his only extant writing—is an account of a Muslim-Christian encounter. Ignatios mentions no writings by Gregory Dekapolites, not even this historical sermon which explicitly bears his name. However this omission, by itself, ought not to be taken as sufficient proof that the writing is not by Gregory Dekapolites.

The *Sermon* is based on a story which, as the text claims, was related to Gregory by a certain *strategos*[14] Nicholas. The incident took place in the strategos' own town of Al-Kurūm[15] in the Thebaid, lower Egypt. Here is the text:

A HISTORICAL SPEECH OF GREGORY DEKAPOLITES, VERY PROFITABLE AND MOST PLEASING IN MANY WAYS, ABOUT A VISION WHICH A SARRACEN ONCE HAD, AND WHO, AS A RESULT OF THIS, BELIEVED AND BECAME A MARTYR FOR OUR LORD JESUS CHRIST.

[1201A] Father, give your blessing.

Nicholas the *strategos,* called Joulas, has related to me that in

---

[13]Dvornik, *La vie,* p. 58; 1.15-9.

[14]A Byzantine high military official in charge of administration of a *thema,* or large territory or province.

[15]The Arabic name of the town means "vineyard," and Gregory has translated it in Greek as *Ampelos.*

his town, which the Sarracens[16] call in their language "Vineyard", the Emir[17] of Syria sent his nephew to administer some works

[16]The name "Sarracen" (actually, Saracen) is used here meaning "Muslim." It occurs frequently in Byzantine literature. Philip K. Hitti has suggested that the name derives from the Arabic *sharq* and sharqīyūn (East, and Easterners) and refers to the land and the tribes east of Palestine (*History of the Arabs* [10th ed., New York, 1973, p. 43.]). Other evidence, which I am presently examining, suggest that the use of the name "Saracen" contained also derogatory connotations, for Easterners, who were living far away from the main centers of civilization and who were led astray from accepted religious beliefs and practices. After the emergence of Islam the name "Saracen" in the Byzantine anti-Islamic literature was used with the meaning of "Muslim." John of Damascus is perhaps the earliest Byzantine writer who attempted to give an etymological explanation, and a polemic one, to the name. Such an explanation required a change in the spelling from Saracen to Sarracen. John of Damascus suggested that "Saracen" derives from the name Sarrah and the adjective κενός (empty) and as such it applies to "those who were expelled by Sarah empty," without grace; that is to the *illegitimate* sons of Abraham. A synonym for Sarracens used by Muslims according to John of Damascus, is the name Hagarenes (the sons of Hagar, Abraham's concubine, rather than a legitimate wife) and Ishmaelites (the descendants of Ishmael, the illegitimate son of Abraham)! John of Damascus, *On the Heresies,* in *Die Schriften des Johannes von Damaskos,* P. Bonifatius Kotter (Berlin, 1981), 4, p. 60. See also Daniel, J. Sahas, *John of Damascus on Islam, the "Heresy of the Ishmaelites"* (Leiden, 1972), pp. 70-71. V. Christides has missed all this evidence when he concludes that "a Byzantine explanation of the origin of Saracen which has escaped the attention of modern scholars is found in the writings of the fifthteenth-century Byzantine author Georgios Phrantzes who asserts that the Arabs were called *Sarakenoi* because they were sent out by Sarah devoid of inheritance and empty-handed"; see "The names Ἄραβες, Σαρακηνοί etc. and their false Byzantine etymologies," *Byzantinische Zeitschrift* 65 (1972) 329-33, at 331.

[17]The word used here is Ἀμερουμνής, an obvious Hellenization of the Arabic title *Amīr al-mu'minīn,* "Ruler of the Faithful". The first to assume this title was 'Umar, the second caliph (634-644). Other Umayyad and subsequently Abbasid caliphs followed his example, as did some rival smaller rulers. The title was assumed more frequently by rulers in the West. Since the text specifically calls this *amīr al-mu'minīn* "Emir of Syria," the reference must be to one of the Umayyad caliphs ruling from Damascus from 661 to 750. The Hellenized title Ἀμερουμνής occurs also in the writing of Arethas of Caesarea (850-932): "To the Emir in Damascus at the request of Romanos the Emperor"; *Arethae Archiepiscopi Caesariensis. Scripta Minora,* ed. L. G. Westerink (Leipzig, 1968), 1, p. 242. On Arethas, see Daniel J. Sahas "Arethas's 'Letter to the Emir at Damascus': Official or popular views on Islam in the 10th century Byzantium?" *The Patristic and Byzantine Review* 3 (1984) 69-81.

under construction in the said castle. In that place there is also a big church, old and splendid, dedicated to Saint, the most glorious martyr, George.[18] When the Sarracen saw the church from a distance he ordered his servants to bring his belongings and the camels themselves, twelve of them, inside the church so that he may be able to supervise them from a high place as they were fed.[19]

[1201B] As for the priests of that venerable church, they pleaded with him saying: "Master, do not do such things; this is a church of God. Do not show disrespect towards it and do not bring the camels inside the holy altar of God." But the Sarracen, who was pitiless and stubborn, did not want even to listen to the pleas of the presbyters. Instead he said to his servants, in Arabic: "Do you not do what you have been commanded to do?" Immediately his servants did as he commanded them. But suddenly the camels, as they were led into the church, all, by the command of God, fell down

---

[18]The affection of Muslims for Saint George is very interesting, although not yet thoroughly explained. The Muslim Arabs of the Middle East, especially those who have lived in co-existence with Orthodox Christians, have shown a remarkable reverence for Saint George, the military saint, who is depicted riding a horse and killing the dragon. Perhaps the link between the Muslims and Saint George is Abyssinian Christianity. This pre-Chalcedonian Coptic Church with its many Jewish and Semitic practices (arks, circumcision, observance of the Sabbath, claims of its emperors as being "sons of David and Solomon," etc.) respects Saint George as its patron saint. Ancient texts indicate that the Ethiopians were partly under Mosaic law and in part they worshiped the Serpent. No wonder, therefore, that Saint George is a patron saint of Ethiopia; Ninian Smart, *The Phenomenon of Christianity* (London, 1979), p. 60. The encounter of Islam with Abyssinia goes back to the time of Muhammad himself. *The Life of Muhammad* (A translation of Ishāq's *Sīrat Rasūl Allāh,* by A. Guillaume [Oxford, 1969]), pp. 146-55. Heroes who defeat superhuman creatures and evil powers seem to have attracted people of various cultures and religious traditions. There is such a hero also in Islam, Abū Zayd, known as Bu Zīd il-Hilāli in Zafar and North Arabia. The Muslim fascination with him is because he defeated a huge monster, plaguing the country, whom no one else had managed to contain. For the text of this story with an introduction and commentary, see T. M. Johnstone, "A St. George of Dhofar" *Arabian Studies,* 5 (1978) 59-65.

[19]The description suggests that the church, being big and spendid, had a balcony usually reserved for women, which the Emir occupied for his private quarters, while he had planned to use the nave as a stable for the camels.

dead.[20] When the Sarracen saw the extraordinary miracle he became ecstatic[21] and ordered his servants to take away the dead camels and throw them away from the church; and they did so.

[1201C] As it was a holiday on that day and the time for the Divine Liturgy was approaching, the priest who was to start the holy service of the preparation of the gifts was very much afraid of the Sarracen; how could he start the bloodless sacrifice in front of him! Another priest, co-communicant to him, said to the priest who was to celebrate the Liturgy: "Do not be afraid. Did you not see the extraordinary miracle? Why are you hesitant?" Thus the said priest, without fear, started the holy service of offering.[22]

The Sarracen noticed all these and waited to see what the priest

---

[20]Theophanes the Chronographer (d. 818) mentions a similar case in which "the camels of the chief minister were burned in the church of Saint Elijah; *Chronographia*, ed. De Boor, 1, 404.14-15. This incident reportedly took place in Caesarea, Cappadocia in the second year of Hisham's reign, i.e. in 726. Do these similar reports by two independent sources suggest a usual Muslim practice? They perhaps suggest a more hostile attitude toward and treament of the Christians by the Muslims, uncharacteristic of the earliest Umayyad caliphs. Hishām was the son of 'Abd-al-Malik (684-705), the caliph who initiated hostile measures against the Christians under his rule.

[21]The expression "to become, or be ecstatic" occurs frequently and characteristically in this text. It is an expression of a mystical disposition, rather than of an ordinary way of speaking. *"Ecstasy,"* etymologically speaking, is the state of being in which a person is removed from (ἐκ) the place on which one "stands" (στάσις), to a different state, or "world." It is the state of being transcendent from the empirical world to a higher level of consciousness and spirituality. Ecstasy is the state which a mystic strives to attain in his process towards a union with God. Frequency of such expressions and the theme itself of the sermon, which is about a vision, manifest clearly the mystical character of the text. Ecstasy and "ecstatic utterances" (*shaṭḥiyāt*) are also ingredients of Islamic mysticism, documented and defended by the theorists of Sufism. See, for example, the *Kitāb al-Luma'* of *Abū Naṣr al-Sarrāj* (d. 988); A. J. Arberry, *Sufism: An Account of the Mystics of Islam* (New York, 1970), p. 67.

[22]This service is called προσκομιδὴ literally meaning "offering" of the gifts. It is the service prior to the divine Liturgy itself and to the communion service, during which the gifts for the communion are received and prepared. The rites of the προσκομιδή commemorate the nativity of Christ, "who, from the first moment of his incarnation, was the Lamb destined to be sacrificed for the sons of men"; D. Sokolof, *A Manual of the Orthodox Church's Divine Services* (Jordanville, N.Y., 1962), p. 62. The subsequent vision of the Saracen seems to support this meaning of the προσκομιδή.

The Sarracen noticed all these and waited to see what the priest [1204A] was going to do. The priest began the holy service of offering and took the loaf of bread to prepare the holy sacrifice. But the Sarracen saw that the priest took in his hand a child which he slaughtered, drained the blood inside the cup, cut the body into pieces and placed them on the tray![23]

As the Sarracen saw these things he became furious with anger and, enraged at the priest, he wanted to kill him. When the time of the Great Entrance approached, the Sarracen saw again, and more manifestly, the child cut into four pieces on the tray, his blood in the cup. He became again ecstatic with rage. Towards the end of the Divine Liturgy, as some of the Christians wanted to receive [1204B] the holy communion and as the priest said, "With the fear of God and with faith draw near,"[24] all the Christians bent their

---

[23]The priest extracts from a loaf of bread small pieces and particles. These various pieces represent Christ himself, the Theotokos, the angels, the apostles, the martyrs, the saints, the living members of the Church and those who have passed away. These pieces of bread are subsequently mixed in the chalice with the wine, consecrated during the Liturgy and offered as communion. Thus, communion in the Orthodox Church is a sacrament of an existential union between each individual and the entire Church, visible and invisible, past and present, within the body of Christ.

The προσκομιδή rites commemorate the Nativity. See note above. The eucharistic service also, in spite of its predominant paschal character, is closely related to the Nativity as well. John Chrysostom, the modifier of the Divine Liturgy, which is the most often celebrated one in the Orthodox Church, has identified frequently the altar with a spiritual cradle, and the Eucharist with a memorial of Christ's passion but also with his infancy; thus, the existence of a number of parallel edifying anecdotes and sermons such as this, presenting Christ as an infant being sacrificed physically in the place of elements. For such references, see Christopher Walter, *Art and Ritual of the Byzantine Church* (London, 1982), pp. 209-10.

The tradition of the Christ child standing out from inside the chalice, before dismemberment, surrounded by angels and the Fathers-authors of the Divine Liturgy, has been preserved by the iconography in the theme of *Melismos* (literally, dismemberment). Such an icon can be seen, for example, in a fresco in the niche of the sanctuary in the abbot's tower at the Monastery of Saint Panteleimon in Thessaly, Greece. See John T. A. Koumoulides, *Byzantine and Post-Byzantine Monuments at Aghia in Thessaly, Greece: The Art and Architecture of the Monastery of Saint Panteleimon* (London, 1975), pp. 35 and 36, fig. 15 and 15a.

[24]The full liturgical invitation to receive communion is: "With the fear of God, with faith, and with love, draw near."

heads in reverence. Some of them went forward to receive the holy sacrament. Again, for a third time, the Sarracen saw that the priest, with a spoon, was offering to the communicants from the body and the blood of the child. The repentant Christians received the holy sacrament. But the Sarracen saw that they had received communion from the body and the blood of the child, and at that he became filled with anger and rage against everybody.

At the end of the Divine Liturgy the priest distributed the antidoron, to all Christians.[25] He then took off his priestly vestments and offered to the Sarracen a piece from the bread.[26] But he said, [1204C] in Arabic: "What is this?" The priest answered: "Master, it is from the bread from which we celebrated the liturgy." And the Sarracen said angrily: "Did you celebrate the Liturgy from that, you dog, impure, dirty, and killer? Didn't I see that you took and slaughtered a child, and that you poured his blood into the cup, and mutilated his body and placed on the plate members of his, here and there? Didn't I see all these, you polluted one and killer? Didn't I see you eating and drinking from the body and blood of the child, and that you even offered the same to the attendants? They now have in their mouths pieces of flesh dripping blood."

When the priest heard this he became ecstatic and said: "Master, [1204D] I am a sinner and I am not able to see such a mystery. But since your Lordship saw such a mystery I believe in God that you, indeed, are a great man."

And the Sarracen said: "Is this not what I saw?" And the priest: "Yes, my Lord, this is how it is; but myself, being a sinner, I am not able to see such a mystery, but only bread and wine. Indeed, we believe we hold and we sacrifice this bread and wine as a figuration of the body and blood of our Lord Jesus Christ. Thus, even

---

[25]Ἀντίδωρον means that which is offered "instead of the gift." These are small pieces of bread of the non-consecrated part of the loaf, which the priest distributes, at the end of the Liturgy, to those who for whatever reason did not receive the sacrament. The ἀντίδωρον is not a substitute for the communion, but a pastoral gesture of the Church acknowledging and, in a way, rewarding, the presence of everybody in the celebration of the Eucharist.

[26]This detail ("he took off his priestly vestments and offered . . .") clarifies the distinction that the Orthodox Church makes between partaking in communion with members of the one Church, and participating in a religious service or prayer with members from different churches; even with people from different religious traditions!

the great and marvelous Fathers, the stars and teachers of the
[1205A] Church, like the divine Basil the Great, and the memorable
Chrysostom and Gregory the Theologian, were unable to see this
awesome and terrifying mystery. How can I see it?"

When the Sarracen heard this he became ecstatic and he ordered
his servants and everybody who was inside to leave the church.
He then took the priest by the hand and said: "As I see and as I
have heard, great is the faith of the Christians. So, if you so will,
Father, baptize me." And the priest said to the Sarracen: "Master,
we believe in and we confess our Lord Jesus Christ, the Son of
God, who came to the world for our salvation. We also believe in
[1205B] the Holy Trinity, the consubstantial and undivided one,
Father, Son, and Holy Spirit, the one Godhead. We believe also in
Mary, the ever-virgin mother of light, who has given birth to the
fruit of life, our pre-announced Lord, Jesus Christ. She was virgin
before, virgin during, and virgin after giving birth. We believe also
that all the holy apostles, prophets, martyrs, saints, and righteous
men are servants of God. Do you not realize, therefore, my master,
that the greatest faith is that of the Orthodox Christians?"

And the Sarracen said again: "I beg you, Father, baptize me."
But the priest answered: "Far from that. I cannot do such a thing;
for if I do and your nephew[27] the Emir hears of that, he will kill
[1205C] me and destroy this church, too.[28] But if it is, indeed,
your wish to be baptized, go to that place in the Sinai mountain.
There, there is the bishop; he will baptize you."[29]

---

[27]At the beginning of the sermon the Sarracen was stated as the nephew
of the Emir; PG 100.1201A. See also 1208B and 1208C.

[28]Regulating the rights and obligations of Christians, whose cities had
fallen under Muslim domination, an early ordinance attributed to 'Umar
(although in all probability it belongs to the era of 'Umar II, 717-720) explicitly prohibits the conversion of a Muslim to Christianity: "We will not
show off our religion, nor invite any one to embrace it."

The same ordinance prohibits even the repair of any old religious institution, let alone the erection of any new church, monastery or hermitage.
It prohibits also the display of crosses and sacred books in the streets and
market places where Muslims live; the ringing of bells loudly; religious pro-
cessions on Palm and Easter Sundays and prayers sung in loud voices near
Muslim quarters!

[29]The reference here is, obviously, to the Monastery of the Transfiguration, known as the Monastery of Saint Catherine, in Sinai. This monastery
erected as a monastery-fortress during the reign of Justinian (527-565)

The Sarracen prostrated himself in front of the presbyter and walked out of the church. Then, one hour after nightfall, he came back to the priest, took off his royal golden clothes, put on a poor sack of wool,[30] and he left in secret by night. He walked to Mount Sinai and there he received the holy baptism from the bishop.

---

encompassed older hermitages going back to the early fourth century and to Empress Helen, the mother of the first Roman Christian Emperor Constantine (324-337). By a Justinian law (PG 86.1149) respected until today, the abbot of the monastery holds the office of the bishop with the title of "archbishop." The monastery had in its possession also a number of *metochia*, or dependencies. These were scattered throughout the Sinai peninsula, Cairo, Gaza, in various parts of Syria, Crete, the mainland Greece, and possibly in Rumania and Russia. Some of these *metochia* are still in existence and active. The history of the monastery, famous for its wealth in icons, manuscripts (including the Codex Sinaiticus now in the British Museum), and for its long tradition in monastic spirituality, is one of the most fascinating places and examples of Muslim-Eastern Christian relations. Bedouin Muslims are still surrounding the monastery serving as guardians. They hold the authority of the Christian archbishop in high respect, demonstrate their devotion to Christian saints, especially to Saint Catherine and to Saint George, and defend their allegiance to the monastery; a strange type of "citizenship" which remains unaffected by the shifting national borders between Israel and Egypt in recent years! For a brief excursus through the history of the monastery, see K. Amantos, Σύντομος Ἱστορία τῆς Ἱερᾶς Μονῆς τοῦ Σινᾶ (Thessalonike, 1953); Evangelos Papaioannou, *The Monastery of St. Catherine* (Athens, 1976); George H. Forsyth and K. Weitzmann, *The Monastery of Saint Catherine at Mount Sinai. The Church and Fortress of Justinian* (Ann Arbor, 1973).

The monks still today show an Arabic manuscript, which they claim to be an ordinance written by Muhammad himself, ordering the Muslims to preserve the inviolability of the monastery.

The words of the priest in this story seem to confirm an early tradition giving immunity to the monastery of Sinai from any interference of the Islamic state.

[30]This was the characteristic garment of Christian ascetics. One of the explanations given to the name *ṣūfī* for a Muslim mystic is that it is a derivative of the word *ṣūf* (wool). The name *ṣūfī* related to the woolen gown worn by early *ṣūfī* is related to Muslim ascetics influenced by their Christian counterparts. That such a practice was prevalent in early Islam is evident by the debate on the appropriateness of such a gown between two contemporary Muslims. The ascetic Ḥasan al-Baṣrī (d.110/728) justified the woolen gown of the ascetics as an act of imitation of such prophets as Jesus and David, while Ibn Sīrin (d.110/728) condemned it as contrary to the tradition of the Prophet "who clothed himself in cotton"! Arberry, *Sufism*, p. 35.

He also learned from the Psalter, and he recited verses from it every day.[31]

[1205D] One day three years later he [the former Sarracen] said to the bishop: "Forgive me, Master, what am I supposed to do in order to see Christ?" And the bishop said: "Pray with the right faith and one of these days you will see Christ, according to your wish."[32] But the former Sarracen said again: "Master, give me your consent to go to the priest who offered me instruction when I saw the awesome vision in the church of the most glorious martyr George."[33] The bishop said: "Go, in peace."

[1208A] Thus, he went to the priest, prostrated himself in front of him, embraced him and said to him: "Do you know, Father, who I am?" And the priest: "How can I recognize a man whom I have never seen before?" But, again, the former Sarracen said: "Am I not the nephew of the Emir, who brought the camels inside the church and they all died, and who during the Divine Liturgy saw that terrifying vision?" When the priest looked at him he was amazed and praised God seeing that the former Arab wolf had become a most calm sheep of Christ. He embraced him with passion and invited him to his cell to eat bread.

---

[31]See below, footnote 37-39.

[32]The definite answer of the abbot and its emphasis on *prayer* betrays, perhaps, a direct influence on him of John Klimakos, a mystic of the Christian East. John (+ ca. 649) is the well-known abbot of the Monastery of Sinai and the author of the spiritual writing *The Ladder* (in Greek Κλίμαξ,) after which he was surnamed. The text of *The Ladder of Paradise,* in PG 88.631-1210; trans. Colm Luibheid and Norman Russell, as *The Ladder of Divine Ascent* (New York, 1982). John of the Ladder is a major "witness of monastic spirituality based upon the invocation of the 'name of Jesus.' " John Meyendorff, *Byzantine Theology, Historical Trends and Doctrinal Themes* (New York, 1979), p. 70. Most likely the "prayer of the heart," as the prayer of Jesus is otherwise called, was already practiced in Sinai prior to John of the Ladder. The invocation of the name of Jesus or "Jesus prayer" ("Lord Jesus Christ, son of God, have mercy on me the sinner") is a kind of *dhikr,* aiming at concentrating the mind, collecting it from wandering around and bringing about an experience of and a union with the divine presence. As taught by John of the Ladder, the Jesus prayer was not meant to be an exercise of the mind alone, but one of the whole human being remembering and participating in the experience of the transfigured Christ.

[33]Does the request reflect, perhaps, a dissatisfaction of a novice monk with the contemplative hesychastic practices at Sinai and his search for a more immediate and direct spiritual experience?

And the former Sarracen said: "Forgive me, Master and Father, but I want and have a desire to see Christ. How can I do that?" [1208B] And the priest said: "If you wish to see Christ go to your nephew[34] and preach Christ to him. Curse and anathematize the faith of the Sarracens and their false prophet Muhammad and preach correctly the true faith of the Christians without fear, and thus you will see Christ."[35]

[1208C] The former Sarracen left in earnest. By night he was knocking at the door of the Sarracen forcefully. The guards at the gate of the house of the Emir asked: "Who is yelling and knocking at the door?" And he answered: "I am the nephew of the Emir who left some time ago and was lost. Now I want to see my nephew[36] and tell him something." The guards of the gate conveyed this to the Sarracen immediately: "Master, it is your nephew who left some time ago and was lost." The Emir, heaving a sigh, said: "Where is he?" They said: "At the gate of the palace." He then ordered his servants to go and meet him with lights and candles. They all did as the king, Emir, commanded and they took the monk, the former Sarracen by the hand and presented him to the Emir, his nephew.

When the Emir saw him, he was very glad. He embraced him with tears in his eyes and said to him: "What is this? Where were [1208D] you living all this time? Aren't you my nephew?" And the monk said: "Don't you recognize me, your nephew? Now, as you see, by the grace of God the Most High I have become a Christian and a monk. I have been living in desert places so that I may inherit

---

[34]The priest continues treating the Sarracen as the uncle, instead of the nephew of the Emir! See above n. 27 and below n. 36.

[35]In reality the priest is inviting the convert to become a martyr! Monasticism, as a way of "dying" for the world and offering a witness to the world, and martyrdom, have been viewed by the early Christian East as two sides of the same coin—that of witness (in Greek μαρτυρία) and of imitation of Christ. Earliest ascetics saw monasticism as an alternative to martyrdom where martyrdom, resulting from persecution by the State, was not possible. Thus, while ascetics sought to experience a union with Christ in the flesh, martyrs sought to achieve a union with Christ beyond and in spite of the flesh.

[36]From this evidence it becomes evident that either there is a confusion in the terms, or an uncle and a nephew are both called in relationship to each other "nephew." The word "uncle" occurs nowhere in the text; see above notes 27 and 34.

the Kingdom of Heaven. I hope in the unspeakable compassion of the All-sovereign God to inherit his kingdom. Why are you hesitating yourself, too, Emir? Receive the holy baptism of the Orthodox Christians in order to inherit eternal life, as I hope to do."

The Emir laughed, scratched his head and said: "What are you chattering about, you miserable one; what are you chattering? What has happened to you? Alas, you pitiful one! How did you abandon [1209A] your life and the sceptres of reign and roam around as a beggar, dressed in these filthy clothes made of hair?"

The monk responded to him: "By the grace of God. As far as all the things I used to have when I was a Sarracen, these were [material] property and were of the devil. But these things that you see me wearing are a glory and pride, and an engagement with the future and eternal life. I anathematize the religion of the Sarracens and their false prophet."

Then the Emir said: "Take him out, for he does not know what he is chattering about." They took him away and put him in a place in the palace where they gave him food and drink. And he spent three days there, but he took neither food nor drink. He was pray-[1209B] ing to God earnestly and with faith. Going down to his knees he said: "O Lord, I have hoped in thee; let me never be ashamed,[37] neither let mine enemies laugh at me to scorn."[38] And again: "Have mercy on me, O God, according to thy steadfast love; according to thy abundant mercy blot out my transgressions."[39] And again: "Enlighten my eyes, Lord God, that I may not fall asleep into death; that my enemy may never say 'I have overpowered him'. 'Strengthen my heart, O Lord,' so that I may be able to fight the visible deceiver, the Sarracen; so that the evil devil may not stamp on me and make me fear death, for your holy name." He then made the sign of the cross and said: "The Lord is my enlightenment and [1209C] my savior. Whom shall I fear? The Lord is the protector of my life. From whom will I hesitate?" And again he cried out to the Emir: "Receive holy baptism in order to gain the immeasurable kingdom of God."

Again the Emir gave orders for him to be brought in front of him. He had prepared for him clothes exceedingly beautiful. And

---

[37]Ps. 30 (31) 1; 70 (71).1
[38]Ps. 24 (25) 2.
[39]Ps. 50 (51) 1.

the Emir spoke: "Enjoy, you pitiful one, enjoy and rejoice for being a king. Do not disdain your life and your youth which is so beautiful, walking instead mindlessly like a beggar and a penniless one. Alas you pitiful one. What do you think?"

The monk laughed and replied to the Emir: "Do not weep at what I have in mind. I am thinking of how to be able to fulfil the [1209D] work of my Christ and that of the Father priest who has sent me, and has been my teacher. As far as the clothes you have prepared for me, sell them and give the money to the poor. You, too, should abandon the temporary sceptres of the reign, so that you may receive sceptres of an eternal life. Do not rest your hope on things of the present but on things which are of the future, and do not believe in the pseudo-prophet Muhammad, the impure, the detestable one, the son of hell. Believe, rather, in Jesus Christ of Nazareth, the crucified one. Believe that the one Godhead is a consubstantial Trinity; Father, Son and Holy Spirit, a Trinity of the same essence, and undivided."

The Emir laughed again and said to the officials who had [1212A] gathered in the palace: "This man is mindless. What shall we do with him? Take him out and expel him." Those, however, sitting by the king said: "He meant to desecrate and corrupt the religion of the Sarracens. Do you not hear how he curses and anathematizes our great prophet?"

The monk and former Sarracen cried out loudly: "I feel sorry for you Emir because you, unfortunate one, do not want to be saved. Believe in our Lord Jesus Christ, the crucified one, and anathematize the religion of the Sarracens and their false prophet, as I did."

And the Sarracen Emir said: "Take him out as I am ordering [1212B] you. He is mindless and does not know what he is talking about."

Those sitting by with him said: "Well, you heard that he anathematized the religion of the Sarracens and that he is blaspheming against the great prophet, and you say, 'He does not know what he is talking about?' If you do not have him killed we will also go and become Christians."

And the Emir said: "I cannot have him killed because he is my nephew and I feel sorry for him. But you take him and do as you please."

And they got hold of the monk with great anger, they dragged [1212C] him out of the palace and submitted him to many tortures to try to make him return to the previous religion of the Sarracens. But he did not. Instead he was teaching everybody in the name of Jesus Christ of Nazareth to believe and be saved.

The Sarracens dragged him out of the city, and there they stoned him to death[40] this most pious monk, whose name was Pachomios.

On that night a star came down from heaven and rested on top of the most pious martyr, and everybody was able to see it for forty days;[41] and many of them became believers.

With the prayers of the most blessed martyr, of the all-pure [1212D] Mother of God Mary, who is ever-virgin, and of all the saints; for the remission of our sins. Amen.

Summary of Remarks

The story is attractive, imaginative and with a characteristic Oriental plot. It is motivated by monastic ideals, and a desire to witness to one's faith boldly, making converts to the Christian faith, becoming a martyr for one's faith and being united with Christ as imminently as possible. If the text does not prove the historicity of the episode, it does ascertain the historical reality of its time. Thus, the story allows us to make the following observations:

1. The whole incident rides on the miraculous and mystical; elements which lie at the heart of monastic spirituality. Preoccupied by these ideals, the author does not seem particularly concerned about

---

[40]Denouncing Islam (*ridda,* apostasy) has traditionally been met in Islam by the death penalty. The practice goes back to Abū Bakr the first caliph (632-634) who brought the tribes, which apostacized after the death of Muhammad, by force back to the central authority of Medina. See also Fazlur Rahman, "The Law of Rebellion in Islam," in *Islam in the Modern World* (1983 Paine Lectures in Religion, the University of Missouri-Columbia, 1983), pp. 1-10, at 1-2. Most neomartyrs of the Orthodox Church were actually converts to Christianity from Islam, or crypto-Christians. On the neomartyrs, see R. M. Dawkins, "The crypto-Christians of Turkey," *Byzantion* 8 (1933) 247-75; N. Russell, "Neomartyrs of the Greek Calendar," *Sobornost* 5 (1983) 36-62; Demetrios J. Constantelos, "The Neomartyrs as Evidence for Methods and Motives Leading to Conversion and Martyrdom in the Ottoman Empire," *The Greek Orthodox Theological Review,* 23 (1978) 216-31.

[41]Since the word "star" and "martyr" in Greek are of masculine gender, it is not clear from the text whether "everyone was able to see him" (the martyr), or "it" (the star).

certain inconsistencies which his story contains. For example, while the priest is once depicted reserved, even afraid, of the Emir, not daring to even baptize the Saracen, later the same priest urges the convert to preach directly to the Emir, and curse and anathematize Muḥammad in front of him! Also, while the author portrays the priest as being modest, humble and convincing in front of the Saracen prince, he portrays the convert monk as arrogant and combative. Finally, the Emir himself appears as being good-hearted and compassionate, while the monk (nephew) appears as intransigent and confrontational.

2. The story is a good example of a meaningful interfaith "dialogue" in words and action, but a bad example of martyrdom! The earliest Church did not reward cases of martyrdoms which resulted from open and unwarranted provocations. This story—if it reflects a historical reality—tends to suggest that later Christendom condoned and perhaps encouraged such martyrdoms; a sign of a Church growing tired of, and intolerant towards, Islam.

The vision itself, which should be taken as the focal point of the sermon, signifies the importance of worship in general, and of the liturgy in particular, as a means of an interfaith encounter in experience and action, rather than in words by themselves. Verbal encounters alone can, as in this particular story, easily deteriorate into polemics.

3. The central and suprising figure in the story is the Saracen prince. He is able to see with his eyes what a Christian believes in his heart, but is unable to see. The Saracen appears to be a mystic by disposition, one of those who flees the secularism and the luxuries of the Umayyad court at Damascus. His example seems to represent the trend of the earliest Muslim ascetics; a trend which gave rise to Sufism. Thus, the story fits well with the extravagant Umayyad administration and the emergence of Islamic asceticism.

The prince converts to Christianity easily. He goes to Sinai without hesitation, where he becomes a disciplined and accomplished monk. He demonstrates a particular passion for mystical, hesychastic experiences. He wants to "see Christ," immediately. This is what he felt was missing from Sinai. He was not even reluctant to die in order to be able to see Christ! The early mystics of Islam also had set for themselves a similar goal: transmutation in God even by the extinction (*fanā'*) of their own self or individuality; an insult to the orthodox Islamic doctrine and sensibility. This clash between orthodox Islam and mysticism reached its culmination in al-Junayd (d. 910) and especially in the case of his celebrated contemporary al-Ḥallāj. The latter was executed on the cross (d. 922) for claiming "*ana 'l-ḥaqq*" ("I am the truth") after having achieved a mystical union with God.

4. All external and internal indications point to a text which reflects life in the eighth century, rather than in late medieval times. Not all evidences are of the same value but, collectively, they present a rather convincing case:

a) The name of the author is clearly stated as Gregory Dekapolites, a figure well-identified (780/790-842) whose life has been narrated by a contemporary and well-known biographer Ignatios (780-?).

b) The caliph is called *Amīr al-mu'minīn* an ancient title introduced by 'Umar, the second caliph (634-644), and preserved by the Umayyads and the 'Abbasid caliphs. Furthermore the text calls this emir *Amīr al-mu'minīn* "of Syria." This designation suggests an Ummayyad caliph governing from Damascus.

c) With regard to the relations between Muslims and Christians, the text seems to imply the terms of the "Ordinance of 'Umar." The Christian priest refrains from baptizing the Saracen because such an act could have resulted in death for him and in destruction of the church. The Church of Saint George is in the hands of Christians for purposes of worship, although the Muslim prince easily takes the liberty of invading and occupying it; an allusion to a hardening position of later Caliphs compared to the earliest Ummayads. The text depicts an atmosphere of co-existence between the two religious communities, with the Christians being the subordinate and protected community (*dhimmīs*). The Saracen prince is put to death, not for being a Christian but for having apostacized from Islam and for blaspheming Muḥammad. There is no indication, however, that either the bishop who baptized him or the priest who instructed him were punished for their actions.

5. The text is, of course, an hagiological sermon. Its purpose is to praise the virtues, the faith and the self-renunciation of the martyr. However, the central event of the story and the catalyst to the process of the hero's conversion and his ultimate martyrdom is a vision! This vision obviously has a eucharistic meaning. But considered in this particular historical context, the scope of the sermon and the meaning of the vision go beyond that. In the context of the Iconoclastic controversy the iconoclasts maintained that the only icon of Christ that the Church knows is the Eucharist, rather than painted icons made by the hands of men. The one who articulated this thesis was none other than the theologically-inclined iconoclast Emperor

Constantine V the Kopronymos (741-775) who made this thesis the subject of one of his pointed and provocative theological "Inquiries" (*Peūseis*). These "Inquiries" became the backbone of the theology adopted by the Iconoclastic Council of Constantinople (754).[42] For the iconophiles, however, the perception of the Eucharist as the "icon" of Christ, or Christ's own body "by participation and convention," is tantamount to blasphemy. For the iconophiles the Eucharist is an act established by Christ himself who offered the bread as "his [my] body", not as an icon of his body, and the cup as "his [my] blood" not as an icon of his blood. The Seventh Ecumenical Synod (Nicaea, 787), which refuted the iconoclastic Definition of the Council of 754, and on this particular eucharistic argument of the iconoclasts, states the following: "Thus, it has been clearly demonstrated that nowhere did either the Lord, or the Apostles, or the Fathers call the bloodless sacrifice offered through the priest "an icon," but rather they called it "this very body" and "this very blood.""[43] Is it not the story of the sermon, a narrative depicting precisely the wording and the spirit of this Orthodox (and iconophile) eucharistic theology? Knowing Gregory Dekapolites as a theologically ardent iconophile monk who left the contemplative and ascetic life in order to fight against iconoclasm and support the iconophiles, one has little difficulty in accepting this story as a sermon on the iconophile eucharistic theology. Perhaps the *Sermon* as a whole is iconophile apologetics: the fact that even a Muslim, guided by the providence of God, is able to see the stark ontological reality of the Eucharist, represents a judgment against the *Christian iconoclasts,* and it exposes their effort at diluting the sacrament into a mere "image," or icon, of Christ in the place of a real sacrifice!

6. If there is no compelling reason to question the authorship of the text as being indeed "a historical sermon of Gregory Dekapolites,"

---

[42]On the *Peūseis* of Emperor Constantine, and on the eucharistic theology in the context of iconoclasm, see Stephen Gero, "Notes on Byzantine Iconoclasm in the Eighth Century," *Byzantion* 44 (1974) 23-42, and his "The Eucharistic Doctrine of the Byzantine Iconoclasts and its Sources," *Byzantinische Zeitschrift* 68 (1975) 4-22.

[43]G. D. Mansi, *Sacrorum Conciliorum Nova et Amplissima Collectio* (Florence, 1867), 13, 265B. The texts of the iconoclastic Definition of 754, its Refutation and the iconophile Definition of 787 can be found in Daniel J. Sahas, *Icon and Logos. Sources in the Eighth-century Iconoclasm* (Toronto, 1986).

who is, then, this Emir-al-Muminin of Syria? The text offers us little
evidence with which to determine the possible historical figures im-
plicated in the sermon. Of various possible caliphs two seem to be
the more probable ones, 'Umar II (717-720), and Hishām (724-743).
'Umar, (the fifth caliph), was the son of 'Abd al-Azīz who served as
governor of al-Ḥulwān in Egypt in 61 or 63 A.H. 'Umar himself was
born in Egypt.[44] As Sūyūtī describes 'Umar II as a man of "justice,
removing grievances and establishing good laws":[45] The people addressed him as "Amīr al-Mu'minīn," and 'Umar himself assumed
this title. The relationship of 'Umar to Egypt, his title, as well as the
above stated traits of his personality are characteristics congenial to
the information provided by the text.

Another possible case in Hishām (724-743). Theophanes, the Chronographer, himself an iconophile like Gregory, who died in exile as
a confessor for his faith, reports that after the death of Yazīd (Yazīd II
720-724) Hishām, the latter's brother, became emir "and he started
building in every country and city palaces, making plantations and
gardens, and extracting water."[46] This piece of information corro-
borates the information regarding the building of a castle in Kurūm.

Incidents of desecration of churches were attributed to iconoclasts,
as well as to Muslim officials whom the iconophile writers considered
as forerunners and instigators of the Christian iconoclasm.[47] The incident that Theophanes mentions and the dates of Hishām's reign
coincide with the violent iconoclastic actions of the Byzantine Emperor
Leo III "the Isaurian" (717-741). The sermon of Gregory Dekapolites,
therefore, might also be a product of the same turbulent period.

The questions of locality of the village or town of Kurûm,[48] the
castle in this town, the identity of the *strategos* and especially the
name of the Muslim caliph are still open questions. Less obscure questions, however, seem to be the period and the context of the text:
the writing presupposes an iconoclastic climate and an iconophile

---

[44]On 'Umar, see Jalalu'ddin As Sūyūtī, *History of the Caliphs*, trans. H. S.
Jargett (Amsterdam, 1970) pp. 233-49.

[45]Ibid. p. 235.

[46]*Chronographia*, ed. C. de Boor, 1,403.24-27.

[47]On the bibliography referring to Islam and Byzantine iconoclasm see
Sahas, *John of Damascus*, pp. 10-13; *Icon and Logos*, pp. 18-21.

[48]Neither this name, nor its Greek translation, Ampelos, appear in Theophanes.

author; it reflects early Muslim-Christian relations; it betrays the growing anti-Christian policies of the later Umayyads, and it points to the rising Muslim discontent with a secularized caliphate.

However, beyond the historical and theological information and implications of the text, the text in itself and its content seem to contain a moral: "dialogue" in the context, or through the means, of worship, existential religious experience and mysticism—that is, meeting of hearts within the context of a mutual encounter with the divine—does bear fruit. Irrespective even of the question of whether the text is authentic or not, the fact remains that such a text *has found* a place in the Byzantine anti-Islamic literature! Among so many other pieces of anti-Islamic literature, such as refutations, formulas of abjuration, decrees, heresiological writings, responses, dialogues and condemnations, here is a short writing which is a "story"; something less encephalic and more experiental and miraculous. It is this fact which compels us to notice it as a suggestion of another kind of Muslim-Christian encounters; at least, as a possibility.

This text, as a piece of spiritual literature of Christianity, points to a significant trait in the attitude of the Christian East towards Islam, and, by extension, towards other non-Christian religious traditions: that *it is possible* for an "infidel" to see things that a faithful has been accustomed to believe but unable to experience; and that these things are not simply "things" but the very essence, the core and the mystery of Christianity. Once such a possibility has been acknowledged, a major breakthrough has been accomplished. Then an interfaith encounter can be lifted up to a level of relationship higher than merely polemics.

The Word of God in Islam

MAHMOUD MUSTAFA AYOUB

I WOULD LIKE TO REITERATE a point which I have made several times already in this conference: that this meeting is historic moment in the history of Muslim-Christian relations. After the fruitful exchanges in philosophy and science between Byzantium and the Arab Muslim empire, after the acceptance by early Muslim thinkers of Aristotle as the "First Teacher," after many wars and much bloodshed, we come to the moment in our history in which we can, at least in North America, talk as the people of God, as people of faith, across the differences and similarities of our traditions. I believe that we need to tell the world again that Christ was a Palestinian, and that Christianity started not in Rome but in our area of the Middle East. We cannot therefore study and understand the culture of either group without understanding the culture and history of the other. Islam was born in a Christian spiritual milieu, a fact which is recognized in the Qur'ān and early Christian tradition.[1]

Let me begin by relating a little anecdote. One of my favorite dramatic moments every year is to attend what we call in Lebanon the *hajma*, that is, the Easter vigil where at midnight the priest and everyone else reenacts the descent of Christ to Hades to save the souls of those who were before him. So I went while in Boston to the Cathedral of Saint John of Damascus. The priest was, I believe, Father

---

[1] See for example Qur'ān 5.82. For the role of Christianity in Arabia before Islam, see Spencer J. Trimingham, *Christianity Among the Arabs in Pre-Islamic Times* (London, 1979) and Tor Andrae, *Islamische Mystiker* (Stuttgart, 1960), pp. 13-43.

Murphy. At the end we all went up to have sandwiches, and Father Murphy saw me, a new face sitting there. He came up to me and asked, "What is your faith?" I didn't want to disappoint him, so I said, "I'm from Lebanon." He said, "Yes, that's good, but what is your faith?" "I study at Harvard," I said, but he persisted. "Father," I said, "I'm not a Christian, but I love your traditions. May I now please have my roast beef sandwich?"

The word of God in Islam includes a great deal of meanings and significances. Linguistically, the term *kalima* may mean one word, a discourse, or even a poem. When applied to God, *kalima* means decree or ordinance, a source of blessing or of judgment, or, finally, revelation. It is these three aspects of the Word of God which I wish to discuss here.

In many places the Qur'ān speaks of the word, or decree, of God being confirmed against a people as a judgment or a punishment.[2] In this sense the Word of God as divine judgment, ordinance, or decree is at the same time an affirmation of his absolute sovereignty and majesty. As a source of blessing the word of God is used in the Qur'ān as the good, salutory, or beautiful divine word (*kalimat al-ḥusnā*). The word of God in this sense is used in the Qur'ān to signify a source of reward for the Children of Israel for their patience.[3] Another instance is the reference to Adam, Abraham, and other prophets in which the word of God also denotes selection.[4]

Most importantly, however the word of God is that word of guidance and salvation which he promised to humanity in the primordial covenant. The Qur'ān tells us that God "drew out of the loins of the Children of Israel their progenies, and made them bear witness against themselves, saying, 'Am I not your Lord?' " They said, "Yes, we bear witness . . . "[5] This divine question and our human answer to it constitute both God's covenant with humanity and his promise of guidance through revelation. This divine covenant is the affirmation of divine Oneness (*tawḥīd*) by humanity. Yet because we forget, God took it upon himself to remind us of this affirmation—or rather guide us to it—in every epoch of our history through revelation. The word of revelation, however, is not only that which God communicates to

---

[2] See Qur'ān 10.33.
[3] See Qur'ān 7.137.
[4] See Qur'ān 2.37 and 2.124.
[5] Qur'ān 7.172.

us; it means or includes that which we share with God. What do we in fact share with God as his word? The Qur'ān states that, "God has borne witness that there is no god but he. Likewise did the angels and those who are endowed with knowledge." The word we share with God is the word of witness that he is one. The verse, however, goes on to say, "There is no god but he, maintaining (his creation) in justice. He is the Mighty, the Wise."[6]

In its true meaning, salvation means healing or wholesomeness through divine succor and providence. Revelation, I wish therefore to argue, is the Islamic way to salvation. For to say that there exists no salvation in Islam would be to deny a reality on which the Qur'ān concentrates throughout. How otherwise is a human being to escape eternal torment and to attain eternal bliss? While the Qur'ān does not deny that Adam sinned, it regards sin simply as a protypical act to which we are all open—to think of ourselves as equal to God. Satan, we are told in the Qur'ān, tempted Adam and his spouse with eternal life and unending dominion.[7]

But as with all of us, the Qur'ān declares, Adam repented. This repentance, however, was not enough. Adam's salvation came again through revelation, through the divine word. Thus Adam, the Qur'ān tells us, "received certain words from his Lord, and he turned toward him, for he is truly Relenting Compassionate."[8] Adam therefore becomes the first sinner. Yes, but also the first prophet. It is thus in these two roles that Adam and his descendants become the representatives of God in his earth. Adam was followed by other prophets in affirmation of God's promise to him and his wife when God said to him (as related in the Qur'ān), "Yet guidance from me will surely come to you, and whosoever follows my guidance, no fear will come upon them, nor shall they grieve."[9]

Abraham, the father of prophets, was also tried by words from his Lord, and he fulfilled them. Hence he becomes the chief monotheist, the first Muslim, and the father of all prophets to come. Moses likewise was favored by being directly addressed by God, and was

---

[6] Qur'ān 3.18.

[7] Qur'ān 20.120.

[8] Qur'ān 2.37. For a discussion of the various interpretations of these verses of the Qur'ān by commentators, see M. Ayoub, *The Qur'ān and its Interpreters* (Albany, 1984), pp. 84-93.

[9] Qur'ān 2.38.

commanded with his people to "take with strength" the revelation vouchsafed them by God.[10] While other prophets received the word of God in the form of divine revelation or communication, Christ is the word of God which he sent to Mary, the "righteous woman" who guarded well her chastity. She therefore became worthy of God's spirit and Word, Jesus the Christ.[11] Is there a sense in which we can speak of Christ as the divine Logos in Islam? God's creative act is expressed in both the Bible and the Qur'ān by words of command. Hence in Genesis we read that the first act of creation was the divine resounding word, "Let there be light." In the Qur'ān the Word of God as the creative command is expressed in the divine *kun* ("be"), the fiat of creation out of nothing. The Qur'ān says, "Surely, the likeness of Jesus with God is as that of Adam. He created him from dust and said to him: 'Be,' and thus he was."[12] Similarly, Jesus was created by the same divine fiat or creative command, and thus he is like Adam, an original creation. In his case as in that of Adam, the operative divine power of creation is the word of command (*amr*) and not the word of *khalq* (creative act).

Adam, the Qur'ān says, had no resolve (*'azm*).[13] Jesus, however, is one of the prophets of power, or resolve (*'ulū al-'azm*). Jesus moreover was, unlike Adam, not affected by the touch of Satan. He is like Adam, but without sin. According to a tradition related from the Prophet, every child when born is touched by Satan and he bursts out crying because of Satan's touch, but not so in the cases of Jesus and his mother.[14] Christ, in a sense, completes Adam. Adam was both prophet and sinner, but Jesus was a prophet without sin, immune from sin, protected by God from the touch of Satan. Is this not the view of many of the early Greek Fathers?

Even though the Qur'ān speaks of Christ as the Word of God, this does not mean from the point of view of Islam revelation properly speaking. Rather revelation is, following the ancient Semitic pattern, a divine sound, an uttered word which may also be contained

---

[10]See Qur'ān 4.164.

[11]See Qur'ān 4.171 and 21.91.

[12]Qur'ān 3.59.

[13]Qur'ān 20.115.

[14]Aḥmad ibn Ḥanbal, *Musnad,* ed. Aḥmad Muḥammad Shākir (Cairo, 1375/1955), 15, H. 7902ff.

in a book, broadly understood. It may be instructive to read the beginning of the first chapter of the Fourth Gospel both Christianly and Islamically, if you will. John declares: "In the beginning was the Word (Logos), and the Word was with God, and the Word was God." Muslims have also for the most part affirmed that the Qur'ān in its essence is the eternal and uncreated Word of God. John tells us further that the Word was with God, but where we differ is with John's next statement, that is, that the Word is God. The great theological controversy over the Qur'ān, a controversy which remains unresolved to this day, concerns the relationship of the Qur'ān, as the Word of God, to God himself. To my knowledge, no one has asserted that the Qur'ān is God. Another important difference is that while for John the divine Logos is the agent of creation—"all things were made through him . . . ";[15] the eternal Qur'ān is the source of salvation or guidance. But perhaps the most concrete difference is that while John declares "And the Word was made flesh and dwelt among us,"[16] the eternal Qur'ān was made a book and entered into our time and history.

That the Word was made flesh affirms the humanity of Christ not only in theological theory, but in actual fact of his life here on earth. That the Qur'ān is a book "contained between two covers" affirms its human dimension as it shares our history, shaping it and being shaped by it. Thus the humanity of God's revelation in both Christianity and Islam has not, I believe, been taken as seriously as it deserves to be taken by either of the two communities of faith.

The Qur'ān was communicated to the Prophet in two ways. Both are important, although usually one is given prominence. It was communicated through the angel Gabriel to the Prophet when Islam began, not in the bustle of Mecca or the clamor of Medina, but rather in the solitude of one human being with his Lord, in the cave of Mount Hira outside Mecca. Then the angel came with the first revelation of the Qur'ān, which was the command to "recite in the Name of your Lord who created, created man from a bloodclot . . . and taught him what he knew not."[17] For nearly twenty-two years the angel came with subsequent revelations which made Muslim history. But there was another mode of revelation which is crucial for the understanding

---

[15] John 1.1-3.
[16] John 1.14.
[17] Qur'ān, Sura 96.

of the profundity of the Prophet's mission, personality and faith. We are told on the authority of 'A'ishah, the Prophet's wife, that at times the Prophet would fall into something like a trance. He would hear in his ears a sound like the ringing of bells. If this happened on a hot summer day often he would shiver as if it were cold, and when it happened on a cold winter day, his face would drip with sweat as if it were hot. Then he would ask to be covered with a mantle, and when he woke up he would understand the sound that was communicated to him not as words but as divine "logoi," unbound by letters and sounds. The Qur'ān was communicated to a man whom, Islam insists, had no education in the formal sense, in that he could not read or write. This does not mean, of course, that he was not a highly gifted individual, but that his mind, as a pure receptacle of the divine Word, could not be contaminated with human wisdom. The Qur'ān was gathered on bones, stones, palm leaves, and in the minds and hearts of men. It shaped our history, but it was waiting for us to shape it and make it the Book that it remains to this day. Through the collections and the final recension of the Qur'ān, prepared under the direction of the third Caliph Othman, the Qur'ān not only did shape our history, but was also shaped by it.

I have earlier argued for the humanity of divine revelation. Two important principles may be cited in support of this argument. The principle of abrogation, which means that God can suppress the ordinance laid down in a verse or even remove[18] the verse altogether as the general welfare of the community demands, is an indication of the close relationship of the Qur'ān to the life of the Muslim community. Muslims have been concerned with the reason or occasion for the revelation of many verses of the Qur'ān. Many verses were revealed in answer to a particular problem in the life of the community. Thus *asbāb al-nuzūl* or "occasions of revelation" have bound the Qur'ān to human history, and even its mundane experiences. I therefore conclude that the Qur'ān shares in our humanity in entering fully into history in the same way that Christ the eternal Logos entered into our humanity as well. It is this which makes the Qur'ān open for study and exegesis at all times.

In this conference parallels have already been drawn between Christ and the Qur'ān and the Prophet and the Virgin Mary. Let me carry them a little further. There are two kinds of prayers in Islam:

---

[18]See Qur'ān 2.106.

that which we call *du'ā*, the supplicatory prayer, a free prayer, and
that which we call *ṣalāt*, which denotes the official canonical five daily
prayers. The latter is obligatory worship. Muslims pray with the Qur'ān
and through it. In this way, therefore, the eternal Word of God is
interiorized by us and and fulfilled in our lives through prayer. The
Prophet is said to have declared that God has praised himself from
all eternity, and he could not teach us better praise than to praise
him with the words with which he praised himself: "All praise be
to God, the Lord of all beings." Christ shared his word with humanity as he taught his disciples to pray, "O Father, thou who art in
heaven." God has likewise shared his word with us when he taught
us to pray with the Fātiḥa, the opening Sura of the Qur'ān. We are
told in a divine utterance (*ḥadīth qudsī*) that, "I have divided the
prayer (*ṣalāt*, in which the Fātiḥa is recited repeatedly) between me
and my servant, and my servant shall have what he prays for. For
when the servant says, "All praise be to God, the Lord of all beings,"
God says, "My servant has praised me." When the servant says, "The
All-Merciful, the Compassionate," God says, "My servant has mag-
nified me." When the servant says, "Master of the day of judgment,"
God says, "My servant has glorified me . . . this is my portion and
to him belongs what remains."[19] Islamic prayer, again echoing that
primordial divine promise of revelation and guidance, becomes a re-
creation of that covenant, in the words of the Fātiḥa, "Guide us on
the straight way." The five daily prayers of Islam may therefore be
considered to be the sacrament of Islam. As you appropriate and interiorize Christ through the bread and wine, so do we interiorize and
appropriate God's word through recitation and prayer. It is our communion with God.

The transcendence of the divine Word in Islam goes beyond mere
prayer and supplication. Like God, his Word is infinite in meaning
and significance for our lives. Thus the Qur'ān declares, "Say, 'Were
the oceans to be ink for the words of my Lord, the oceans would be
exhausted before the words of my Lord are exhausted, even if we
were to bring many oceans like it without end.' "[20]

God's word in Islam is the link between ephemeral humanity and

---

[19]Abū Ja'far Muḥammad ibn Jarīr al-Ṭabarī, *Jami' al-Bayān 'an Ta'wīl
al-Qur'ān*, ed. Maḥmūd Muḥammad and Aḥmad Muṣṭafā Shākir (Cairo,
1332/1954), 1, p. 201.
[20]Qur'ān 18.109.

divine transcendence. The insistence on divine transcendence in both the Qur'ān sharing in this absolute divine transcendence. Therefore the Islamic objection to the Trinity is not a doctrinal objection, but rather it is an objection against violating the divine transcendence or what we call in Arabic *tanzīh*. Islam therefore insists that God must be God. Yet the Trinity in Christianity as I understand it is in reality not a doctrine, but a mystery. It remains a mystery in spite of the many treatises, dialogues, church councils, credal statements, and the attempts of Christians to understand it for themselves and to explain it to others. Whatever else the Trinity is, it signifies God's operation in the world to create, to save, and to guide humanity back to him, who is its source and ultimate end. Many have written that what is analogous in the Islamic tradition to the Trinity in Christianity are the divine attributes. From the theological point of view this may be true, because, as al-Ash'arī reminded us, they are "neither he nor are they other than he." Therefore, divine attributes share in that aspect of mystery; they are that divine mystery which we can only know in the concretely created things.

But may I suggest another, and perhaps in the final analysis a more fruitful, analogue in Islam to the Trinity. It is the word or words (*logoi*) of God—the word of command, of creation, and of revelation and guidance.

We Muslims and Christians share a common commitment of faith to the One and only God, who made himself known as he spoke "in many and various ways."[21] He spoke through Greek philosophy and the Greek idiom, through the Hebrew language, and through Arabic, and also through many other languages. For the Qur'ān puts the divine challenge to humankind in the assertion that "there is not community but that a warner was sent to us," this "in order that humankind shall have no argument against God after messengers have come."[22] This challenge is fulfilled in all of us again through the word of God in all its diverse expressions.

All human beings, the Qur'ān says, were once one nation and one community. But "had it not been for a word which proceeded from your Lord, judgment would have been passed over them concerning the things in which they had differed."[23] Humanity is one in all its

---

[21]Hebrews 1.1.
[22]Qur'ān 35.24 and 4.165.
[23]Qur'ān 10.19.

elemental needs. It is one in its capacity to know God, but it is diverse in its culture and expression of faith.

In a world now dominated by material concerns and the threat of total annihilation, if we have these things in common, then what ought to be the purpose of our dialogue? First our dialogue must not assume that we are one in our expression of faith and therefore ask for disappointment and frustration when we discover that we are not. Muslims assume that Christians ought to be at least like them. This is why they judge Christianity by the criterion of Islam. Muslims will not be able to understand the Christian concept of revelation —God revealing himself in the flesh—as long as they insist that revelation must be as in Islam another book. We must realize that for the Christian community over its two thousand years of history, revelation has meant incarnation and redemption. Even where this doctrine does and will clash with our Islamic understanding of revelation, we have to start from it if we are to "know the truth," and reap the fruits of our dialogue. Similarly on the other side, Christians cannot continue to deny Muḥammad the role of prophet. Nor would it do to be generous and say that he is a prophet, but only like those of the Old Testament, when we know he did not play that role. Muhammad is a prophet like Moses; he brought to the world a new dispensation and founded a community which changed the course of history. Can the Christian community today accept that revelation was not only *preparatio evangelica* before Christ, but that post-Christian revelation may yet have something to say to the world.

If we then approach Islam and Christianity on their own terms and try to understand them through their own doctrines and history, our dialogue will achieve its desired end. We must strive for fellowship of faith and not simply a means by which we can understand and tolerate in differently the existence of one another as two communities of faith. I am convinced—and in this perhaps I am a heretic in the view of both communities—that the multiplicity of expressions of faith from ancient China to Iran, to Palestine, Byzantium and Rome, to Arabia and then to the New World is willed by God to show that the truth is larger than any of its expressions. Yet in this global human family there are small clans or tribes, and we are all the tribes of Abraham, some physically, but all of us spiritually.

Because the Qur'ān recognized revelation as universal and historic and so because the Prophet saw in the Christian community that fellowship of faith, he ordered the weak and defenseless of his nascent community to make their first *hijra* or migration to Ethiopia, the then chief Christian country of the area. Thus Islam began not only in a physical exile of faith but in a spiritual exile, which we now all share. Our meeting of dialogue here in North America ought to have been held in Istanbul, in Beirut or in Athens. Both our traditions of faith are universal in their scope and history. They are both Eastern and Western, both heirs to Abraham and Aristotle. Both communities are, more importantly, heirs to God's revelation, and if we are pure in heart, perhaps heirs of God's kingdom.

The Word of God in Orthodox Christianity

BISHOP MAXIMOS AGHIORGOUSSIS

IN THE BEGINNING was the Word: the Word was with God and the Word was God. He was with God in the beginning. Through him all things came to be, not one thing had its being but through him. All that came to be had life in him and that life was the light of men, a light that shines in the dark, a light that darkness could not overpower.

A man came, sent by God. His name was John. He came as a witness, as a witness to speak for the light, so that everyone might believe through him. He was not the light, only a witness to speak for the light.

The Word was the true light that enlightens all men; and he was coming into the world. He was in the world that had its being through him, and the world did not know him. He came to his own domain and his own people did not accept him. But to all who did accept him he gave power to become children of God, to all who believe in the name of him who was born not out of human stock or urge of the flesh or will of man but of God himself. The Word was made flesh, he lived among us, and we saw his glory, the glory that is his as the only Son of the Father, full of grace and truth.

John appears as his witness. He proclaims: 'This is the one of whom I said: He who comes after me ranks before me because he existed before me.'

Indeed, from his fulness we have, all of us, received yes, grace in return for grace, since, through the Law was given through Moses, grace and truth have come through Jesus Christ. No one has ever seen God; it is the only Son, who is nearest the Father's heart, who has made him known [Jn 1.1-18].

This text, the prologue of the Fourth Gospel is at the basis of the Christian understanding of Logos (Word of God) in relation to God and creation. It is the text that constitutes the heart of Christian theology and spirituality. Saint John, to whom Christian tradition attributes the Fourth Gospel, is called the Theologian, because of this text, for the author of the Fourth Gospel deals with the Word of God who became flesh in such a unique way that it gives Christianity its distinctive character among the other monotheistic religions, including Judaism and Islam.

This text, which is the great Easter proclamation of the Eastern Orthodox Church, and which is in many ways utilized by the Eastern Orthodox Liturgy, was also utilized in the defense of the Christian doctrine against the Gnostics (by Saint Irenaios), the Arians (by Saint Athanasios and the Cappadocian Fathers, among others), and later in the dialogue with Islam. Along with the doctrine of the image of God, the Logos/Word of God doctrine was utilized to defend Christian monotheism "against those who accuse us of venerating three Gods." The basic Christian defense was that the Word of God, as well as the Spirit of God, were always with God, one in essence with him, constituting, however, distinct hypostases from him. Thus, by using the Logos doctrine, Christian apologists preserved the mystery of God's unity and distinctiveness, as affirmed in Christian revelation. The apologists were conscious that with the Logos doctrine, they kept the unity of God as they also revered the mystery of God as trinity of hypostases, without introducing multiplicity in God. One in his essence and energies, God is triune in his hypostases, for there was no time when God did not have Reason/Word, and there was no time when God was not Spirit.

The same apologetic doctrine was utilized by Christian apologists against Islam, as one discovers by reading the documents of those old polemics. Today's dialogue has a completely different character, as it was stated more than once in the context of this symposium.

The scope of this presentation will be a limited one: unfortunately, there is not much room in it for the patristic, liturgical, and spiritual witness regarding the Logos/Word of God doctrine in Orthodox Christianity. Since the dialogue partners are also People of the Book, I will limit myself to the sayings of the Book, with only one exception:

I believe that the Greek antecedents of the Logos doctrine in general are a necessary introduction to the Judaeo-Christian understanding of the same doctrine. Also, from a Christian point of view which considers the Old Covenant as the first stage of God's revelation completed by the New, the Old Testament doctrine on the Word of God is a necessary introduction to the Christian understanding of the Logos/Word of God. Thus, I will review the Greek and Old Testament antecedents first, before presenting the New Testament doctrine regarding the Logos/Word of God, a doctrine that culminates in the Johannine understanding of a "Christological Logos," as we read it in the prologue of the Fourth Gospel.

This presentation intends to be an academic one, in the context of the dialogue as given to us by our eminent keynoter, and as prescribed in the *Dialogue Decalogue* distributed to the patriciants of this symposium.[1] With this word of introduction, I can now proceed in the presentation of my materials.

One more thing should be said here: Since I am not a biblical scholar per se—my specialization is in the field of systematic theology —I had to heavily rely upon the work of specialists, with some personal investigation and examination of the sources used.[2]

THE GREEK ANTECEDENTS

Etymologically speaking, the word λόγος (word) comes from the verb λέγειν, which means to gather, count, enumerate, and narrate. In turn, λόγος, exactly parallel to λέγειν, means collection, counting, reckoning, calculation, account, consideration, review, evaluation, value, reflection, ground, condition, narrative, word, and speech.[3]

From the second part of the fifth century B.C., logos is subjectively

---

[1]Leonard Swidler, "The Dialogue Decalogue," *Journal of Ecumenical Studies,* 20.1 (Winter, 1983) 1-4 (revised, September, 1984).

[2]My presentation heavily relies on the excellent work by Gerhard Kittel on the scriptural understanding of the words λέγω, λόγος, ῥῆμα, λαλέω, Λόγος Θεοῦ in *Theological Dictionary of the New Testament* (Ann Arbor, 1967), 4, pp. 68-137. Henceforth, Kittel. Also the articles on Λόγος and Λόγος Θεοῦ by Socrates Gikas and Markos Siotis in *Θρησκευτικὴ καὶ Ἠθικὴ Ἐγκυκλοπαιδεία,* ed. Vasileios Moustakis (Athens, 1962), 8, pp. 334-46 were most helpful. Henceforth, ΘΗΕ.

[3]Kittel, pp. 71-78.

used to mean man's *ratio*, his ability to think. Thus logos is synonymous with νοῦς, reason, the human mind or spirit, and thought. However, Plato maintains the distinction between mind (διάνοια) and word
(λόγος), which is the expression of mind in words.

The term logos played an important role in Greek philosophy.
Before we review the various developments, let us begin with the
general statement that for the Greeks logos always implies a connected
rational element in speech. It has no "creative power," as is the case
in the Judaeo-Christian tradition.[4]

The logos concept in Greek philosophy and religion (or theology)
develops according to two aspects, one logical and one metaphysical.
To quote Kittel,

> First, we have in view the use of logos for word, speech, utterance,
> revelation, not in the sense of something proclaimed and heard,
> but rather in that of something displayed, clarified, recognized,
> and understood, logos as the rational power of calculation in vir-
> tue of which man can see himself and his place in the cosmos;
> logos as the indication of an existing and significant context which
> is assumed to be intelligible; logos as the content itself in terms
> of its meaning and law, its basis and structure. Secondly, we have
> in view logos as a metaphysical reality and an established term
> in philosophy and theology, from which there finally develops
> in later antiquity, under alien influences, a cosmological entity
> and hypostasis of deity, a δεύτερος θεός.[5]

The starting point of the development of the logos concept is
Heraklitos (± 500 B.C.). In Heraklitos, the two aspects of the logos
concept are still significantly undivided. For Heraklitos, logos is the
transcendent and lasting order in which the flux of things and events
occurs, binding the individual to the whole. It is the principle by which
all things behave, the connecting link between cosmos, man, and God.
Also, this same logos when it applies to man, is man's power of thought,
reason and speech, part of the universal spirit and common Logos.[6]

For the Sophists (fifth and fourth century B.C.), the unity of meaning which distinguishes Heraklitos is disrupted. Logos now becomes

---

[4]Ibid. pp. 78-79.
[5]Ibid. pp. 80-81.
[6]Ibid. p. 81; ΘΗΕ pp. 334, 342.

"predominantly the rational power set in man, the power of speech and thought."[7] Gorgias Leontinos extols the "psychagogic" power of logos which is here almost personified: "Logos is a great ruler; in a small and insignificant body he achieves most divine works: he can make fear cease, dispel sadness, cause joy, and augment compassion."[8] Plato (c. 428-348/7 B.C.) identifies logos with the "supreme form" (or idea) that constitutes the "soul of the world." For Plato, "thought, word, matter, nature, being and norm . . . are all brought into a comprehensive interrelation in the logos concept."[9] Plato transcends the individualistic logos of the Sophists to discover the power of logos, which only emerges when this logos is linked to the common reason (κοινὸς λόγος). There is a pre-existent harmony between the logos of the thinking individual soul and the logos of things in general.

Aristotle (384-322 B.C.) sums up the classical understanding of human existence in his statement: "man is the only reason-endowed animal." By logos Artistotle understands both reason and speech.[10]

In the Hellenistic times, the Stoics used the term logos to signify "the ordered and teleologically oriented nature of the world."[11] It is the "cosmic law of reason," identified with god/Zeus with providence and fate (πρόνοια, εἱμαρμένη). It is the "power that extends throughout the matter, and works immanently in all things."[12] It is the organic power that gives shape to the unformed and inorganic matter, and that gives growth to plants and movement to animals. It is seminal reason (λόγος σπερματικός) according to Zeno: that is, it is "a seed which unfolds itself, and this seed is by nature reason."[13] It is this "seminal reason" present in the seeds of plants and animals that gives to each of them their particular shape.

---

[7]Kittel, p. 82.
[8]"Λόγος δυνάστης μέγας ἐστίν, ὃς σμικροτάτῳ σώματι καὶ ἀφανεστάτῳ θειότατα ἔργα ἀποτελεῖ· δύναται γὰρ καὶ φόβον παῦσαι καὶ λύπην ἀφελεῖν καὶ χαρὰν ἐνεργάσασθαι καὶ ἔλεον ἐπαυξῆσαι." Ibid. p. 82; ΘΗΕ p. 342.
[9]Kittel, p. 83.
[10]Ibid. p. 84.
[11]Ibid.
[12]Ibid. p. 85.
[13]Ibid.

Man's reason (logos) is only part of the great general logos. The duality of logos as reason and speech is expressed in the Stoic language, inwardly as inward reason (λόγος ἐνδιάθετος) and outwardly as spoken word (λόγος προφορικός).

In Neoplatonism, logos is also a "shaping power which lends form and life to things and is thus closely related to shape (εἶδος) and form (μορφή), light (φῶς), and life (ζωή)." Life is artistically fashioning power. Where it works, everything is shaped by the logos (λελόγωται). Nature is life and logos, the working power of form. Logos is the origin of all things; the world is logos, and all that is in it is logos (ἀρχὴ οὖν λόγος, καὶ πάντα λόγος).

This logos is an emanation from the nous, which in turn in an emanation from the One. Thus, logos is regarded both as a principle of unity (as an emanation from the one nous), and also as a principle of multiplicity that explains and justifies the variety of phenomena in the world. "This universe derives from and is shaped after the one Nous and the logos that emanates from it . . . and the logos is the one who brings harmony among all things and establishes only one order."[14]

The logos concept is enhanced with a religious significance in the Hellenistic Mysteries. The concept of sacred word (ἱερὸς λόγος) is introduced to signify "sacred history," "holy and mysterious doctrine," and "revelation." Logos is also identified with prayer here, thus becoming the worthy way to enter into relation with God.

In Hermetism, all aspects of the philosophical logos concept are gathered together, personified, and comprehended in the figure of the god Hermes. Hermes is called logos and son of God. However, "there is no implied incarnation" of this logos, "but the equation of a revealing and cosmogonic principle with one of the deities of popular religion . . . In other words, a concept is hypostatised as a god, or identified with a god. There is no question of the divine word of power and creation becoming man, incarnate."[15] It is interesting to note that Hermes takes the role of a mediator and revealer who declares and makes known to men the will of the gods. He thus

---

[14]"Ἐξ ἑνὸς νοῦ καὶ τοῦ ἀπ' αὐτοῦ λόγου ἀνέστη τόδε τὸ πᾶν καὶ διέστη . . . τοῦ δὲ λόγου ἐπ' αὐτοῖς τὴν ἁρμονίαν καὶ μίαν τὴν σύνταξιν εἰς τὰ ὅλα ποιουμένου." See Plotinos, *Ennead* 3. 2.2; Kittel, pp. 85-86.

[15]Kittel, p. 87.

He thus undertakes a soteriological role, "insofar as the logos is present for σώζειν. Thus, in Hellenistic mysticism logos is essentially a cosmic and creative potency, the guide and agent of knowledge, increasingly represented as a religious doctrine of salvation."[16]

The question arises: how much has this doctrine of the Greek philosophers and religion influenced the Christian doctrine of logos, as found in the prologue of Saint John's Gospel? This rich logos doctrine has certainly played a role in the life of the Church, since many of the Greek Fathers used much of this doctrine after making the proper adjustments. Some of this doctrine, and especially that of the Stoics, was also used by Philo Judaeus.

However, both the Old Testament and the New Testament logos doctrine is in contrast with the Greek logos doctrine as delineated above. The Old Testament and New Testament logos doctrine includes more than a logical or "dianoetic" element. Furthermore, the Judaeo-Christian doctrine of logos excludes its understanding as a "hypostatized concept," except in the Wisdom literature, where a power (the wisdom, or even the logos of God as a power of God) receives this hypostatization.

More specifically concerning the prologue of the Fourth Gospel, there is no parallel whatsoever between the Greek logos doctrine and that of Saint John; for Saint John's doctrine regarding the pre-existing Logos, who exists eternally by God and becomes flesh in time, is a completely new doctrine, which according to the Christian understanding can only come from direct revelation given by God himself.

PHILO JUDAEUS

In his writings, Philo of Alexandria (c. 20 B.C.-54 A.D.) uses the term logos over 300 times. The importance of the logos concept for Philo is more than obvious. Philo is certainly dependent upon the Greek philosophers, namely the Stoics, as he tries to harmonize his Jewish faith with Greek philosophy.

According to scholars, the Stoic λόγος τῆς φύσεως is the root of Philo's λόγος Θεοῦ or θεῖος λόγος, to be understood as "divine reason," and "the epitome of divine wisdom."[17] However, Philo gives a new, personalized interpretation to this divine reason, which

---

[16]Ibid.
[17]Ibid. p. 88.

is different from that of the Stoics. This divine reason is not a god himself, as it was in the case of the Stoics. For Philo, this logos is "second after God, through whom all things were made" (τὸ δὲ γενικώτατόν ἐστιν ὁ Θεός, καὶ δεύτερος ὁ Θεοῦ λόγος, τὰ δ᾽ ἄλλα λόγῳ μόνον ὑπάρχει). This logos is the "son of God" (ὁ τῶν πάντων λόγος ἐστὶ κατὰ μὲν Κέλσον αὐτὸς ὁ Θεός, κατὰ δὲ ἡμᾶς ὁ υἱὸς αὐτοῦ). As such this logos-Son of God is called the image of God through whom the world was created (Λόγος δ᾽ ἐστὶν εἰκὼν Θεοῦ δι᾽ οὗ ὁ σύμπας κόσμος δεδημιούργηται or ἐδημουργεῖτο).

Thus, for Philo, this divine reason is a mediating figure between God and man, and God and the world. Through him, a link is established between the remotely transcendent God and his creation.[18]

In his effort to reconcile Greek philosophy with his Jewish faith, Philo becomes the natural bridge between the Greek world and that of the Judaeo-Christian revelation.

In terms of the influence that Philo may have exercised upon Christian thought, and especially in terms of the Fourth Gospel, one realizes that there are some similarities between the two. For example, the mediation of Philonian logos, its being an image of God and a link between God and his creation, and its being a creator logos and a "son of God," remind us very much of the Johannine logos doctrine, as found in the prologue of the Fourth Gospel. However, it is not at all clear that the Philonian logos is a pre-existing divine hypostasis, as in the prologue of John. Instead, the Philonian logos seems to be the personification of a divine energy, probably the creative power of God, to which Philo gave the name logos.

OLD TESTAMENT

The main Hebrew equivalents of the Greek logos are the roots *amar* and *dabar*. More rare is the word *millah* mostly restricted to Job. Etymologically speaking, in *dabar* "one is to seek the 'back' or 'background' of a matter." Everything has a *dabar*, a "background," a "meaning." Thus, in Hebrew speech the meaning or concept stands for the thing, "so that the thing as an event, has in its *dabar*, its historical element, and history is thus enclosed in the *debarim* as the background of things."[19] Since the meaning of the thing is included

---

[18]Ibid. p. 89.
[19]Ibid. p. 92.

in its *dabar,* word and thing are co-extensive. Hence, the most important attribute of *dabar* and its translations as logos and *rhema* is truth: "In every spoken word, there should be a relation of truth between the word and thing, and a relation of fidelity between the one who speaks and the one who hears. Hence, the word belongs to the moral sphere, in which it must be a witness to something for the two persons concerned."[20]

One more thing should be said about the Hebrew *dabar,* which in itself is of great theological significance: besides the intellectual, "dianoetic" element in *dabar* there is one more element, the so-called "dynamic" element. To quote Kittel:

> Dianoetically, *dabar* always contains a νοῦς, a thought. In it is displayed the meaning of a thing, so that *dabar* always belongs to the field of knowledge. By its *dabar* a thing is known and becomes subject to thought. To grasp the *dabar* of a thing is to grasp the thing itself. It becomes clear and transparent; its nature is brought to light. . . . But along with the dianoetic element is the dynamic, even if this is not always so evident. Every *dabar* is filled with power which can be manifested in the most diverse energies. This power is felt by the one who receives the word and takes it to himself. But it is present independently of this reception in the objective effects that the word has in history. The two elements, the dianoetic and the dynamic, may be seen most forcefully in the word of God, and the prophets had a profound grasp of this from both sides, so that in this respect they are the teachers of all theology.[21]

It should be noted that in the Septuagint logos and *rhema,* being Greek words, naturally have a mainly dianoetic value. They receive their dynamic element from the Hebrew *dabar.* To quote Kittel once more:

> Only in the Hebrew *dabar* is the material concept with its energy felt so vitally in the verbal concept that the word appears as a material force which is always present and at work, which runs and has the power to make alive . . . *Rhemata* in 3 Kings 11.41 or Genesis 15.1/27.1 stands for the Hebrew *debarim* which actually

---

[20]Ibid. p. 93.
[21]Ibid. p. 92.

means history. History is the event established and narrated in the word, so that the thing and its meaning may both be seen, as expressed in the Hebrew *debarim* in the plural. From these examples it may be seen that the LXX concept cannot be wholly explained in terms of the Greek logos or *rhema,* but can be fully understood only against the background of the Hebrew *dabar.*[22]

Prophetic Revelation

According to Old Testament scholars, the history of the theological development of the *dabar* concept has its roots in prophesy. There is a progressive development from revelation given in sign and a pictorial language, to direct revelation given to the writing prophets in direct speech from God.

In the first instance, the prophet is seized by God, by his Spirit (*ruah*) and Word (*millah,* logos). Visions given to the prophet by God, and voices heard by him in his own heart, find expression on his lips, thus translating them to express the word of God. At this stage, the prophet is the speaker and not God. Old Testament scholars give two such cases, the case of David the King (2 Sam [2 Kgs] 23.1ff.) and the case of the Balaam oracles (Num 24.4,15; cf. Prov 30.1).

This pictorial revelation, through signs and visions, does not disappear completely, for even in the classical age of the writing of the prophets it is still known as containing the revelation of the Word of God. The visions related to the call of *Isaiah* and *Ezekiel,* for example, present images through which the word of God is announced.

A second stage of the Old Testament prophesy is that of a combined sign and word given to the prophet by God. The voice that the prophet perceives in himself is not revealed any more as his own voice (*neum david*) in 2 Sam 23.1, but the voice of God himself (*neum Jahweh*). The original whispering in *neum* that could not be regarded as articulate speech, is now developed with increasing clarity and energy in the (*dabar Jahweh*).

In the case of interconnection of image and word, the word of God, *dabar* is the background and meaning of the sign (see Amos 8.2, and Jer 1.11ff.). However, the word does not have to be combined with an image. Instead, it can be received as a voice, the voice of God speaking directly to the prophet.

In the history of Old Testament prophesy, the *dabar* increasingly

---

[22]Ibid. p. 93.

freed itself from the image and sign and became a pure expression of divine revelation. The prophet realized that God himself was speaking to him from within. God prepares him to receive his message, which the prophet expresses through his own means of expression as a divine message and God's word. The process is very beautifully described in the case of Samuel (1 Sam 3.1ff.).

From the days of Samuel, God's word is a decisive force in the history of Israel. The word of God is given to David the king through Nathan the prophet (2 Sam 7.4), and it is given to Elijah (1 Kgs 17.2,8). The word of God plays a constructive historical part in the parade of events, it is fulfilled; it comes to pass, and it stands forever without any cooperation on man's part. The Word of God expresses God's mystery, and its content is irresistible (2 Kgs 1.17; 9.36; Is 9.7; 53.10ff.)[23]

Finally in the books of the writing prophets, the transition is made to the final view regarding Old Testament prophesy and the inspiration of the entire Old Testament, as representing the word of God. The books of the writing prophets are often opened by the statement: The Word of God that was revealed to Hosea (*debar-Jahweh asher haya el hoshea*) (see Hos 1.1; Mic 1.1; Zeph 1.1; Mal 1.1). It is on this basis that the books of the Old Testament were collected, that is, as representing the Word of God revealed to man. Besides *dabar*, which was a dynamic, creative, and, at times, destructive element (see Is 9.7, for example) *Torah* is also part of divine revelation (see Is 1.10; 2.3; 30.9; 12; Jer 18.18). This *Torah*, God's teaching, is originally conceived as the doctrine of God mediated by the priest.

Jeremiah offers the most theological understanding of the word of God, with his speculations on that word, which is entrusted to the prophet rather than to the priest. Jeremiah is committed to the dynamic content of the word of God. He feels compelled to preach God's word, which is the joy and the delight of his heart (15.16). Inwardly aflame with the word of God, he feels that he will perish if he does not speak. Jeremiah has to preach God's word for his own soul's salvation.

Whereas Jeremiah's wrestling with the Word of God is a matter of personal destiny, Deutero-Isaiah sees the Word of God in a different light: for Deutero-Isaiah *debar Jahweh* is a historical force. Deutero-Isaiah also stresses the dynamic aspect of God's Word. Nature may pass away, but the Word of Jahweh endures forever (Is 40.8).

---

[23]Ibid. p. 96.

God's word carries its fulfilment in itself. As rain and snow always produce results in terms of soaking the earth and making seeds sprout, so the Word of Jahweh cannot return to heaven unless it accomplishes its mission (Is 55.10ff.).

Revelation of the Law

Debar Yahweh applies to prophesy, but also to *Torah,* the teachings of God, or the Law of God. Whereas prophesy establishes a personal and moral relationship between God and the prophet, the revelation of the Law, more frequently called the *debarim* of God, is a revelation for all. As we can see in Jeremiah, "the legal *dabar* is valid for the whole people in every age quite independently of the prophetic recipient."[24]

The best examples of the "legal *dabar*" are, first, the Decalogue, which is called *asereth hadebarim,* in Exodus 34.28 (cf. Deutoronomy 4.13; 10.4); second, the Book of the Covenant (Exodus 20.23—chapter 23), read by Moses on the making of the covenant to which the chosen people pledged itself, and which is also called *debarim* of God; and third, Deuteronomy, the *sepher haberith* in 2 Kings 23.2ff., 21, whose purpose is to proclaim as Moses' testament the divine words he received on the Mount of God (*elleh hadebarim*), in Deuteronomy 1.1.

The Divine Word of Creation and Poetry

In the post-exilic times, the Pentateuch and the Prophets were put together to represent the One Word of God as a single whole. Both the legal and the prophetic Word of God reveal the will of God contained in them. A third sphere of revelation besides the legal and the prophetic, is that of the creation of nature, which is everywhere attributed to the Word of God.

Finally, in the Old Testament poetry, revelation is affected by the Word of God (Job 4.12), as creation is also the result of the creative power of the *dabar* of God (Ps 33). *Dabar* in poetry (Psalms) keeps its double character: prophetic and legal. Besides containing revelation, it keeps both of its elements: dianoetic and dynamic.

Where does this Old Testament logos doctrine lead us, in terms of the New Testament, and especially the Johannine logos doctrine?

The dynamic content given to the Word of God, besides the

---

[24]Ibid. p. 98.

dianoetic content, certainly makes a great difference in comparison with the Greek logos doctrine. The Old Testament doctrine is certainly on the way toward a doctrine of the word of God which presents this word as reflecting not only the will of God, but also his essence. It is certainly the predecessor of the Christian doctrine, as we have it in the Johannine Logos doctrine, and especially the prologue of the Fourth Gospel. God spoke to the prophets and the fathers in various ways throughout the Old Testament salvation history. He finally spoke through and in his own Son, his Logos who became flesh in order for him to fully reveal to us God the Father, according to the favored expression of the Greek Fathers.

The creative word of God through whom God creates the world; the efficient word of God who achieves what he announces; the irresistible word of God that compelled the prophets to action, is not a mere energy of God, which only partially reveals the Father. Instead, he is the one who is always with God, being everything that God the Father is, however distinct from the Father.

The Wisdom literature, omitted by Kittel and other Protestant scholars in their otherwise outstanding scholarly work, gives us more insights and even more striking parallels which go in the direction of Saint John's doctrine. In the Wisdom literature, the Word of God is described as a creative principle, that which preserves the world, the one which is the source of life, the νοῦς (mind) that governs and directs history, the salvation of men, and the one which punishes God's enemies.[25] This logos proceeding from God's essence (Is 44.26, Lam 2.17), is eternal, infallible, almighty, and self-sufficient; however, this word of God in the Old Testament doctrine is never personified.

In the *Targoumim* (commentators) of the Old Testament, we also find an anthropomorphic expression regarding the word of God: namely, the word of God is identified with the *memra Jahweh*, that is God's thought and will (or thought-will), which is ultimately identified with God. However, this word of God is not an intermediate being between God and the world, as is at times the case in Greek philosophy and religion. This word of God is the poetically hypostatized thought-will of God, which is not a divine hypostasis.

One can say as much of the hypostatized Wisdom of God, as we find it in Proverbs (3.19; 8.1-21; 9.1-9), in Ecclesiasticus (2.3,9; 7.20; 9.16), and in Wisdom of Solomon (7.22,23-chapter 8).

---

[25]See ΘHE, p. 341.

It is only in the New Testament doctrine, based upon the experience of the Word of God becoming flesh, that we can find the revelation of the true nature of the logos of God, gradually reaching its apex in the Fourth Gospel.

THE NEW TESTAMENT LOGOS DOCTRINE

The New Testament places its emphasis on hearing (ἀκούω). This hearing presupposes a preceeding speaking. The φωνὴ of God that accompanies some events in the life of Christ, such as his baptism and his transfiguration, is not just an accompanying phenomenon; it gives the event its theme and content.

As one reviews the various usages of the word (λόγος) in the New Testament, one realizes that the whole gamut of meanings is given to this word, beginning with the more negative to the most positive ones. At times no judgment is given regarding the content of the word. At all times, the word has something to say whether negative or positive.

The most profound meaning of the word is that of the word of God. The word is never an independent entity. It is spoken by a person. Its authority depends on the person who speaks. For the word points out towards the person that speaks it. What makes the distinctiveness of the New Testament logos statements is their relation to the one who speaks them, God himself, of God in Jesus.

It is true that throughout the New Testament Jesus calls upon his own authority: but I say to you (Ἐγὼ δὲ λέγω ὑμῖν). However, what makes these statements of Jesus authoritative is not the calling upon his own authority as such, but "the content which sets aside traditional authorities . . . and the fact that this content is offered through Christ."[26]

More Specific Meanings

One group of texts where the word logos is to be found uses the word in the various classical meanings described above. Thus, one may group various New Testament texts under the following specific categories of logos meaning and content: "reckoning," "account," "ground," "matter," and "reason why" this is so or happens so.[27]

---

[26]Kittel, p. 103.
[27]Ibid. pp. 103-05.

Sayings of Jesus

The sayings of Jesus (λόγοι or ῥήματα) are by far more important than any previous category:

a) Quotations: The New Testament gives an ample amount of quotations of these sayings, especially in the Synoptic Gospels. Collections of these sayings of Jesus were preceded by the apostolic witness. The Gospels are the authoritative collection of these sayings.

b) Authority: As for the authority of these sayings of Jesus, this authority is based upon the kind of person that Jesus is: His authority is not that of the rabbis, but that of the Son of God.

What was said of the word of God in the Old Testament also applies to the word of Jesus: "heaven and earth will pass away; but my words will not pass away" (Mk 13.31).

As it is with his acts, Jesus' word also demands faith in the one whom God sent. This is nothing else but the heart of the Word of God according to the Synoptic tradition (Mt 8.9ff.; Lk 5.5).

The Synoptic tradition is taken up by John. Receiving or rejecting the words of Jesus is a matter of life or death: receiving or rejecting the word makes one worthy of eternal life or eternal judgment and damnation.[28] For the word of Jesus is equivalent to that of scripture (γραφή): "they believed in the scripture and in the word spoken by Jesus . . ." (Jn 2.22; 5.47).

However, to believe or not to believe in the Scripture and in the word spoken by Jesus, to know or not to know the secrets of God's Kingdom, is a given (Mt 19.11; Mk 4.11; Lk 18.34; 9.45), which absolves from responsibility and guilt.

c) The Appeal to Words of Jesus Outside the Gospels: It is surprising that outside the gospels the direct quotations of the sayings of Jesus play a less important role that one would expect. However, there are many ways of quoting the Lord's sayings without direct reference to them. In Saint Paul and Saint James we find the example of such quotations, as we do in *Didache*.

Also, it should be noted that there is no evidence of autonomous collections of the words of Jesus (λόγια), as some scholars may suppose. The words of Jesus cannot be separated from his works, and are always seen in a Christological context. They are seen in the light of his crucifixion and resurrection, and his ascension into heaven.

Furthermore, in primitive Christianity, as in post-prophetic

---

[28]Ibid. p. 107.

Judaism, the entire Christian message becomes word of God, word of the Lord, or even just simply logos to indicate the revealed message of God spoken in and through his only begotten Son and Word of God, Jesus.

Quotation of the Old Testament as the Word of God

The New Testament refers to the Old Testament either as the Scripture or the word of God. There is a variety of rabbinic formulae that refer to the Old Testament, reflected in a variety of forms of the Greek verb λέγω such as λέγει, φησίν, εἶπεν, λέγων, ἐρρέθη, εἰρημένον and ῥηθέν.

It seems that the predominant tenses are two, whether present or perfect, on the basis of the Hebrew *omer-amar*. These tenses are normally used to indicate a past event or statement made in the salvation history, which, however "is just as directly alive and active in the present."[29]

In the above traditional formulae no definite subject is given. However, there is also a variety of subjects mentioned, for example: a human subject, Moses, the prophet Isaiah, someone, a superhuman subject, the pre-existent Christ, referred to in a variety of texts besides the prologue of Saint John; finally, God himself, in a variety of ways, such as ὁ Θεὸς εἶπεν τὸ ῥηθὲν ὑπὸ τοῦ Κυρίου (διὰ τοῦ προφήτου) and so on.

In some instances the mention of the divine subject is facilitated by the presence in the quotation of an "I-saying" (Mt 22.31ff.: "I am the God of Abraham . . ."). But the quotations go further by giving God as the author of the entire Old Testament, for it is God who speaks in the Scripture, (and more so according to the Alexandrian view of inspiration). However, the human factor does not disappear, for it is the true subject of what is said. Thus, most of the time the quotation formulae that refer to the human subject are freely interchangeable with those which refer to the divine subject.

The same principle applies to the words of logos or *rhema*. Both aspects of divine inspiration, divine and human, are well emphasized. The Scripture (Old Testament) is both a human word (λόγοι Ἡσαΐου, Jn 13.38, Lk 3.4), and also a divine word (λόγος Θεοῦ, Mk 7.13; Jn 10.35; 2 Pet 3.5-7).

When the New Testament quotes the Old Testament, it maintains

---

[29]Ibid. p. 109.

original reference to it as *debar-Jahweh.* God spoke in a concrete historical situation. However, in view of the totality of God's revelation, the Old and the New Covenant are combined as the one word of God (Col 1.25; Heb 4.13).

This is the reason that in some instances it is hard to decide if the word of God quoted in the New Testament text is that of the Old Testament or that of the early Christian message (see Heb 4.12: ζῶν ὁ λόγος τοῦ Θεοῦ, καὶ ἐναργής, καὶ τομώτερος ὑπὲρ πᾶσαν μάχαιραν δίστομον," and Eph 6.17: "καὶ τὴν μάχαιραν τοῦ πνεύματος, ὅ ἐστι ῥῆμα Θεοῦ").

The Word of God as Spoken to Individuals

a) Simeon, John the Baptist: The Old Testament formula regarding the word of God specifically given to a man (e.g. 1 Kings 15.10, "ῥῆμα Κυρίου"; 2 Kings 24.11) "λόγος Κυρίου," is very rare in the New Testament. However, we have two specific cases in the New Testament; that of Simeon who received the Messianic promise (Lk 2.29), and that of Saint John the Baptist (Lk 3.2, "ἐγένετο ῥῆμα Θεοῦ ἐπὶ Ἰωάννην τὸν Ζαχαρίου υἱόν").

b) The Apostolic Period: Besides these two cases, in which the word of God is spoken to individuals, there is no other case in the New Testament where the "word of God" (λόγος Θεοῦ, Κυρίου, ῥῆμα Κυρίου) is used to give special divine directions to special people. These directions are given; however the expressions used for them are different (ἀποκάλυψις, πνεῦμα, φωνή, λόγος προφητείας, οἱ λόγοι οὗτοι).[30]

The reason for this is that the word of God takes a new and irrevocable meaning for primitive Christianity: it is the word of God finally, definitively and irrevocably spoken once and for all (ἐφάπαξ) in his Son, in what took place in him and in the message concerning it. This Son of God is the historical Jesus of Nazareth, the Lord of the faith, the Word of God made flesh. It is the primitive Christian conviction that the revelation of God in his Son is final (Heb 1.1ff.), and that "a new age has been inaugurated therewith (καινός, καινά)."[31]

c) Jesus of Nazareth: Because of the consciousness in early Christianity that Jesus of Nazareth is the Son of God and the Lord of the

---

[30]Ibid. p. 113.
[31]Ibid.

faith, in whom and through whom the last word of God's revelation is given, no reference is made to Jesus as having imparted a "word of God" of any kind, as was the case with the Old Testament prophets. In two instances, the baptism of Jesus and his transfiguration, a voice is heard from heaven. However, this voice is an attestation of the divine sonship of Christ to the hearers, just in case there is any doubt left in them regarding this divine sonship.

Such phrases as "everything was handed to me by my Father" (πάντα μοι παρεδόθη ὑπὸ τοῦ πατρός μου) and "he knows the Father" (τὸν πατέρα ἐπιγιγνώσκει Mt 11.27) set the unity of Jesus with the Father, and also with the word of God, on a completely different basis which goes far beyond isolated impartation.[32]

The Early Christian Message as the Word of God (Outside the Johannine Writings)

a) Statistics: The expression "word of God," "word of the Lord," and logos are used by the New Testament corpus (without any differentiation in usage in Paul, Acts or elsewhere), to indicate the complex of New Testament events around Jesus and the message bears witness to this complex.

b) Content: As far as the content of this word of God in the New Testament is concerned, the following remarks should be made:

The content of the word of God preached by the apostles is only one: to witness about Jesus and the word and work of God in him and through him. The disciples were the eye-witnesses of the events that took place in the life of Jesus; they were the eye-witnesses of his miracles, his teachings, his sufferings, death, and resurrection. Their unforsakable task is to be witnesses to all these things, and proclaim Jesus of Nazareth that was put to death as the risen Lord of the faith. This proclamation is made to both the Jews and the Gentiles. For the disciples of Jesus, the word of God is the word about Jesus.

Saint Paul's message is the same: he is called to proclaim the message about Christ. So it is with the late epistles. In one of them the content of God's logos is given in these terms: "that Christ came into the world to save sinners" (ὅτι Χριστὸς ἦλθεν εἰς τὸν κόσμον ἁμαρτωλοὺς σῶσαι 1 Tim 1.15).

---

[32]Ibid. p. 114.

The Character and Efficiency of the Early Christian Word/Message
The early Christian message is the message of salvation in Christ, a message about Christ the Savior, the good tidings of God's *magnalia* in Jesus, the Gospel.

Since this message is the word of God, it corresponds to a reality for the one who speaks the word of God. This is why the Gospel is called the Gospel of truth (see 2 Cor 1.18; Eph 1.13; Col 1.5.; 2 Tim 2.15; Jas 1.18).

This word of truth is a given by God (Tit 1.3). Its efficacy depends upon its author who is God; it is also assured by his will (Jas 1.18), and by God's power (Acts 19.20; 2 Col 6.7). It cannot be bound (2 Tim 2.9); and only God can open the door for the word to enter (θύρα τοῦ λόγου Col 4.3).

Being a non-magical entity, the word of God only produces its effects in those who receive it in faith, and are saved and sanctified by it (1 Tim 4.5); whereas the same word is blasphemed by those Christians of an unholy walk and conduct (Tit 2.5). For those who accept the word, this word "does not simply point to grace, salvation and life; it affects salvation and life, for it is grace, salvation and life."[33]

b) Relation of Man to the Word: We have already indicated that the word of God is relational or, to use the expression coined recently by an Orthodox theologian, it is a "relational entity." Being God's word, God speaks, and man hears.

Man is passive at the beginning: the term "birth" and "rebirth" gives this message (see Jas 1.8: βουληθεὶς ἀπεκύησεν ἡμᾶς λόγῳ ἀληθείας, and 1 Pet 1.23: ἀναγεγεννημένοι . . . διὰ λόγου . . . τοῦ Θεοῦ).

However, the word of God must be received through faith, and must be acted upon by the hearer, in order for it to achieve its purpose, salvation in Christ.[34]

c) The Word as Spoken Word: Finally, the word of the early Christian message is a spoken word. It is heard and known, lived and experienced, so that it may also be proclaimed. It was the responsibility of the first Christians to proclaim in faithfulness (ἀσφάλεια) the event that has happened in Jesus "the word of God which has been established by God and spoken in the event" (Lk 1.1-4; cf. Tit 1.9).[35]

---

[33]Ibid. p. 118.
[34]Ibid. p. 119.
[35]Ibid.

The Word in the Synoptic Account of Jesus

The Synoptic Gospels are in direct continuity with the primitive Christian message regarding the word of God and expressed by it. It continues the message and witness about Jesus (see Lk 1.2). Once more, Jesus in the Synoptic account is not called the word of God, which is the contribution of Johannine theology. Neither is there a reference to him as a "prophet," or a "transmitter" of the word.

There are only four difficult passages to consider, two in Mark (2.2, 4.33), one in the Gospel of Luke (5.1) and one in the Book of Acts (10.36) where it is said that Jesus is a preacher of the word. Jesus preaches the same word as the apostles. However, his vision is not to simply "pass on" the word. The word that Jesus preaches is not the object of mere talking (λαλεῖν). It is a word that is spoken in power, and presented in the works of Jesus as well as in his speech: miraculous healings that accompany it are part of his word, not only spoken, but also enacted (see Mt 11.4).

The Word in the Synoptic Sayings of Jesus

The occurrence of logos in the case of the sayings of Jesus in the Synoptics is minimal. Besides the parable of the Sower, common in all three Synoptics, there are only two passages in Luke where the expression word of God (λόγος τοῦ Θεοῦ) occurs. Luke 8.21, which tells us of the relatives of Jesus as being those who "hear God's word and do it," is rendered differently by Matthew (3.5) and Mark (12.50). Where Luke says "word of God," the others say "will of God." It seems that "word of God" is a Lucan construction; it is possible that the Aramaic substratum used "will of God." As for Luke 11.28, which is peculiar to Luke, "blessed are those who hear the word of God and keep it" (μακάριοι οἱ ἀκούοντες τὸν λόγον τοῦ Θεοῦ καὶ φυλάσσοντες αὐτόν), it is not clear that Jesus actually used the word and applied it to his own preaching.[36]

As for the parable of the Sower, present in all three synoptics (Mt 13.18-23; Mk 4.13-20; Lk 8.11-15), the use of the expression "word of God" is in the interpretation section of the parable and in its allegory. It is possible that the Christian community laid the words on the lips of Jesus.[37]

---

[36]Ibid. p. 121.
[37]Ibid. pp. 121-22.

Word of God in Revelation

In the group of sayings that refer to the content of the Book of Revelation, the phrase "word of God" is not used.[38]

In two instances, (Revelation 19.9 and 17.7) the phrase (λόγοι Θεοῦ) is used in plural to indicate the promises spoken to the prophets.

In another case (Rev 1.2; 1.9; 6.9), λόγος Θεοῦ is paralleled with μαρτυρία 'Ιησοῦ. The two are a tautology; the word of God is witness about Jesus the Christ. This statement is in perfect continuity with the logos doctrine of primitive Christianity.

The only problematic passage is Revelation 19.13: "and his name is called the logos of God" (κέκληται τὸ ὄνομα αὐτοῦ ὁ Λόγος τοῦ Θεοῦ). However, this statement cannot be seen apart from the total New Testament picture. It belongs to the series of primitive Christian logos sayings, and is a part of the primitive Christian view of Christ.

Jesus Christ, the Logos of God

We have established that in primitive Christianity there is an awareness reflected in the use of the term logos, that preaching of what has taken place in the person of Jesus is preaching of the word. Also, reception of the word implies faith in Jesus. The preachers of the word, are not people who simply repeat old sayings (*tannaites*), but then are eye-witnesses of those saving events—Christ's death and Ressurection—that have taken place.

The point of the Sower parable of the Synoptics is that the seed in actually the Christ event which has taken place in Jesus. The word of God is the hidden mystery of Christ made manifest to the saints. Christ is the word of God, which God has spoken to the saints (Col 1.25-27).

It is obvious that the New Testament word theology is in continuity with the Old Testament, when it does not rest the logos statements on a "concept" of the word. The word is not a concept, but an event, which is given in the person of Jesus the Christ. In him, God enacted yes to man's salvation (2 Cor 1.19). He is the word yes in his historical person. According to Revelation 3.14, he is the word Amen (τάδε λέγει ὁ 'Αμήν). The promises of God regarding man's salvation are decisively realized in him. This is the meaning of Revelation 19.13: "Whose name is the Word of God," a "succinct expression

---

[38]Ibid. p. 123.

to something present in the whole outlook and utterance of the primitive church."[39]

The historical person of Jesus is the only one who can meet the qualification of "Word of God." He is the only one to teach with authority, for "His authoritative word is the word of one who knows that the fully authority of God is present in his person Mt 9.1ff.)."[40] Jesus is not just the one who brings the word, but the one who incorporates it in his person, in the historical process of his speech and action, of his life and being."[41] It is this Word who is "King of Kings and Lord of Lords" (Rev 19.16). As the Word of God, he is witness and bears witness, even the "faithful witness" (ὁ μάρτυς ὁ πιστός: Rev 1.5; 3.14), who came to "bear witness" (Jn 1.7) and explain the Father (Jn 1.18). He is the word of God spoken by God.

The Word of God Spoken by God in 1 John 1.1ff.

By now we have enough historical background to appreciate and understand the statement made in 1 Jn 1.1 ff., regarding the Logos/ Word of God. He is the Logos of Life who became manifest, whom we touched and saw: He is the Christ event in the historical figure of Jesus.

The words used are those known from primitive Christianity: witness and announce (μαρτυροῦμεν καὶ ἀπαγγέλλομεν) (Acts 6.4; 1.22); λόγος ζωῆς is parallel to ῥήματα ζωῆς (Acts 5.20).

It is to be noted that the equation of Logos with Jesus in 1 Jn 1.1 is still dynamic. There is no personification whether conceptually or "mythically," a danger not avoided by some of the trinitarian heresies later in history.

The whole statement in 1 Jn 1.1ff. is in continuity with other New Testament statements concerning the word. However, there are two new elements added which make this text comparable to the prologue of the Fourth Gospel: "ὃ ἦν ἀπ᾽ ἀρχῆς" (verse 1), and "ἥτις ἦν πρὸς τὸν πατέρα" (verse 2).

The Distinctiveness of the Logos Saying in John 1.1

We are now ready for the most important logos theology text, the prologue of Saint John's Gospel. The use of logos in the prologue of the Fourth Gospel is absolutely unique, even in terms of

---

[39]Ibid. p. 125.
[40]Ibid. p. 124.
[41]Ibid.

the rest of the Gospel.

All the other uses of logos are in continuity with the primitive Christian tradition, as established above.[42] In the prologue, the Fourth Gospel breaks with the Synoptic tradition that hesitated to apply the word Logos to Jesus' teachings, in order to avoid making Jesus a mere transmitter of the message at the same level with the Apostles. However, in the Fourth Gospel, and especially its parting discourses, it is clear that this is no longer a problem: Jesus speaks, and refers to his doctrine with "I have said unto you," and also speaks of his mission. The unity of action and speech is established once and for all in the prologue, with the proclamation of Jesus as the pre-existent, eternal word of God who became flesh.

The point of transition, making the Fourth Gospel (which is in agreement with the prologue statement on the Logos) unique, is verse 1.14: "the word became flesh" (ὁ Λόγος σὰρξ ἐγένετο). This is only implied in 1 Jn 1.1.ff., whereas it is clearly enunciated here: Jesus, in his historical person, is the Word of God: Jesus is not partially, but unconditionally identified with the eternal word of God, a word who entered our history, became incarnate, became flesh (σάρξ).

The essential point of the prologue is that (as in 1 Jn 1.1ff.) the logos is the pre-existent Christ, and that (as distinct from 1 Jn 1.1ff.) the true theme of the Gospel is the transition of logos from pre-existence to history. The theme of the pre-existence of logos underlies the entire Fourth Gospel. It should be noted that the theme of the pre-existence of Christ is not unique to the Fourth Gospel. Saint Paul, for example, dealt with the topic on many occasions (especially Phil 2.1ff., Col 1.12ff.). What makes the Fourth Gospel unique is that its Christology is well stated at the beginning (prologue), and that its Christological doctrine is grouped under the catchword the Logos.

Interest and Derivation of the Logos Sayings in the Prologue of John
a) The Lack of Speculative Concern: The Logos statement in the Johannine prologue is not a speculative one, in spite of the appearances: the statement was not derived from a speculation on the pre-existence of logos, but from seeing, contemplating (θεᾶσθαι) his glory (δόξα) in the historical figure of Jesus.

For the same reason, it is wrong to speak of personification of logos in Jn 1.1, 14, if by this "personification" is understood the

---

[42]Ibid. p. 128.

non-biblical interest in a "world of reason or a semi-divine intermediate being, the Logos, . . . which . . . entered one day into the
person of an earthly man."[43]

b) The Allusion to Genesis 1.1: There is an obvious allusion to
Genesis 1.1, in the ἐν ἀρχῇ statement regarding logos: it reminds us
of "the beginning" (*bereshith*) of God's creation. God spoke in the historical person of Jesus of Nazareth, the eternal and pre-existing Word
of God who became flesh. It is only logical to identify the historical
figure of Jesus—the word of God—with the word of the divine Creator.

A new element introduced by the prologue of John as compared
with Genesis is that the word of God who is always by God and who
proceeds from God without being detached from him, is a distinct
person, or, better, a hypostasis, with regard to God. Once more, this
is not the result of a speculative concern of the evangelist: he con-
templates God's glory in a person, the incarnate Son of God, Jesus
of Nazareth, in whom the word took place (σὰρξ ἐγένετο).

c) Logos and Torah: Scholars looked for other connections between the prologue of John and its environment: four concepts were
brought to be compared with that of Johannine Logos: the Hellenistic
Gnostic Logos; the oriental Gnostic man; the Hellenistic Jewish *hoch-
mah* (σοφία) and the Palestinian Jewish Torah. There is certainly
parallelism with all these concepts, but no real connection with the
Johannine Logos, for the reasons stated above.

Regarding the last one, the rabbinic Torah, there is a direct
reference in the prologue: "The Law (Torah) was given by Moses;
grace and truth came through Jesus Christ" (Jn 1.14). The contrast
is obvious: Torah was passed on by Moses. The content of the revelation given by Jesus, and that which replaces the law of Moses is "grace
and truth."

As a parallel to the Καινὴ Διαθήκη of the Lord's supper, one
might speak of Καινὸς Νόμος, with reference to the word of God
which has gone forth and become an event, flesh, and history, in his
divine person.[44]

* * *

---

[43]Ibid. p. 131.
[44]Ibid. p. 136.

The Logos doctrine, as delineated above, and culminating in the prologue of the Fourth Gospel, has profoundly left its mark on Eastern Christianity. It permeates its entire liturgical life, with meaningful liturgical statements regarding the eternal Logos of God, who manifests "all of the Father in himself" (ὅλον ἐν ἑαυτῷ δεικνὺς τὸν Πατέρα).

The Logos doctrine, doubled with that of the "image of the invisible God," became the basis of the refutation of Gnosticism by Saint Irenaios, Arianism and tritheism by Saint Athanasios and the Cappadocian Fathers. It holds a special place in the systematic speculations of the Christian doctrine regarding Christology throughout the ages.

Since the Logos doctrine is also present in the Qur'ān, one may hope that it can be considered to be one of the elements that we Christians and Muslims may cherish together as a common patrimony, at least to a certain extent. But even if and when do we decide to differ, let us hope that we do in the mutual respect of one another's convictions. We commend ourselves and one another to the common Father in heaven, praying to him that his divine Word may always have the last word.

Jews, Christians, and Muslims According to the Qur'ān

ABDULAZIZ A. SACHEDINA

IN THIS PAPER I PROPOSE to examine the Qur'ānic references to the believers—the Muslims, and the People of the Book—the Christians and the Jews in the context of their response to the message from God in the form of "guidance" (*hudā* and *hidāya*) sent through the prophets. The Qur'ān makes numerous references to the Old and New Testament religious personalities who had come to different peoples and nations at different times with a revealed scripture. All these messages, according to the Qur'ān, emanate from a single source, and are universal and identical. Accordingly, human beings have the responsibility to believe in the divine message and act according to its requirements. It is within the context of such a responsibility that human beings are obligated to accept God's religion and prophethood as the source of "guidance" to the life of "prosperity."

"Guidance" in the Qur'ān is constitutive of God's purpose in creating human beings. There is in the world, "for those who reflect," a moral purpose—a purpose which will be fulfilled in the Last Judgment:

> By the soul; and that which shaped it and inspired it to [know the difference between] lewdness and Godfearing! Prosperous is he who purifies it, and failed has he who seduces it [91.7-8].

In order for human beings to attain the purpose for which they are created, they need to be adequately guided. Thus, God, according to this verse, has endowed human beings with the necessary cognition and volition to further their comprehension of the purpose for which they are created and to realize it by using their knowledge. Moreover, the verse also makes it plain that the distinction between "lewdness" (evil) and "Godfearing" (good) is ingrained in the soul in the form of "inspiration," a form of "guidance" with which God has favored human beings. It is through this "guidance" that human beings are expected to develop the ability to judge their actions and to choose that which will lead them to prosperity. But this is not an easy goal to achieve. It involves spiritual and moral development, something that is most challenging in the light of the basic human weaknesses indicated by the Qur'ān:

> Surely man was created fretful,
> when evil visits him, impatient,
> when good visits him, grudging [70.19-20].

Humanity, the Qur'ān shows, was created as God's vicegerent; was given "trust" (*amāna*), so as to live purposively in the world and to exercise authority over creation with justice:

> Lo! We offered the trust unto the heavens and the earth and the hills, but they shrank from bearing it and were afraid of it. And man assumed it [33.72].

This trust makes human beings the agents of God in relation to the creation. It also, of course, implies that there is a standard of correct behavior and of governance which humanity is to follow to attain "prosperity." The tragedy, according to the Qur'ān, is that humanity has not lived up to its office; has not, by and large, submitted to following the "guidance" which God has proffered. Human beings assumed the *amāna*. But, "Lo! He hath proved a tyrant and a fool" (33.72).

This human weakness reveals a basic tension that must be resolved by further acts of "guidance" by God. It is at this point that God sends the prophets and the "Books" (revealed messages) to show human beings how to change their character and bring it to conformity with the divine plan for human conduct:

> That is the Book, wherein is no doubt, a guidance to Godfearing. Those rely upon guidance from their Lord. Those are ones who prosper [2.2,5].

"Guidance" from God signifies the "direction" He provides to procure that which is desirable, first by creating in the soul a disposition that can guard against spiritual peril, if a person hearkens to its warnings, and then, by further strengthening this natural guidance through the Book and the Prophet. "Guidance" signifying "showing the path" is a fundamental feature of the Qur'ān and is reiterated throughout to emphasize the fact that this form of guidance is not only part of normative human nature, but is also "universal" and available to all who aspire to become "Godfearing" and "prosperous."

However, human beings can reject this "guidance," although they cannot produce any valid excuse for the rejection. Still, rejection pertains to the "procuring" or appropriating of that which is desirable, and not to the act of apprehending in the first place what is desirable. Thus, when God denies "guidance" to those who do not believe in his revelations (16.104), the denial pertains to the procurement of the desirable end, and *not* to the initial guidance that is originally engraved upon the hearts of all human beings. The verse 4.70: "And we guide them to a straight path" points to the "guidance" signifying the procurement of the good end. It implies that this guidance is available to an individual after that person has consented to lead a life of uprightness (*taqwā*). In another place, the Qur'ān makes even more explicit that this latter aspect of "guidance" enables a person to achieve that which is desirable:

> Whomsoever God desires to guide, he expands his breast to *Islam* [to submit himself to the will of God in order to procure the desirable goal]; whomsoever he desires to lead astray [because of his personal choice not to "submit"] he makes his breast narrow, tight, as if he were climbing to heaven. So God lays admonition upon those who believe not [6.125].

It becomes evident, then, that the Qur'ān is speaking about two forms of "guidance." As a matter of fact, all the exegetes in their commentaries on verse 2.2, "That is the Book wherein is no doubt, a guidance to the Godfearing," distinguished the two forms in response to the question as to why the Book should be revealed as "guidance" to the Godfearing, for they have presumably already attained guidance in order to become "Godfearing" in the first place. The first form is the one by which means an individual becomes

"Godfearing" (*muttaqī*), while the second form is the one which God bestows *after* the attainment of "piety" or "moral consciousness" (*taqwā*). This latter "guidance" helps the individual to remain unshakable when encountering the unbelievers and the hypocrites. *Taqwā*, which is "keen, spiritual and moral perception and motivation," is a comprehensive attribute that touches all aspects of faith, when faith is put into practice.

However, human beings can reject faith, and that results in "misguidance" (*iḍlāl*). It is important to note that the Qur'ān considers "misguidance" or "leading astray" as God's activity in response to unsatisfactory actions or attitudes on the part of the individuals who have chosen to reject the faith. As such, they deserve it:

> How shall God guide a people who have disbelieved after they believed. . . . God guides not the people of evildoers [3.86]. Surely those who disbelieve after they have believed and then increase in unbelief—their repentance shall but be accepted; those are the ones astray [3.90].

The above passage implies human responsibility for being led astray. Human beings are given the choice to accept or reject the faith and bear the consequences of their choice. However, the Qur'ān makes frequent reference to the effect that:

> They [the unbelievers] say: "What did God desire by this for a similitude?" Thereby he leads many astray, and thereby he guides many; and thereby he leads none astray save the ungodly such as break covenant of God . . . [2.24-26].

This verse imputes the responsibility of "leading astray" to God. The Muslim exegetes have correctly distinguished between two kinds of "misguidance" so as to explicate statements of this nature. The first kind of "misguidance" follows from the choice made by an individual. It causes corrupt attributes such as disbelief (*kufr*) and hypocrisy (*nifāq*), whereas the second kind of "misguidance" confirms these attributes in that person. This is the point of the following verse:

> In their heart is a sickness, and God has increased their sickness, and there awaits them a painful chastisement for that they have cried lies [2.10].

The first kind of "sickness" is imputed to the person, implying a willful act which results in spiritual affliction, while the second stage of "sickness" is imputed to God who "caused their hearts to swerve when they swerved" (61.5). This means that God does not guide the people who have neglected to respond to "universal guidance" ingrained in the human soul (91.7), by means which human beings could have helped themselves to understand their true role on earth.

From the above observations about the "guidance" and "misguidance" it would be accurate to visualize people who possess *taqwā*—as being situated between the "universal guidance," and the "revelational guidance." In other words, being equipped with the necessary cognition and volition, they are ready to follow the commands of God to attain "prosperity." On the other hand, the "unbelievers" and the "hypocrites" can be visualized as being situated between the two forms of "misguidance." By having allowed the "heart" to become "sick," they have allowed correct judgment and the sharp sense of personal responsibility to become dull.

Since the question of "guidance" is related to the question of the source of knowledge of ethical values, in the classical as well as modern works on the Qur'ānic exegesis, we have taken some care to explicate the various forms of guidance in the Qur'ān. Significantly, it is at this point that theological differences become explicitly marked. These differences, as pointed out earlier in our brief remarks about the Mu'tazilī and Ash'arī theological standpoints, are rooted in two conflicting conceptions of human responsibility. The Mu'tazila, who emphasized the complete responsibility of human beings, upheld the concept of human free will in responding to the call of both natural guidance as well as guidance through revelation. On the other hand, the Ash'arī, who upheld the omnipotence of God, denied man any role in responding to divine guidance. As a matter of fact, according to them, it was impossible for a individual to accept or reject faith unless God willed it. Nevertheless, the Qur'ān undoubted contains a complex view of human responsibility. It allows both for human decision and divine omnipotence in the matter of guidance.

Actually, the concept of "universal guidance" has wider implications than merely demonstrating the existence of volitional capacity in the human soul (91.7), and proving human responsibility as regards developing a keen sense of spiritual and moral perception and motivation. It appears that the Qur'ān regards humanity as one nation in reference to "universal guidance" ("prior" [*sābiqa*] guidance), before "particular guidance" through revelation ("subsequent" [lāḥiqa] guidance) was sent:

> The people were one nation; then God sent forth Prophets, good tidings to bear and warning, and he sent down with them the Book with the truth, that he might decide between the people touching their differences [2.213].

God's "universal guidance" treats all human beings as equal and potentially believers in him before they become distinguished through the particular "guidance" as believers, unbelievers, hypocrites, and so on.

The verse 2.213 also points to divine mystery in dividing humanity into communities and even recognizes Jews and Christians as such, although, they too were invited to "submit" to the will of God, *Islām*. Such a recognition on the part of the Qur'ān was based on the awareness that Jewish and Christian communities existed as exclusive religious groups just as the Muslim community did under the leadership of the Prophet Muḥammad:

> The Jews say: The Christians stand not on anything; and they recite the Book [2.113].

> And they [the Jews and the Christians] say: None shall enter Paradise except that they be Jews or Christians. Such are their fancies [2.111].

The Qur'ān's rejection of these exclusivist claims is based on the very notion of "guidance," namely, that "guidance" comes from God and he guides whom he wishes to guide. Hence, no community may regard itself as uniquely guided and elected. God has provided "guidance" out of his bounty for which humanity ought to give thanks.

On the basis of the notion of "universal guidance," it is possible to speak of natural-moral ground of human conduct in the Qur'ān. These passages refer to an objective and universal moral nature on the basis of which all human beings are to be treated equally and held equally accountable to God. In other words, certain moral prescriptions follow from a common human nature, and are regarded as independent of particular spiritual beliefs, even though all practical guidance ultimately springs from the same source, namely, from

God. It is significant to note that the term the Qur'ān uses, for instance, to designate "goodness" (moral virtue)—with which all human beings are exhorted to comply—is *al-ma'rūf*, meaning the "well-known," "generally recognized" and even "universally accepted." In an extremely important passage, the Qur'ān recognizes the universality and objective nature of moral virtue ("goodness"), which transcends different religions and religious communities and admonishes humankind "to be forward in good work":

> To every one of you [religious communities] we have appointed a law and a way [of conduct]. If God had willed, he would have made you all one nation [on the basis of that law and that way]; but [he did not do so] that he may try you in what has come to you; therefore, be you forward [i.e., compete with one another] in good works. Unto God shall you return all together; and he will tell you [the Truth] about what you have been disputing [5.48].

There is a clear assumption in this verse that certain basic moral requirements find all human beings, regardless of differences in religious beliefs. Interestingly enough, the ideal human being is conceived of as combining moral virtue with complete religious surrender:

> Nay, but whosoever submits his will to God, while being a good-doer, his wage is with his Lord, and no fear shall be on them, neither shall they sorrow [2.112].

It is indeed in the realm of universal moral truth that human beings are treated equally and held equally accountable for responding to "universal guidance."

But, do human beings respond to divine "guidance," whether in its "universal" or "particular" form? This is the tragedy. Humanity has not, by and large, submitted to the Divine Will by following the guidance that God has proffered. The Qur'ān indicates that the answer to the problem of unbelief, of failure to respond to the guidance is tied to the narrow-mindedness and stupidity (self-cultivated) of human beings who do not reflect on the signs that come their way. Preoccupied with worldly affairs, they do not see that their life and all that they have is given by the Beneficient and Merciful Lord to whom they will have to render an account on the Day of Reckoning. They live for the pleasure of the moment, not considering that the pleasures of the next world (not to mention the punishments) will exceed their wildest dreams.

On the other hand, the Qur'ān also asserts the lordship of the sovereign God by indicating that God has the power and could, if he so willed, make unbelievers into believers (6.107). In other places the Qur'ān says that those who go astray have been led astray by God, while those who follow the "straight path" are able to do so because God helps them (2.6-7). These verses stand alongside those which indicate that humanity has been afforded all the power it needs to follow the way of truth. There are, moreover, those passages which evidently resolve the tension, indicating that those whom God has misled, he did so because they had already rejected him (59.19).

The relationship of this Qur'ānic treatment to the problem of unbelief, or failure to respond to God, was the object of intense discussion among Muslim scholars in the centuries following the establishment of the Islamic empire. It is not possible to take up these discussions in this paper. But for the present, it suffices to say that the problem of human persistence in unbelief and ingratitude is a major concern; even a preoccupation for the Qur'ān. Such unbelief became for the Qur'ān and its Messenger not only a denial of truth, to be punished on the Day of Judgment, but also a threat to the community of the faithful, to be subdued in the present, by the use of force, if necessary. The faithful are told in *sūrat al-tawba* (9) to fight the unbelievers; even to fight the peoples of the Book "until they pay the tribute readily," submitting to Islamic polity (9.29). The sense is that there is a growing need for security on the part of the Muslim *umma* which calls for armed resistance to the threat posed by those who do not share its faith. This move, it seems, is a part of the transition from Mecca to Medina; it is the movement from a minority and missionary religious movement to a community with power to shape the political and economic forces which affect its existence.

This focus on the problem of unbelief on the part of humanity in its religious and political dimensions serves to introduce a more specific analysis of the situational dimension of Islamic revelation. In what follows, I shall take up that dimension especially, though not exclusively, in relation to the *sūrat al-Baqara*, which is a unique example of the ways in which the Qur'ānic message indicates the responsibility of humanity to respond to divine guidance. It is this divine guidance that constitutes the situational dimension in this discussion.

The problem of unbelief, particularly on the part of the peoples of the Book, the Jews and Christians, is a concern of *al-Baqara* from its outset. This problem, and the various reflections to which it leads, can be traced through the *sūra* as follows: (1) establishment of God's claim; (2) the fact of unbelief; (3) exploration of causes of this fact (religious problem); (4) encouragement and guidance for the Muslims in relation to the problem (political problem). This set of reflections may be taken as a kind of reflection of the progressive nature of the problem of unbelief for the *umma*, from a more or less purely religious problem to a political threat which has bearing on the safety of the new community.

(1) Establishment of God's Claim

The Qur'ān speaks about signs of God's power and lordship in creation and in history. These are said to be confirmed, or human beings reminded of them, through the particular guidance of the prophets, the greatest of whom not only "warn" or "remind," but bring a "book," a scripture. If the "universal guidance" is enough to establish responsibility, the "particular guidance" through the revelation intensifies God's claims considerably. This is so because the Qur'ān is, according to 2.2. "the Scripture wherein there is no doubt, a guidance unto those who ward off (evil) . . . " It is, then, a guidance which is clear and full; it is worthy of the faith which it promises will be rewarded. This is the faith of those:

> Who believe in the unseen, and establish worship, and spend of that we have bestowed upon them;
>
> And who believe in that which is revealed unto thee [Muḥammad] and that which was revealed before thee, and are certain of the Hereafter. These depend on guidance from their Lord. These are the successful [2.2-5].

The indubitability of the Qur'ān as the guidance of God through the Prophet establishes the divine claim to human response.

(2) The Fact of Unbelief

But all do not respond, of course. Some resist the messenger of God, presenting him and those who submit with a religious and political problem of the first order. This is especially true for the Peoples of the Book, whose reception of previous prophecy should, according to the Qur'ān, make them more aware of God, and more able to recognize the marks of true prophecy—namely, Muḥammad's. Their continued resistance, especially in the case of the Jewish tribes at Medina, developed into a problem which could not be resolved except through political action. Similarly, the opposition of the Meccan tribes was increasingly as a political problem, or a religious and moral problem which called for political action. The distinctions and relationship between these two dimensions are the points of (3) and (4) below.

(3) Religious Problem

As a religious problem, unbelief is, in a sense, beyond the jurisdiction of the Muslim community and its Prophet. Belief and its opposite may be construed as the work of God, who is merciful and compassionate, but also the Sovereign Lord of the Worlds. Thus 2.6-7 of the Qur'ān states:

> As for the unbelievers, whether thou warn them or thou warn them not it is all one for them; they believe not.

> God hath sealed their hearing and their hearts, and on their eyes there is a covering. Theirs will be an awful doom.

At the same time, unbelief can be malicious—a kind of free action on the part of human beings who think to deceive God, or to deprive him of his right. It is even possible for such to attempt a deception of greater dimensions by feigning faith when it is not their true posture:

> And of mankind are some who say, We believe in God and the Last Day, when they believe not.

> They think to beguile God and those who believe, and they beguile none save themselves; but they perceive not. In their hearts is a disease, and God increaseth their disease. A painful doom is theirs because they lie [2.8-10].

Here the action of God simply confirms choices already made. In other words, God entrenches one in the position one has taken.

The unbelief of Medinan Jews is the opposite case. For *al-Baqara,* while maintaining the mystery of God's involvement in unbelief to a certain extent, places greater stress on Jewish responsibility for deceit and wrongdoing, both historically and in the present. Thus, in the verses from which the *sūra* takes its name, a story is told in which Moses, faced with the unbelief of his people, is able to answer question after question about a cow which is to be sacrificed as a sin offering (2.67ff.). In 2.72-73, this historic prophet gives further demonstration for the unbelieving, taking a portion of the sacrifice and using it to bring a murdered man back to life. But the response of Israel, says *al-Baqara,* was not faith: they were hardened and their hearts "became as rocks, or worse than rocks, for hardness" (2.74). To the Prophet and the believers, then, God says:

> Have ye any hope that they will be true to you when a party of them used to listen to the Word of God, then used to change it, after they had understood it, knowingly [2.75]?

The notion of treachery is thus extended to the realm of morality— it is not only that these unbelievers are untrue to God; they are such in relation to the Prophet and his community, as well. The discussion builds to the higher and higher levels of accusation: the Jews of Medina are accused of deceit in verses 76 and 77. Their knowledge of Torah is impugned in verse 78, where it is said that many know it only by hearsay; and in verse 79 their leaders, those who should know the Book, are accused of changing it or making up portions for the sake of petty profits. In succeeding verses, the punishment of God is promised to such persons. The Jews are described as cursed for their unbelief (88); they begrudge the fact that God should reveal himself "unto whom he will" (90). Finally, the accusation reaches a fever of pitch in verses 91-93:

> And when it is said unto them (i.e. the Jewish tribes): Believe in that which God hath revealed, they say: We believe in that which was revealed unto us. And they disbelieve in that which cometh after it, though it is the truth confirming that which they possess.

Say [unto them, O Muḥammad]:

> Why then slew ye the Prophets of God aforetime, if ye are [indeed] believers? And Moses came unto you with clear proofs [of God's sovereignty], yet, while he was away, ye chose the calf [for worship] and ye were wrongdoers.
>
> And when he made with you a covenant and caused the Mount to tower above you, [saying]: Hold fast by that which We have given you, and hear [Our Word], they said: We hear and we rebel. And [worship of] the calf was made to sink into their hearts because of their rejection [of the covenant]. Say [unto them]: Evil is that which your belief enjoineth on you, if ye are unbelievers.

Jewish unbelief, then, refers to the deceit, pride, and hardness of heart said to be characteristic of that people's relationship with God and his prophets. Their unbelief is ultimately rebellion against God, and is thus subject to his judgment, which may be executed in this world or the next (verses 98, 10, 27, 39, 79, 81, and 85).

(4) Political Problem

This is the problem of unbelief with moral and political dimensions. *Al-Baqara* indicates that various kinds of action are appropriate, on the part of the Prophet and the Muslim community. The interesting fact to observe here is that the more the moral aspects of the problem are stressed, the more the use of force as a form of political action is indicated.

The first form of action appropriate to the Muslim community may be summarized in terms of "steadfastness" (*ṣabr*). This response is indeed implicit throughout *al-Baqara,* as believers are exhorted through the promise of God's favor, in opposition to the curses promised for the unbelievers. It is explicitly present in the verses on trials (verses 153ff.):

> O ye who believe! Seek help in steadfastness and prayer. Lo! God is with the steadfast.

"Steadfastness," one may say, is a "keeping on" or "continuing" in God's way. It is a reminder that one belongs to God; comes from him and will return to him. And it is this reminder which God will reward: "remember me; I will remember you" (152). In sum, it is continued trust in him and adherence to his guidance.

The second action given for the Muslims in the face of unbelief is more readily thought of as political than "steadfastness." It is symbolized in the change of *qibla*—the direction of prayer. Particularly in relation to Jewish unbelief, this alteration in Muslim patterns is significant as a proclamation of independence from the worship and, in a sense, the way of believing of that older community of faith. The change is justified in *al-Baqara* through an appeal to God's sovereignty and to the deviance of the Jewish community from the straight path. Thus, if it be said that the changing of the *qibla* from Jerusalem to Mecca is an alteration of a previously revealed pattern, then:

Such of our revelations as we abrogate or cause to be forgotten, we bring (in place) one better or the like thereof.

Knowest thou not that God is able to do all things [2.106].

As a matter of fact, true revelation affirms that Abraham, the forebearer of those who believe and the example of true faith (the faith that is summarized in the term Islam, and which is not, or at least not exclusively to be defined in Jewish or Christian terms) and his son Ishmael, established the Ka'ba at Mecca as a place of worship. Muslims, then, do not need to follow the precedent set by Jews or Christians. They are to be followers of "the religion of Abraham" (verses 124-29, 136). Challenges to the place of Mecca in God's plan are answered in this manner:

Dispute ye with us concerning God when he is our Lord and your Lord? Our works are our works and yours are your works. We look to him alone:

Or, say ye that Abraham, and Ishmael, and Isaac, and Jacob, and the tribes were Jews or Christians [2.139-40]?

The change in *qibla* is finally justified with the claim that "unto God belong the East and the West" [2.142, 115, and 177]. It is, in one sense, not the kind of change in practice which is calculated to bring about the collapse of relations between the *umma* and other peoples of the Book who do not recognize the claims of the Qur'ān. Thus, the Qur'ān declares that this is not the most significant point of religion, for "each has a goal toward which he turneth; so vie with one another in good works. Wheresoever ye may be, God will bring you together" (2.148). However, in the context in *al-Baqara's* stress on unbelief, and in particular Jewish unbelief, the change of direction is definitely a form of political action calculated to dissociate the Muslims from the Jewish tribes, and to emphasize the standing of Islam as a way independent of the practices of these tribes. The claim is, as through the Qur'ān, that Muḥammad's message is truly consistent with that of the former prophets, and that differences between the Prophet of the Muslims and the Peoples of the Book are due to the departure of the latter from the straight path.

It is possible, however, for unbelief to take on actively hostile aspects, in relation to the community of faith—to be perceived as a threat which is aggressively seeking to harm the *umma* and its members. When this is emphasized, the Qur'ān justifies the use of force; even, commands it. In verses 190ff. we read:

> Fight in the way of God against those who fight against you, but begin not hostilities. Lo! God loveth not aggressors.

> And slay them wherever ye find them, and drive them out of the places whence they drove you out, for persecution is worse than slaughter.

Reluctance to fight, which may be understood in terms of the priority of the rule against killing, is overcome by the security needs of a community which is presented as persecuted and outnumbered. Muslims are urged to spend their wealth and even their lives in support of such fighting (e.g. verses 195 and 245). God has promised to reward those investing in the effort. The one who makes the "goodly loan" does so that God may "give it increase manifold." Those who lose their lives in the cause are really not dead—"Nay, they are living" (153). And even superior numbers of the enemy's side should not frighten the Muslims, as *al-Baqara* recalls the story of David and Goliath (243-51).

Consequently, against the aggressively hostile unbelief of the Meccan Arabs (as in 191: "they drove you out"), the Muslims are commanded to fight. This command connotes an overriding of the normal prohibitions against killing. It is also given in such a way that it overrides certain rules about times and places of fighting which are tied to religious duties. For instance, in verse 191, following the justification for warfare in cases of persecution, the Qur'ān commands:

Fight not with them at the Inviolable Place of Worship until they first attack you there, but if they attack you (there) then slay them. Such is the reward of disbelievers.

Similarly in verse 194:

The forbidden month for the forbidden month, and forbidden things in retaliation. And one who attacketh you, attack him in like manner as he attacked you. Observe your duty to God, and know that God is with those who ward off (evil).

The above passages are meant to convey that the security needs of the Muslim community, and the demands of justice in verse 194, can override even certain religious obligations. The "Inviolable Place of Worship," for instance, signifies the Ka'aba, established by Abraham as a place of worship and by the Qur'ān as the *qibla* for Muslims. Indeed, pre-Islamic Arab culture regarded all Mecca, and the area surrounding it, as *ḥaram* ("inviolable") and killing was prohibited there and still is. Similarly, pre-Islamic Arabia regarded certain months of the year as *ḥaram*, and these were observed as "truce" months, for the sake of economic transactions and the making of pilgrimages.

When unbelief threatens the existence of faith, however, such customary religious observances are overridden. One does whatever is necessary to stop aggression—even, it is implied, customary rules of warfare may be overridden at such a time. Once that aggression occurs, survival of the just community dictates a response, governed by the *lex talionis* ("one who attacketh you, attack him in like manner," verse 194) until the aggressors desist:

If they desist, then lo! God is Forgiving, Merciful. And fight them until persecution is no more, and religion is for God. But if they desist, then let there be no hostility except against wrongdoers [2.192-93].

Thus, the just community, which is steadfast to God and receptive of his guidance, may fight to defend itself and thus to establish justice (or perhaps, to reestablish a violated justice) in the face of aggressive unbelief. The qualities of that just community are specified in the long verse in which Muslims are provided with guidance in reference to a number of life-situations. Verse 177 speaks of the characteristics of the "righteous" who have accepted divine guidance:

> Righteous is he who believeth in God and the Last Day and the angels and the Scripture and the Prophets; and giveth his wealth, for love of him, to kinsfolk and to orphans and the needy and the wayfarer and to those who ask, and to set slaves free; and observeth proper worship and payeth the poor-due. And those who keep their treaty when they make one, and the patient in tribulation and adversity and time of stress. Such are they who are sincere. Such are the Godfearing.

It is important to point out that such "righteousness" is regarded as a possibility among the followers of other Books. As a result, consistent with its rejection of exclusivism and election, the Qur'ān acknowledges the existence of righteous people in other communities who can expect to be saved:

> Surely those that believe [the Muslims], and those of Jewry, and the Christians, and those Sabaeans, whoso believe in God and the Last Day, and work righteousness—their wage awaits them with their Lord, and no fear shall be on them, neither shall they sorrow [2.62].

It is with this recognition of universal goodness, with belief in one God and the Last Day, that whole question of faith has been treated in the Qur'ān, where humanity is held responsible to respond actively to the "universal" as well as "particular" guidance. All humanity is called upon to "compete in goodness" and produce the best community on earth (5.48).

Philoponos and Avicenna
on the Separability of the Intellect:
A Case of Orthodox Christian-Muslim Agreement

DIMITRI GUTAS

ARISTOTELIANISM, the longest lived and historically the most influential philosophical tradition in the West and the Near East, provided the common ground where philosophers of all religions—pagans, Christians, Muslims, and Jews, and schismatics of all sorts—could conduct a meaningful dialogue across the centuries. In this paper I wish to study an instance in which the affiliation of Ioannes Philoponos (d. after 560), an Orthodox Christian,[1] and of Avicenna (d. 1037), a Sunnī Muslim,[2] with this tradition led to their agreement in the solution of a particularly difficult philosophical problem with serious implications for their respective monotheistic religions.

The problem concerns the interpretation of Aristotle's opening words in his examination of the intellect, *De Anima* 429a10-12:

> Concerning the part of the soul with which the soul knows and thinks, whether this part is separable or inseparable with respect to magnitude but in theory only . . . (Περὶ δὲ τοῦ μορίου τοῦ τῆς ψυχῆς ᾧ γινώσκει τε ἡ ψυχὴ καὶ φρονεῖ εἴτε χωριστοῦ

---

[1]See H.-D. Saffrey, "Le chrétien Jean Philopon et la survivance de l'école d'Alexandrie au VIe siècle," *Revue des Études Grecques* 67 (1954) 396-410. Philoponos was considered orthodox in his time; he was condemned as a tritheist only in retrospect (680). See ibid. p. 408, n. 2.

[2]For the purposes of this paper the question of Avicenna's sectarian affiliation is irrelevant. Suffice it to say that I believe that there is enough evidence to indicate that he was a Sunnī Muslim of the Ḥanafī rite.

ὄντος εἴτε καὶ μὴ χωριστοῦ κατὰ μέγεθος ἀλλὰ κατὰ
λόγον . . .).

In his *Marginal Notes on De Anima,* a relatively late work, Avicenna interprets the above passage as follows:[3]

Aristotle begins [here] the investigation of the theoretical faculty about which he asks whether its essence subsists separately.[4] By his statement, "or inseparable with respect to magnitude," Aristotle means, "inseparable from magnitude."
Themistios understood Aristotle to mean "or it is inseparable
with respect to location,"[5] but this is incorrect because Aristotle's discussion in this passage about whether it is separable or
not does not concern location, nor is he occupied with it at the
moment; rather, the extent of his discussion and investigation
is devoted to [the subject of] subsistence. In another translation
[of the same passage into Arabic we read]: "or inseparable, like
the separation of a body from another body,"[6] that is, without
needing it to subsist.[7] It appears as if this translation is more
correct.

---

[3]'Abd al-Raḥmān Badawī, *Arisṭū 'inda' l-'Arab,* Cairo 1947, p. 98.17-22.
For the title and origin of the work, see my *Avicenna and the Aristotelian
Tradition* (forthcoming), Chapter 2, Work 9.

[4]Literally, "whether it is separable with respect to the subsistence of its
essence" (*hal hiya mufāriqa fī qiwām ḏātihi* [sic]). This literal rendering
highlights the parallelism between Avicenna's paraphrase and Aristotle's
words, "inseparable with respect to magnitude" whereby it is seen that the
Aristotelian "magnitude" is interpreted by Avicenna as "essence." See the
discussion further below.

[5]Themistios, *In Libros Aristotelis De Anima Paraphrasis* [Commentaria
in Aristotelem Graeca 5, 3], ed. R. Heinze (Berlin, 1899), p. 93.33; *An Arabic Translation of Themistius, Commentary on Aristoteles De Anima,* ed.
M. C. Lyons (Oxford 1973), p. 163 has a different text.

[6]This is the poor Arabic translation, wrongly attributed in the manuscript
to Isḥāq b. Ḥunayn, and published by 'Abd al-Raḥmān Badawī, *Arisṭū fī 'l-
nafs* (Cairo, 1954). See R. M. Frank, "Some Fragments of Isḥāq's Translation of the *De Anima,"* *Cahiers de Byrsa* 8 (1958-59) 232, n. 7, last line.

[7]The unique manuscript of the text, Cairo Dār al-Kutub Hikma 6M, has
qiwām on the line. It was crossed over and *qiyām* was written over it by
the same hand. Although the original reading appears to be the correct one,
both would give approximately the same sense.

In the *De Anima* translation by Isḥāq b. Ḥunayn that Avicenna was using, the Greek text εἴτε καὶ μὴ χωριστοῦ κατὰ μέγεθος ("or inseparable with respect to magnitude") was rendered by *aw ghayr mufāriq bi'l-'iẓam.*[8] As far as the Arabic construction of the phrase itself is concerned, the preposition *bi-* is ambiguous in that it could mean a number of things, none of them completely satisfactory for the sense. Avicenna interpreted it as the particle introducing the object, *li-* (i.e., *ghayr mufāriq li'l-'iẓam*) thus understanding *'iẓam* ("magnitude") as the object of the participle *mufāriq* ("separable"), and elicited the sense, "inseparable from magnitude." This interpretation is unwarranted on the basis of the Arabic phrase alone, for despite its ambiguity, the preposition *bi-* in the present context cannot yield this sense. It is therefore obvious that Avicenna is following here traditional ways of interpretation, a brief review of which will reveal his precedents.

To start with some general observations: the discussion is about whether the rational (part of the) soul—or the intellect—is separable or not. The question, however, is, separable from what? The answers that were given by the Greek commentators whose works are extant can be classified into three categories:

    (1) separable from the body;
    (2) separable from the other faculties of the soul (i.e., the nutritive, etc.) (a) in essence (τῇ οὐσίᾳ) or (b) in theory (κατὰ λόγον, τῷ λόγῳ);
    3) separable from the other parts of the intellect (a) in essence, or (b) in theory.

Alexander's theory of the soul is quite consistent as a whole with that of Aristotle; he considers the soul to be the form of the body. At the end of the discussion about the presence of the soul in the body as its form he states,

If then the soul is, as it has been shown, a form, then it is necessary that it be inseparable (ἀχώριστον) from the body whose [form] it is, and also that it be incorporeal and immovable in

---

[8]See Frank, "Some Fragments," p. 224, frg. 35. The first line of this fragment, as printed, should be deleted. It is not Isḥāq's text but Avicenna's paraphrase; see n. 4 above.

itself;[9]

and concludes,

> Since the soul is the form of a body, as already stated, such a
> form, by being inseparable from the body, would also perish to-
> gether with it; that much of it, at any rate, which is the form
> of a perishable body.[10]

The last qualification was made with the "intellect from outside"
(νοῦς θύραθεν) in mind, which, not being the form of a perishable
body, is not perishable itself. This is stated more explicitly in another
passage where Alexander says about the active intellect (νοῦς ποιη-
τικός) that it exists without matter:

> It is for this reason [*scil.* that it has no matter] that it is also
> separable in itself; for none of the forms in matter (ἔνυλα εἴδη)
> is separable, except in theory only, as they perish when they be-
> come separated from matter.[11]

The same theory is also expressed in Alexander's *De Intellectu.*
The active intellect, coming to humans from the outside, is not a part
or faculty of the soul.[12] As for the other two parts of the intellect,
they are described as mere potentiality (passive intellect) and as potentiality with a certain disposition towards something (intellect *in
habitu*).[13]

Alexander did not discuss their ontological status, but as parts of a
soul which is the form of a body, it is fair to assume from what has
already been said that they are not separable. According to Alexander, then, the soul and all its parts are not separable from the body—
since they are its form—except for the active intellect which, coming from outside, is pure actuality, without a body, and not part of
a soul. His discussion of the separability of the soul thus belongs to

---

[9] Alexander of Aphrodisias, *Scripta Minora. De Anima cum Mantissa*
[Commentaria in Aristotelem Graeca, Suppl. 2, 1], ed. I. Bruns (Berlin, 1887),
p. 17.9-10.

[10] Ibid. p. 21.22-24.

[11] Ibid. p. 89.12-15.

[12] Ibid. p. 108.22-23.

[13] Ibid. pp. 106.19-107.28.

a soul. His discussion of the separability of the soul thus belongs to category (1) in the table above.

It was this kind of separability (from the body) that all the Neoplatonist commentators on Aristotle were against, starting with Plutarch of Athens. In the commentary of Stephanos of Alexandria (Pseudo-Philoponos) we read the following passage:

> Some have interpreted this passage [*scil. De Anima* 429a10-12] as follows: either the intellect is separable from the body, or it is not separable from the body, being separable only in thought (τῇ ἐπινοίᾳ) but not also in actuality. This then is the first problem, whether the intellect is separable and eternal. Plutarch, however, does not like this interpretation at all and condemns it altogether. He himself interprets it by saying that what Aristotle meant by these words is the following: "either the intellect is separable from imagination and sense perception, having, apart from these, another essence (οὐσία), or all three have one essence which is many in theory only."[14]

With regard to the issue of separability, Plutarch was opposed to category (1) (the position of Alexander, to whom the pronoun "some," τινές, in the opening sentence above would appear to refer), and preferred to discuss the matter in terms of category (2). Instead of investigating, with Aristotle, whether the intellect is separable with respect to magnitude or in theory, he asks whether it is separable in essence or in theory from the other parts of the soul. In other words, in this interpretation there is a substitution of essence (οὐσία) for magnitude (μέγεθος).

In Stephanos, continuing from the preceding extract, this substitution is explicitly stated:

> Aristotle is not seeking to find whether the intellect is separable from the body or not. For how could somebody, who believes that [even] imagination is separable from the body, entertain doubts about whether the intellect, which transcends all faculties, is incorporeal or not? But you should take "magnitude" to mean "essence" (μέγεθος δὲ λαβὲ τὴν οὐσίαν). So the first problem,

---

[14]Ioannes Philoponos, *In Aristotelis De Anima Libros Commentaria* [Commentaria in Aristotelem Graeca, 15], ed. M. Hayduck (Berlin, 1897), pp. 520.31-521.3. For the authorship of the third book of this commentary see the references by H. J. Blumenthal, "Neoplatonic Elements in the *De Anima* Commentaries," *Phronesis* 21 (1976) 72, n. 37.

problem, too, is the following: either the intellect is separable from imagination and sense perception in essence, or all three have one essence but are different in theory only.[15]

With Simplikios a further elaboration of the separability theme was effected. For him, as for his predecessors, the kind of separability in category (1) was out of the question. What is novel in him, however, is that he was not content with the second category either. He proposed, instead, yet a third alternative which he considered to be more accurate: separability of one part of the intellect from the other parts in essence or in theory (category [3]). This is what he says:

"Whether it is separable or not" [in the Aristotelian text] should not be understood with reference to the body [category (1)] . . . but to the parts of the soul already mentioned, viz., the nutritive and the imaginative [category (2)]. *Or rather,* since, as it has been said, Aristotle is going to present three aspects (τριχῶς . . . παραδώσει) of that thing which knows rationally, he proposes to investigate whether that thing which thinks in itself is separable *from itself* in magnitude or in theory [category (3)]. The investigation, then, would be whether there are in us three intellects as essences that can be also separated from each other, or only one intellect and one essence which, however, is differentiated in theory, sometimes turned wholly towards itself, sometimes inclining outwards, and being either perfect or imperfect [emphasis added].[16]

In the discussion of the separability of the intellect there is thus discernible in the later stages of Greek Aristotelianism a development towards greater emphasis on the subdivisions within the intellect itself rather than on the distinction among the various parts of the soul. This development points the way to the Arab philosophers and their adoption as a rule of a quadripartite intellect: the potential, the actual, the acquired, and the one *in habitu.*[17]

---

[15]Philoponos, *In De Anima* p. 521.5-10 Hayduck.

[16]Simplikios, *In Libros Aristotelis De Anima* [Commentaria in Aristotelem Graeca, 11], ed. M. Hayduck (Berlin, 1882), p. 222.9-20.

[17]See, in general, J. Finnegan, "Al-Fārābī et le Περὶ νοῦ d'Alexandre d'Aphrodise," *Mélanges Louis Massignon* (Damascus, 1957), 2, pp. 133-52.

In Philoponos' commentary,[18] however, there is a shift in interpretation which is in many ways similar to that of Avicenna. Philoponos says that the Aristotelian passage can be explained in many ways but he actually gives two. The first one he offers is the one of separability in terms of location. He proceeds to give the *Timaeus* as an example, where the various faculties of the soul are given a different bodily seat. This is unique in the commentatorial tradition, and it harks back to Themistios who is the sole commentator to give this analysis only by offering the example of Plato.[19] This explanation is quickly dismissed by Philoponos who now focuses on the second one:

> It could be that "with respect to magnitude" [in the Aristotelian text] . . . means separate from body and magnitude, or "with respect to magnitude" means "with respect to essence and hypostasis," as magnitudes are said to be separated from each other, which is the same as that which follows, namely, that which has a substance separate from body and magnitude. . . . This, then, is the first of the problems, whether the intellect is separate in essence or in theory only.[20]

There are two things to be noted about this passage. First, the discussion is raised to a different, unprecedented level. In Alexander, separability was discussed in terms of category (1), i.e., separation from the body, and the conclusion was that, apart from the active intellect, which is from outside and pure actuality, all the other parts of the soul are inseparable from the body *qua* its form. The later commentators objected to this interpretation in terms of category (1) and centered on categories (2) and (3). Philoponos, however, went back to a discussion of separability from the body[21] (i.e., category [1]), but

---

[18]The third book of Philoponos' commentary, preserved only in a Latin translation, was edited anew by G. Verbeke, *Jean Philopon. Commentaire sur le De Anima d'Aristotle* (Leiden, 1966). Some fragments of the original Greek were recovered by S. van Riet, "Fragments de l'original grec du 'De Intellectu de Philopon dans une compilation de Sophonias," *Revue Philosophique de Louvain* 63 (1965) 5-40. The Greek original of the passages discussed in this paper is not among these fragments.

[19]See n. 5, above.

[20]Verbeke, *Philopon*, pp. 6.32-7.42.

[21]This is also his stated purpose, as expressed in the preface to his commentary. See Blumenthal, "Neoplatonic Elements," p. 70, top.

with two modifications: first, he did not consider whether a part of the intellect only is separable from the body or not, as Alexander had done, but he considered the entire intellect or rational soul; and second, he did not consider this separability in terms of actuality or potentiality, again as Alexander had done, but in terms of substance (*substantia*) and essence (*essentia*) and *hypostasis*. In other words, he transferred the terms in which separability was discussed in categories (2) and (3), i.e., separability in essence or in theory, to category (1). He thereby created a dualism of body/intellect in lieu of the previous triadic divisions of nutrition/sense perception/reasoning, and passive intellect/intellect *in habitu*/active intellect, respectively. This new development in the interpretation of the Aristotelian passage and Philoponos' emphasis can best be understood, I think, against the background of Philoponos' Christianity. It is of vital importance for a religious teaching about a future life that it maintain on a philosophical level the separate existence of the self, the intellect. It is noteworthy, however, that Philoponos was able to effect this shift without any drastic break with the tradition in which he was schooled, but through a mere transposition of the arguments and terms already available.

Second, Avicenna's interpretation relies heavily on that of Philoponos, and his formulation of the issue in Arabic can be understood adequately only by reference to it. Avicenna interpreted "inseparable with respect to magnitude" (*ghayr mufāriq bi'l-'izam*) as "from magnitude" (*li'l-'izam*), just as Philoponos had interpreted the same phrase (*separata secundum magnitudinem*) as "separate from body and magnitude" (*separata a corpore et magnitudine*). Avicenna maintained that separability should not be seen in terms of location but in terms of "subsistence/essence" (*qiwām*), just as Philoponos had interpreted "with respect to magnitude" (*secundum magnitudinem*) as "with respect to essence and hypostasis" (*secundum essentiam et hypostasim*). Finally, Avicenna's preferred translation, ". . . or inseparable, like the separation of a body from another body . . ." (*aw ghayr mufāriqa ka mufāraqat al-jism li'l-jism*) made the same point that Philoponos had made with his illustration ". . . as magnitudes are said to be separated from each other . . . " (*ut magnitudines dicuntur ab invicem separari*). The problem, then, is the same for Avicenna as it is for Philoponos, namely, whether the intellect, separated from the body, is subsistent or separate in essence. And the motivation behind the similar formulation also appears to be the same, namely,

Avicenna's monotheistic (Islamic) frame of reference.

The agreement between Philoponos and Avicenna in both their understanding and solution of the problem does not seem to be accidental. As a matter of fact, there is considerable evidence that Philoponos' commentary on *De Anima,* the Arab bibliographers' total silence on the matter notwithstanding, must have been known in Arabic translation,[22] and that Avicenna must have used it. This, however, is a subject for future research.

---

[22]A good case was recently made about the influence which Philoponos' commentary seems to have exerted on al-Kindī's treatise on the intellect; see J. Jolivet, *L'intellect selon Kindī* (Leiden, 1971), pp. 50-73. As for Avicenna, already in 1959 R. M. Frank had listed a number of passages from his marginal notes on *De Anima* in which Philoponos' commentary appears to have been used ("Some Fragments," p. 236, note, top). The following instance from the same work (Badawī, *Aristū,* p. 101.17-19) may be added to those enumerated by Frank, especially since it is indicative of specific borrowing: it transmits a unique mistake.

Avicenna says in this note that Alexander imputed to Aristotle the doctrine that the material intellect itself was hylic and material. From what we know of Alexander, he could not have made such a statement (J. Finnegan's references in this regard to Alexander's *De Anima,* p. 90.13ff. Bruns, are not to the point; see his "Avicenna's Refutation of Porphyrius," *Avicenna Commemoration Volume,* Calcutta [Iran Society], 1956, p. 192, n. 1, he held that the material intellect is not itself matter but that it is called material because it is, like matter, sheer potentiality (cf. his *De Anima,* p. 106.19-23 Bruns). In all likelihood, Avicenna received his misconception about Alexander in one of two ways: either directly from Stephanos (Pseudo-Philoponos, *In De Anima,* p. 519.23-28 Hayduck), who is the only extant Greek commentator to have attributed to Alexander the opinion that the material intellect is matter, or through a misunderstanding, misreading, or mistranslation of a Philoponos passage in which Alexander *reported* that *Xenarchos,* the first century B.C. Peripatetic, had misunderstood Aristotle and thought that the intellect was primary matter (Verbeke, *Philopon,* p. 15). It is also likely, as a combination of the two alternatives, that Stephanos himself may have been misled by the same passage in Philoponos.

It would seem from the above indications that the problem with regard to Philoponos' commentary on *De Anima* is not whether it was available in Arabic translation, but rather in what form or recension it was available. The Arabic tradition appears to carry traces of both the recension extant in the Latin translation and also the one circulating under the name of Stephanos. Whether these two recensions were available in Arabic separately or together, the names under which they circulated, and the reasons for the silence of the Arab bibliographers regarding them, are questions that have yet to be investigated.

Ottoman Views and Policies Towards the Orthodox Christian Church

KEMAL H. KARPAT

THE CONQUEST of Constantinople by Sultan Mehmet II, the Conquerer (1451-1481), was a turning point in the history of Muslim-Christian relations as well as a landmark of the political and cultural philosophy of the Ottoman state itself.[1] Some scholars have adopted highly subjective views of this event. Hellenists have looked in general upon the fall of the Byzantium as the beginning of the subjection to servility—if not outright slavery—of the Orthodox Christians by the Muslims, the terms "Turk" and "Muslim" having become in their minds synonymous. Turkophiles, on the other hand, have viewed the passing away of the last vestige of the Roman Empire as an inevitable conclusion of the Turkish march towards world domination and invincible primacy among Muslims. Indeed the Turks had triumphed where the Arabs had failed and left behind one of the Prophet's companions entombed in the area which today is one of the largest districts of Istanbul and still bears his name, i.e., Eyub or Ayub.

The truth is that neither of these two subjective views is accurate or even comes close to describing the real situation created by the concordat, the agreement reached by the sultan and the Orthodox patriarch concerning the fate of Orthodox Christianity under Muslim rule. The encounter between the sultan and Gennadios is famous, although its full dimensions and eventful consequences are largely

---

[1]On Mehmet, see Babinger, *Mehmed der Eroberer und seine Zeit* (Munich, 1953). There is also an English translation by W. Hickman.

131

ignored or misunderstood. In fact, the troubled Turkish-Greek political relations that developed after 1821, and especially the rampant nationalist thought which swamped the Ottoman lands after 1856, have blurred and distorted writers' and scholars' intellectual vision and sense of equity toward the history of Ottoman relations with Orthodox Christianity and the Orthodox patriarch.

The history of Orthodox Christianity under Ottoman rule is to a large extent that of the Orthodox Patriarchate of Constantinople. Consequently, a correct appraisal of the history of that Patriarchate after 1453, of its legal, political, and social status in the Ottoman world and of its relations with the government, should shed light on the true situation of the Orthodox Christians and, notably, illuminate the role of the Greek element in Ottoman Christianity. For this reason the encounter of Mehmet II and George Scholarios, who is better known by his monastic name of Gennadios, and the actual content of the agreement reached between them, are of special significance for appraising the Ottoman attitudes and policies towards Orthodox Christianity. It should be noted that in the sixteenth century the Orthodox Patriarchates of Antioch, Alexandria, and Jerusalem also came under Ottoman rule and that the patriarchs of these ancient sees theoretically were equal to the patriarch in Istanbul. However, in due time the Patriarchate of Constantinople acquired supremacy, not only because it was located in the capital and was thus close to the source of imperial power but also because it was a partner of the Ottoman rulers: their new role and consequent ascendency of the Patriarchate of Constantinople was a direct consequence of the agreement with the sultan. The point to be stressed is that the Ottoman expansion into Syria and Egypt brought about also the expansion of the authority of the Constantinopolitan Patriarchate into Asia and united the Orthodox Christians of Europe and the Orient into a single political unit. Thus the unity destroyed by the Arabs in the seventh century was restored by the Turks in the sixteenth century. I shall deal at length later with the topic of the renewed Orthodox unity under the Ottomans.

I return now to the 1453 concordat of Mehmet II and Gennadios, as this agreement shows the true nature of Muslim-Orthodox Christian relations. The known facts briefly are the following. Shortly after the fall of Constantinople on 29 May 1453, Sultan Mehmet II accepted Gennadios as Patriarch, following his election by a duly constituted body (Gregory Mammas, the incumbent unionist patriarch, had fled in 1451, so the position was vacant). It is clear therefore that the patriarch was not appointed by the sultan but elected by the synod, although the approval of the sultan was necessary. Steven Runciman claims that initially Gennadios was captured and sold as a slave but was found one month later in Adrianople (Edirne) and brought before the sultan, who persuaded him to become patriarch.[2] Runciman derived this information chiefly from George Sphrantzes' *Chronicon* and Kritovoulos' history of Mehmet the Conqueror. Hayrullah Efendi, on the other hand, in his history *Kitab-i samin,* gives a different version of what happened. According to Hayrullah, the sultan provided Gennadios with a beautiful horse from the imperial stable, adorned with a silver saddle, and received the patriarch and his suite of Orthodox prelates while standing. For the Sultan to receive someone standing was a very rare display of respect. After discussions with Gennadios, Mehmet II personally gave him a scepter as the symbol of his authority. The Byzantine emperor's symbol of power thus passed to the hands of the Patriarch. According to Hayrullah Efendi, the sultan told Gennadios that "you should implement the [old] patriarch's authority and laws in absolute safety and freedom as well as the new rules [laws]. You may solicit my assistance by appealing directly to me."[3] Other Turkish sources state that the sultan gave Gennadios not only the privileges and freedoms enjoyed by the Orthodox patriarchs under the Byzantine emperors, but far more extensive powers than he ever possessed in the past.[4] Sphrantzes himself stated that the sultan and Gennadios together worked out a constitution for the Greek millet, but the sultan's special decree recognizing the integrity of Christian churches in Constantinople apparently perished in a fire and is thus not available to scholars. After a sumptuous dinner given by the sultan in his honor, the patriarch was conducted to his office—that is, the Church of the Holy Apostles— accompanied by all the viziers and other high Ottoman dignitaries present at the feast. It may be noted that at this point the Church of the Holy Apostles was ranked second only to the Church of Hagia

---

[2]*The Great Church in Captivity* (Cambridge, 1968), p. 169.

[3]Hayrullah Efendi, *Kitab-i Samim,* p. 84. Runciman gives a similar version, writing that the sultan told Gennadios, "Be patriarch with good fortune, and be assured of our friendship keeping all the privileges the patriarchs before you enjoyed" (*Great Church,* p. 155).

[4]See *Yeni Osmanli Tarihi,* vol. 2, p. 127.

Sophia and had been spared from looting by the Sultan's direct orders. A large number of churches, as well as several districts in the city, such as Psamatheia, that surrendered without resistance remained intact. Discounting the obviously inflated tales of Muslim looting and destruction and considering carefully some of the Ottoman survey statistics dating from the time of conquest, one comes to the conclusion that a substantial number of the Orthodox Christians of Constantinople passed peacefully under the Muslim rule and maintained their wealth and religious institutions. It should not be forgotten that at the time of the conquest the population of Constantinople consisted of only about 60,000 people. A century later the population had grown to over half a million, of which at least one third was Christian. It is very well known that Mehmet II would have preferred a peaceful surrender, so as to keep the city intact, rather than a capture by assault, which under Muslim law gave the soldiers the right to loot for a period of three days. In fact, shortly after the conquest a number of Muslims, including even some of the government dignitaries, complained that the sultan had accorded to the Orthodox Christians too generous and too lenient a treatment. The sultan rejected these complaints as not being in accordance with Islam's concept of protection to be given to conquered Peoples of the Book. Later the Muslims in the city complained also about the privileged treatment received by the Christian settlers, who acquired in preference to Muslims land deeds and building sites.

Nevertheless, conquest is a very traumatic experience for the conquered, even under the best of circumstances, and certainly the Christians of Constantinople were not excepted from such shock. To read a few pages from Doukas' *Historia Turko-Byzantina* is to realize the depth of their grief. To Doukas, Mehmet II "even before he was born was a wolf putting on sheep's clothing . . . who, by donning the mask of friendship, transformed himself into a serpent." He also called Mehmet a "disciple of Satan."[5] And yet, what an enormous difference emerges when one compares the conquest of Constantinople by Turks with, say, the conquest of Valencia by the Spanish; in no time at all the latter had destroyed the Muslim culture and religion and made the surviving Muslims into serfs on their own lands, which were given as estates to the army commanders who became the new Spanish

---

[5]See the English version, *The Decline and Fall of Byzantium to the Ottoman Turks*, trans. Harry J. Magoulias (Detroit, 1975), p. 191.

aristocracy.[6] Today, Valencia does not have a single Muslim monument left standing, or even a Muslim ruin, while Istanbul has preserved a large number of Byzantine monuments.

That the situation of the Orthodox Church under the Muslim Turks was, in fact, relatively good becomes more evident when one studies the record of the Fourth Crusade, the armies of which occupied Constantinople with the blessing of Pope Innocent III, despite his overt prohibition against attacking Christian countries. After having occupied the city, the crusaders insulted and abused every symbol of Orthodoxy there, including the patriarch's throne, on which they seated a prostitute who entertained them by singing bawdy French songs. Niketas Choniates contrasted the savagery of these "forerunners of the Antichrist" in thirteenth-century Constantinople with the restraint of the Saracens (Arabs) in Jerusalem who had "respected the Church of the Holy Sepulcher and molested neither the person nor the property of the conquered Christians."[7] Again in contrast to Mehmet II, who respected the Byzantine traditions by accepting Gennadios as the Orthodox Christians' patriarch, the Venetians appointed Thomas Morosini as the first Latin patriarch, and he was confirmed by Rome. As if it were not enough to deprive the Greeks of the Patriarchate, the Latin conquerors of Constantinople allowed the papacy to impose its views, opposed by Orthodox Christianity and the Greek clergy, on some basic matters of doctrine and ritual. To impose the will of Rome became the Latins' basic principle, which Spanish Cardinal Pelagius, who came in Constantinople as a papal legate in 1213, implemented by closing the Orthodox churches and by throwing Orthodox priests in jail. Although there were some Latins who treated the Orthodox Church with respect, the majority of them despised and insulted it.

The Latin treatment of the Orthodox Church is significant for it affected profoundly the later relations of Orthodox Christians to the Muslim Turks. By the time Michael VII Palaiologos was able to retake Constantinople in 1261, the official Orthodox Church, as well as the Christian population of the city, had become fully disenchanted with the West, notably with the Roman Church that had sanctioned

---

[6]See Robert Burns, Jr., *Islam Under the Crusade, Colonial Survival in Thirteenth-Century Valencia* (Princeton, 1973).

[7]*The Cambridge Medieval History*, Vol. 4, *The Byzantine Empire*, Part I (Cambridge, 1966), pp. 280-86.

military conquest of Constantinople and blessed the division of Byzantine lands into fiefs for various Latin lords. Realistically speaking, it was the Latin conquest of Constantinople, not the Turks, that put the *de facto* end to the Byzantine Empire. The remark, attributed sometimes to Princess Irene and sometimes to the Grand Duke Notaras, that the turban of the Turk was preferable to the tiara of the Pope reflected feeling caused by the oppressive treatment of the Orthodox Christians by the western knights of the Fourth Crusade.

I will add here that the social factor independent of the other forces was by itself instrumental in shifting the sympathy of the Orthodox Christian peasantry towards the Muslim Turks. Indeed, the relatively easy Turkish conquest of the Balkans and the relative success of their rule over the vast numbers of Orthodox Christians in the area was the product not only of the absolute freedom they granted to Christians who remained Christian and continued to practice their Orthodox faith, but also of the welcome elimination of the oppressive, Western style feudalism in force there and of the *pronoia* system of land tenure practiced by the Byzantium. The *timar* system introduced by the Muslims favored the peasant, because it gave him, as tenant, various concrete rights over the land and its produce and entitled him to ask protection and redress in the official courts. The peasant no longer dealt with an absolute landlord but with the State and its officials, who were bound by the rule of law. The socioeconomic factors which facilitated the Ottoman conquest and rule of the Balkans have been studied in great detail by the late O. L. Barkan and are too well known to be discussed here.[8] The peasant had his daily bread and his faith assured under the Muslim rule, and in the end these proved to be the essential forces conditioning his attitudes towards his rulers.

Hostility to a varying degree on the part of Christians of Orthodox persuasion toward the Latin branch of the Church—the legacy of European attempts to dominate through military conquest and repression in the thirteenth century—was thus a prominent background condition at the time of the fifteenth-century Gennadios-Mehmet II Concordat. Before proceeding further with my analysis of Ottoman views and policies toward the Orthodox Church after the conquest

---

[8]See Barkan's "Feodal Düzen ve Osmanli Timari" (The Feudal System and the Ottoman Timar) and other articles in *Turkiyede Toprak Meseleleri* (Istanbul, 1980), pp. 725-904.

of Constantinople, I would like to review the events that led to the Ottoman decision to take the city. In the third decade of the fifteenth century the sultans were masters of all the lands around Constantinople. Thus the capture of the city did not seem vital to Ottoman strategic interests as it would have had their hold on the Balkans still been precarious. Already Byzantium had become a tributary of the Ottoman state. Murad II, the predecessor of Mehmet the Conqueror, could thus afford to conclude with the Byzantine emperor agreements accepting the integrity of the Byzantine capital and a few other cities. Murad's policy of maintaining good relations with Byzantium was supported by the viziers of the Candarli family, and Halil Candarli (called by Dukas *"gavur ortagi"*—partner of the infidels") opposed until the last, the proposed conquest of Constantinople,[9] even during the final council held only a day or so before the final assault on the city. Mehmet had been from the beginning in favor of taking the city for strategic military reasons. He considered that as long as the Byzantine emperor held his throne in Constantinople and the Genoese and Venetians held control of the Mediterranean, the Ottoman state would always be in danger either of being attacked from the rear or of facing a frontal assault, as was the case in the crusade that was mounted shortly after the conclusion of the Council of Florence in 1439.

The Council of Florence was called for the purpose of establishing unity between Constantinople and Rome. At the Council it was agreed that the Orthodox Christians would accept the supremacy of the Pope and, in addition, that a new crusade would be mounted to drive the Turks from Europe. This agreement was desired by John III Palaiologos, who sought, through his submission to Rome, to obtain Western help against the Ottomans, while, at the same time, assuring for himself the Byzantine throne. The Ottoman leaders correctly interpreted this as an immediate threat to their position in the Balkans and viewed the union agreement as effectively negating Sultan Murat II's previous agreement to leave Constantinople unconquered. Indeed, the immediate result of the Florence agreement was a crusade headed by Ianos Hunyade of Hungary. Hunyade won a series of initial victories against the Turks in 1443 but was eventually defeated, although with great difficulty, at Varna in 1444 and again in 1448

---

[9]See Halil Inalcik, *Fatih Devri Üzerinde Tetkikler ve Vesikalar* (Research and Documents on the Epoch of the Conqueror) (Ankara, 1954), pp. 11-13.

at Belgrade. During his march through the area that today is northern Bulgaria and Serbia, Hunyade demonstrated that the Latin distrust of and contempt for the Orthodox faith had not diminished: he used such brutal and merciless methods to force the Orthodox Christians to reject their faith and become papists that when the Muslim armies won back the territory they were greeted as liberators and saviors.

Thus the Ottomans were stimulated by the "unity" agreement of the Council of Florence to finish off once and for all the hostile Byzantine power by conquering its capital, despite some fairly powerful voices that continued to urge that Murat II's policy of leaving the city alone be adhered to. In fact, had the final assault of 29 May 1453 failed, the siege would have been lifted, as was continuously demanded by Grand Vizier Candarli. However, the attack succeeded and Constantinople fell. The war party among the Ottoman leadership—including hawks such as Zaganos paşa, Şahabeddin paşa, and Turahan bey—was greatly strengthened and its leaders became more powerful in the government, while the old vizier, Candarli, was jailed and then executed (creating a profound moral crisis among the members of the government).[10] After this conquest of Constantinople, however, Mehmet II himself adopted the policy, advocated by Candarli, of friendship and conciliation toward the Byzantine. Mehmet found that his own fear and mistrust of the Papacy and of the Catholic powers of the West were shared by most of the Orthodox clergy and by the overwhelming majority of the Orthodox subjects. George Gennadios Scholarios was one of the signatories of the union pact at Florence but later, as was so with many of his colleagues, regretted his part in the Council and turned against Rome. He came to view union with Rome as a greater danger to the culture and identity of Orthodox believers and of the Greeks as a whole than the political and military threat posed by the Muslims. Thus, the Muslim Turks and anti-unionist Orthodox Christian Greeks found themselves politically united against the papacy and the Latin states — although for very different reasons. The anti-Latin policy of the Ottomans continued after the Reformation. Sultan Suleyman the Magnificent and his followers became active supporters of the Protestants, including the Huguenots in France, and it was thanks to this sympathy towards the Protestant cause that the Calvinists were able to establish a strong

---

[10]Ibid. p. 135.

foothold in southern Hungary, then under Ottoman rule, and that the British and Dutch were given trading privileges.

I recalled to mind the above facts, which are well known to scholars, simply as a background against which I now set out the fact that I believe to be crucial in explaining the psychological and sociological roots of the concordat between Sultan Mehmet II and Gennadios, the former anti-unionist leader. It is the following. The Christian churches of the Eastern Roman Empire were able, for historical and cultural reasons specific to the eastern Mediterranean area, to blend faith and ethnicity in an amalgam that became the very basis of the identity of their adherents. The Christian Orthodox religion, with its special doctrines, rituals, and costumes, bore the strong imprint of the people who had created its particular religious—ethnic character—i.e. the Greeks—but was not nationally identified with them. However, the acceptance of the supremacy of Rome involved for this Church the imposition of a variety of foreign symbols, customs, and ways of worship upon a whole nation of people known as Christian Orthodox, for whom the spokesmen were the Greeks. Whereas in the West one could be a German, Catalan, or French first and a papist second, in the East a Greek, a Bulgarian, or a Serb, etc. was first an Orthodox Christian and a member of a universal congregation and only second a member of an ethnic group. It was the same for the Muslims, who belonged first to the universal community of Islam and then to some tribal, linguistic, or ethnic group. While in the Hellenic period of the Byzantine empire the emphasis certainly shifted somewhat toward the identification of the faith with "Greekness," this identification did not reach the level of ethnic or racial nationalism until the nineteenth century. For the Muslims, only in the twentieth century did national identity begin to become predominant. When Mehmet II recognized Gennadios, by then head of the anti-unionist forces, as the Orthodox patriarch, he at the same time granted to Orthodox Christians the absolute freedom to retain their identity in the Greek tradition of the Orthodox Church in which Orthodoxy and "Hellenism" were an inseparable, universal whole, without any connotations of Greek national supremacy. The tradition was in many ways similar to that of the Muslim who prayed and studied his religion in Arabic and considered Arabic to be the universal language of Islam—not the language of some superior group—although some contemporary students of Arab nationalism would have us believe otherwise. The grounds for agreement between Gennadios and Sultan

Mehmet II were, therefore, in many ways much more basic and solid than those upon which union with Rome was to be constructed.

As for the sultan himself, he was a ruler of broad imperial vision. He believed that he was bound to act with equity toward and respect for all of his subjects, whatever their religion; this meant that he needed to practice wide tolerance, for he regarded himself not only as the sultan of the Muslims but also as the Caesar of the Romans and, ultimately, the ruler of the world. His conquest of Constantinople, he believed, entitled him to require the obedience of all, including Rome, as whoever was master of Constantinople was master of the world. (Some of these views derived from the writing of George Trapezountes). Mehmet's liberal views on religion, his knowledge of Greek and Latin, and his interest in knowing more about Christianity, as well as about the West, prompted an exchange of letters between him and the pope, who invited him to embrace Catholicism, while George Amiroutzes, the Byzantine philosopher, suggested that Orthodox Christianity and Islam could be blended into one religion, and presented to the sultan a study showing how much the two religions had in common.[11] Thus he seems to have elevated the Christian-Muslim dialogue to a very advanced stage. But the sultan was a Muslim, and a very pious one at that. His treatment of the Orthodox was for the most part in basic conformity with the tenets of Islam. The Qur'ān named the Christians and Jews as the People of the Book and conferred upon them the status of "*Dhimmi*," or "protected people." In according recognition and protection to the Orthodox Christians, Mehmet II was abiding by a divine commandment that had acquired the status of a basic and absolute constitutional principle. He was also following a venerable precedent set by Caliph Omar, who had allowed the Christians of Jerusalem and of other conquered cities to preserve their life, faith, and property, and pay only the *ciziye*, head tax.[12] (The same tax was paid by non-Muslims of the Ottoman Empire often under the name *harac*.)

The freedom and authority granted by Mehmet II to the Orthodox Church went far beyond that granted by his predecessors. Until the conquest of Constantinople and the concordat with Patriarch

---

[11]Runciman, *Great Church*, p. 183.

[12]C. E. Bosworth "The Concept of 'Dhimmi' in Early Islam," in *Christians and Jews in the Ottoman Empire*, ed. B. Braude and B. Lewis (New York, 1982), 1, pp. 37-54.

Gennadios, the Ottoman sultans had treated the conquered Christians within the general framework of Islamic tenets, offering them protection and freedom of faith but no political role in the empire. Mehmet II, on the other hand, institutionalized the status of the Orthodox Christians and broadened their freedoms, granting them nearly complete autonomy in religious and cultural affairs by introducing a new principle of religious representation. The concordat and the later imperial orders that implemented it (the *Kanunnames*)[13] decreed that all the Orthodox Christians were to be considered one *millet*—that is,[14] one nation. The nationality of this *millet* stemmed directly from its faith, which became the primary source of identity of its members. All other identities or loyalties of the Greeks, Serbians, Bulgarians, Vlachs, etc. that derived from race, language, or ethnicity were officially superseded by the Christian Orthodox identity. The head of this *millet,* the patriarch (called the *millet başi* by the Turkish sources), was to promote Christian Orthodoxy—not Hellenism—among his flock, although he was a Greek and it was implicit in the agreement that the Greeks should represent all the national groups included in the Orthodox *millet.* The identity situation of the Orthodox Christian was best described by the first patriarch. When asked his nationality, George Scholarios Gennadios replied that he would not call himself a Hellene, though he was a Hellene by race, nor a Byzantine, though he had been born in Byzantium, but rather a Christian, that is, an Orthodox.[15] If Sultan Mehmet II had been asked the same question, probably he would have answered that although he was an Osmanli through dynastic ties and a Turk because of his language and ancestry, he considered himself first of all a Muslim, and then a sultan and caesar and ruler of a multi-religious, multi-ethnic empire.

As the head and *de facto* ruler of the *millet* the Orthodox patriarch had a lofty position in the Ottoman government, whereas under the

---

[13]The *Kanunnames* were imperial orders that conformed to the Shariat and had the power of law. Those of Mehmet II have been the subject of various studies, notably by H. Inalcik and N. Beldiceanu, the latter being the most recent work; see also Steven Runciman, *The Fall of Constantinople, 1453* (Cambridge, 1965).

[14]See the succinct survey by Richard Clogg, "The Greek Millet in the Ottoman Empire" *Christians and Jews,* 1, pp. 185-208.

[15]Runciman, *Great Church,* p. 379.

Byzantine empire he had been a subordinate of the basileus, or
emperor, who was the head of the Church and the nation. In addition, the Constantinople patriarch had long been subordinate to the
bishop of Herakleia (Thrace) but, although a liaison between the two
was maintained for some time after the new system was put in place,
the Istanbul patriach was in fact no longer truly subordinate to any
other Christian prelate. Under the Ottomans the patriarch in Istanbul acquired greater prestige and authority than he had had at any
time during the Byzantine rule. It may be argued that the Byzantine
Patriarchate maintained not only its historical and institutional continuity under the Ottoman rule (in fact, it was the only Byzantine
institution to do so) but achieved a position of such enhanced authority
and power that it became in effect one of the empire's ruling institutions. The patriarch was given an official high position in the state
hierarchy and enjoyed special privileges normally granted only to
sovereigns. As previously mentioned, he gained the right of direct
access to Sultan Mehmet II and in his presence was entitled to wear
the Palaiologan emblem of twin eagles, representing State and Church.
Turkish historians state that after the patriarch received the title of
millet başi (head of the nation) he transformed the Patriarchate of-
fices (which had been moved to a palace in Balat, the Church of the
Holy Apostles being in bad repair) into a sort of ruler's residence.
Visitors, including Ottoman government envoys, were admitted only
by permission, which had to be obtained through Mehmet II's aides.
In fact, the patriarch's representatives and aides were treated as if
they were ambassadors when they dealt with official Ottoman
bodies.[16] In the nineteenth century the patriarch dealt directly with
the *Adalet Nezareti* (Ministry of Justice).

After 1454 the Orthodox Church took on a number of administrative and executive duties that during the Byzantine times had been
performed by lay bodies, such as the adjudication of marriages, di-
vorces, inheritances, adoptions, etc. (Economic and criminal cases,
as well as cases involving both Muslims and Christians, were dealt
with by the *Kadi* court. Church property enjoyed the same treatment
as that accorded *vakif* properties: autonomy of administration, ex-
emption from taxes, and immunity from confiscation. An Orthodox

---

[16]Mehmet Zeki Pakalin, *Osmanli Tarih Deyimleri ve Terimleri Sözlügü*
(Lexicon of Ottoman Terms and Expressions), s.v. "Patrik" and "Patrik-
hane," p. 762.

Christian could freely turn over funds to a church or monastery that was, in turn, free to use the donation for any of a number of religious or educational purposes. For example, Helena, the daughter of Demetrios (the brother of the Emperor John VIII who went with him to the Council of Florence in 1439), who was taken into the sultan's harem after the conquest but remained a virgin, bequethed all her properties to the Patriarchate.[17] The Patriarchate of Istanbul, like those of Jerusalem and Antioch, held large tracts of land, including extensive estates in Wallachia and Moldavia, the income from which was spent for a variety of educational and administrative services.

A great number of Greek and Balkan nationalist historians, as well as Western scholars with Catholic or Protestant sympathies, have described the Orthodox Patriarchate as a docile tool of the Turkish ruler and a partner in the oppression of non-Greek subjects. These allegations are totally false. The Orthodox Patriarchate dealt strictly with the affairs of the *millet* and was not part of the Ottoman bureaucratic apparatus. Even the *ciziye*, the head tax paid by non-Muslims, was not collected by the Church but by the headman (*ciorbaci, kocabaşi,* etc.) of the village community or town quarter (*mahalle*), although occasionally the Ottoman government would ask the Patriarchate—as a kind of favor—to use its moral influence to get the Christians to pay their taxes.

There is also the much discussed issue of the frequent change of patriarchs, allegedly brought about through the payment of "bribes" to the Porte. Again, this situation has been grossly exaggerated. First, and above all else, it must be stressed that the election and deposition of patriarchs was entrusted to the Synod, the Church administrative body consisting of twelve prelates (equal to the number of the Apostles). There is no question but that the Synod could be influenced to act one way or another, but the fact that the Synod followed well designed procedures which limited its scope for arbitrary decision should not be ignored. The exchange of gifts between two dignitaries or the donation of gifts to the sovereign were not "bribes" but rituals of authority. The *Piş-keş,* for example, was given to the sultan by the recipient of a position as a symbol of his loyalty and a mark of his respect for and dependence on the ruler.[18]

---

[17]Dukas, *Decline and Fall,* p. 181, no. 202.

[18]Halil Inalcik, "Ottoman Archival Materials on Millets," in *Christians and Jews,* Vol. 1, pp. 437-41.

Such gifts were known in Islam as *al-alamat-i mulukiyya* ("expressions of authority"). In fact, the so-called "bribes" did not go into the private treasury of the sultan or the vizier but were registered as state revenues. On the patriarch's side, an office known as *Kalem-i Mukataa-i Peskeopos*, headed by a *hoca* (Muslim clergyman) who was also the secretary of the grand vizier, was established specifically to monitor the revenues of all the patriarchates. After 1837 the appointments of prelates and other religious matters were registered in the *Defter-i Cemaat-i Gayri Muslimin* (Register of the Non-Muslim Communities), since in the nineteenth century the old arrangement underwent considerable change, as shall be discussed later.

The authority of the Orthodox Church was extended to cover practically all Orthodox Christians in the Balkans and the Middle East, as had been the case during the most glorious days of the Byzantine empire. Ruthenians, Vlachs, Greeks, Bulgarians, Serbians, Albanians, etc., in the Balkans and the Bucak were brought under the political sway of the Porte, defusing thus the efforts of Rome to expand its authority into these areas. Only the Russian Church was not under the direct orders of the Istanbul Patriarchate, although it recognized the latter's spiritual leadership. It must be pointed out that during the twelfth and thirteenth centuries the influence of the Byzantine Church in the Balkans had greatly decreased. For instance, Stephen II Nemanja of Serbia (ascended the throne in 1196) and Czar Kalojan of Bulgaria (ascended in 1197) had sought ratification of their rule from Rome, not from Constantinople. However, from 1453 onwards the patriarch, thanks to the Turkish power, had once again established Orthodox rule over almost all of the Balkans, although the fringes, such as Croatia and Dalmatia which were outside the Ottoman rule, remained predominantly Catholic. Moreover, the Patriarchates of Jerusalem, Antioch, and Alexandria were now under the same Ottoman roof, thus consolidating the Church's power for the first time in centuries. Orthodox Christians living in the Ottoman realm were free to communicate with all other Orthodox communities in the world, including those in Poland, Lithuania, and Russia. (However, in the early seventeenth century the Orthodox Church lost most of its followers in Poland and Lithuania to Rome despite the efforts of the Patriarchate of Constantinople to retain their loyalty, because the political and military power of the Ottoman government were not there to provide support as they were in the Balkans.) Cyril (nee Constantine) Loukaris (1572-1638) worked in Lvov among the Orthodox

Christians, but he had to flee the country in order to escape being arrested as a "Turkish spy." His companion was caught and hanged.

There is no question that the political interests of the Church and of the Ottoman government coincided, as did, in many respects, their basic concepts of religion, God, and eternity. For example, paganism was anathema equally to Orthodoxy and Islam. Thus, when there was a resurgence of paganism in Mistra, Gennadios fought fiercely against it and with the assistance of the Ottoman authorities eliminated it. Islam and Orthodox Christianity had, after all, flourished and interacted in the same Mediterranean environment in which the form of society and basic outlook on the world and on human fate were held in common. (Martin Luther considered the Orthodox Church to be much closer in doctrine to early Christianity than the Catholic Church, and Amiroutzes actually wrote a treatise to prove this point.) The Roman Church had evolved under a set of different historical, social, and political conditions that set it apart from Islam and Eastern Christianity. In fact, even after 1453 the Orthodox Church in Istanbul had to continue to defend itself against the intrigues designed by the Western churches to undermine its power and authority. The case of Cyril I Loukaris provides an excellent example of the anti-Orthodox machinations of the Roman Church. We have already mentioned his narrow escape from arrest and execution while visiting Orthodox Christians in Poland. In 1596 the Western Church further demonstrated its hostility towards its Eastern brethren by refusing to allow Loukaris and the Ottoman Christian delegation to participate in the second unionist meeting at Brest-Litowsk. Eventually Loukaris became patriarch of Alexandria, and then of Constantinople. He was a progressive-minded scholar, born in Crete but educated in Venice. He was instrumental in the introduction into Istanbul in 1627 of the printing press, which printed theological works in Greek. The Jesuits suspected him of Calvinist sympathies, however. Thus, when the press published one of his pamphlets in which he stated that certain Islamic dogma could not be accepted by Christians, the Jesuits took the pamphlet to the grand vizier and accused him of anti-government activities. The vizier turned the pamphlet over to the *Şeyhülislâm* (the highest religious official, who was charged with providing religious opinions—*fetva*—on important matters), who declared that Christians were entitled to state their beliefs even if these were contrary to Islam. Thus Loukaris was exonerated. The Jesuits were banned from Ottoman domains (the government having realized full well what was really behind their crocodile concern for its welfare); but the Capucines took their place and eventually succeeded in undermining Loukaris' position within his own *millet* by exploiting the alleged expression of Protestant sympathies in his book *Confession of Faith* (published in Latin at Geneva in 1629), although basically the book simply advocated change that would bring the Orthodox Church up to date.[19] Loukaris occupied the patriarch's throne four times, and the constant efforts to oust him from that position turned into a struggle for power between Catholic and Protestant embassies in Istanbul. The rate of *piş-keş* consequently reached a new high. (It is interesting to note that during this period Russia was becoming the last bastion of the political-ideological type of Christian Orthodoxy—which it exploited in the effort to realize its expansionist aims.)

It is not the purpose of this paper to give a detailed history of the Orthodox Church during the Ottoman era. However, the fact is that this Church survived, and the Orthodox Byzantine culture developed steadily (making such an impact on the Orthodox Christians of the Balkans that the great Romanian historian Nicolas Iorga was inspired to write a book entitled *Byzance aprés Byzance*). The conclusion must be reached that the destiny of the Orthodox Christian Church was intimately bound up with that of the empire itself. The Church's power, authority, and influence reached their zenith during the heyday of Ottoman power and wealth and declined as the empire faded when the classical Ottoman institutions and authority were challenged by European powers from outside and by reformist intellectuals and ambitious bureaucrats from inside.

The rise of the Phanariotes in the eighteenth century came as there began a cycle of economic transformation that shook the political and social foundations of the order on which the Ottoman government and the Patriarchate were based. The new Phanariotes social groups rose to prominence and power as a consequence of the expanded Ottoman commercial and economic relations with Europe and of the intensified trade within its own domains. The classical Ottoman sociopolitical system was undergoing a structural transformation that brought a need for adjustment to new conditions. The young Phanariotes bureaucracy, which filled many of the positions in the hierarchy of the Orthodox Church and its educational system by late in the eighteenth century, took the West as a model and demanded

---

[19]See G. A Hadjiantoniou, *Protestant Patriarch* (Richmond, 1961).

changes accordingly. They and many other Orthodox Christians educated in the West also discovered at that time the roots of their linguistic and national history and called for the overhaul of the existing traditional educational and religious systems. Some became revo-
lutionaries who questioned the whole concept of the Church as the
sole ruler of a society that was rapidly adopting nationalism and
secularism as its ideology and creating a new political identity based
not on a universal faith but on the particularism and localism of language. The Phanariotes sought to create a new Byzantium, working
from the inside by infiltrating the Church administration and gain-
ing influence in the Ottoman government. They also tried to Hellen-
ize the Slavs and the Vlachs in the Balkans. In support of these activities they employed their considerable wealth, derived from trade
and from the taxes collected in Wallachia and Moldavia, which they
ruled from about 1711 or 1716 until 1821 as the appointees of the
Porte. Some voices for change were even heard occasionally from
among the prelates of the Church, such as those of the two monks
who wrote the *New Geography,* bitterly attacking the Church administration therein. (Curiously enough, at about that same time in
the eighteenth century a Muslim scholar, Katip Çelebi, wrote the *Ci-
hanunnuma,* a world geography considered to be the herald of enlightenment among Muslims.)

The sultan also faced demands for change that came not only from
the new intelligentsia but also from the more progressive elements
of the religious establishment and the bureaucracy, notably the bureaucrats in the foreign affairs section, who were in touch with the West
and could read works written in French and other languages. The
patriarch and the sultan were made subject to the criticism of the
modernists within their own establishments on essentially the same
ground: they were regarded as the symbols of the now-scorned tradition and continuity in the old fashion. The patriarch also suffered
the deterioration of his position of prestige and power within the Ottoman State as the Phanariotes became increasingly nationalistic and
vigorous in staking their claims to leadership in the Church. It was
under these circumstances that the *Paternal Exortation,* attributed
to Anthimos II, the patriarch of Jerusalem, was published in 1798,
the very year in which the most formidable strongfold of the Roman
Church—France—invaded Egypt and opened the door to the secu-
larist thinking and political imperialism of Europe as well as to the
Catholic penetration of the Middle East and the Ottoman Empire

as a whole. This book, denounced by Adamantios Koraes, the father of modern Greek nationalism, as unworthy of having been written by a Greek, condemned the French revolution and described the sultan as a gift of God, sent to protect the Orthodox Christians and their Church.[20]

The Orthodox Church, the Muslim religious establishment, and the conservatives within the Ottoman government all were attacked as being against innovation and change, and hence, unheeding of the welfare of their own people. Yet, I dare say the similar positions adopted by the Orthodox Church and the Muslim establishment against the urged "reforms" did not stem from their opposition to change *per se* but, rather from their deeply rooted fear that such changes would undermine the gnostic nature of their societies and destroy their basic identities and historical heritage. Such fears were not without bases, as subsequent events proved.

Drastic structural change, which transformed the traditional Ottoman system into a kind of class society, was forced by the slow but steady penetration of European capitalism that began in the eighteenth century. With the rise of Russia as a major power and its expansion into Ottoman territories, starting with the Peace of Küçük Kaynarca in 1774, the Ottoman economic and political recovery that had begun before the middle of the century was stalled. Hard pressed by the advancing Russian armies, and frequently threatened with total annihilation throughout the period 1792-1829, the Ottoman government sought support from the West in exchange for extensive economic and political concessions that increased the scope and speeded up the rate of Western penetration. The resulting spread of Western culture deeply influenced, first, the Christians and then the Muslim intelligentsia. The non-Muslims became the first agents of Western capitalism and as such received extensive economic rewards and political support, for which they sacrificed their historical, traditional, Christian religious identity, exhanging it for a secular political identity bearing the standard of national revival and, ultimately, of ethnic nationalism and even racism. Through them the European concepts of the territorial state and the nation-state found their way into the Ottoman realm. The ideological manifestation of the new concept

---

[20]For details and bibliography, see Kemal H. Karpat, *The Social Foundations of Nationalism in the Ottoman State: From Social Estates to Classes, from Millets to Nations* (Princeton, 1973).

of political organization was nationalism based on language, ethnicity, race, history, and local or regional attachments. Religion lost its gnostic character and became a secularized ingredient of nationality and nationalism, a mere cultural dimension of national identity rather than a universal fraternity.

In a different paper I argued at length that the principles of territoriality and the European concept of national statehood based on race, language, and history devoid of gnosticism were incompatible with the universality of Islam, as were they with the universality of Christian Orthodoxy. However, once the Church accepted the supremacy of secular nationality, faith and national identity would be reconciled, although the religion would lose its original essence.[21] In a second paper, I stressed the fact that although secular nationalism appeared to favor the Christian states in the Balkans in the initial phase of their search of independence, in the long run the nationalist rivalries that undermined the Ottoman state would destroy the unity of Orthodox Christians and create endless struggle among them.[22] Indeed, the strife-ridden history of the Balkan states after the Berlin Congress of 1878 stands in sharp contrast to the *Pax Ottomanica* which prevailed from the fifteenth to the eighteenth century, when the non-national Orthodox Church reigned supreme among the Ottoman Orthodox Christians.

The Greek revolution of 1821 had a devastating effect on relations between the Orthodox Church and the Ottoman government. The Church had very little to do with the revolution, as the notions of ethnic nationalism and secularism that inspired that revolution were still unaccepted by the Patriarchate. In fact, the Patriarchate of Constantinople recognized the government of independent Greece, where a national church was established, only in 1849 because of pressure of the Ottoman government. Sultan Mahmut II (1808-1839), whose so-called "modern reforms" undermined the socio-cultural foundations of the Ottoman state and quickened its disintegration, did not understand either the dynamics of the Greek revolution or the basic

---

[21]Kemal H. Karpat, "Millets and Nationality. The Roots of the Incongruity of Nation and State in the Post Ottoman Era," *Christians and Jews,* pp. 141-70.

[22]Kemal H. Karpat, "The Social and Political Foundations of Nationalism in South East Europe after 1878: A Reinterpretation," *Die Berlinger Congress Von 1878* (Wiesbaden, 1982), pp. 385-410.

anti-secularist, anti-nationalist position of the Patriarchate. He held the Patriarch responsible for the rebellion of Greeks and hanged him. The sultan also hanged the Şeyhulislam who denounced the punishment of the patriarch as being contrary to Islam. By holding the innocent Patriarch Gregory V responsible for the Greek revolt, the Sultan identified the Church with Hellenism and with the Greeks, thus unwittingly bolstering the claims of the other Orthodox Christian groups that the Patriarchate was Greek and prompting the intensification of their demands for their own national churches. Obviously Sultan Mahmut II had departed from the basic Ottoman traditions of government, and the following governments continued on the same track, further weakening tradition. The Greek revolution of 1821 without question undermined the primacy of the Greeks at the Porte and faced the Patriarchate with the dilemma of how to deal with the government of Greece while remaining at the head of the Orthodox Church, now increasingly referred to as the Greek Church. In fact, after the establishment of the Serbian and then the Bulgarian national church in 1870, the Patriarchate's authority extended only to Ottoman Greeks and a few other communities overseas. After the heat of Ottoman anger over the Greek revolution of 1821 had cooled, the Orthodox Church and the Ottoman government achieved a rapid rapprochement, because each needed the other. However, it was too late to effect a solid, permanent repair of the relationship. The open acceptance of the European concept of reform had undermined the historical foundations of both bodies, especially the Ottoman state, which, after several attempts to establish a concept of universal Ottomanism in the realm, succumbed to the lure of nationalism.

The Orthodox Church lost even more of its influence among Orthodox Christians vis-á-vis the Ottoman government after the so-called reforms introduced through passage of the *Reform Edict of 1856 (Islahat Fermani).*[23] This edict, prepared by the English, French, and Austrian governments, was imposed upon the Ottoman government. Almost the entire edict dealt with the situation of the Christians within the Ottoman Empire. At the first sight, the edict indeed appears to guarantee the Christians "equality" and equitable treatment. However, when studied more closely the edict is seen as aiming at creating the conditions for the rise of a Christian merchant class and giving

---

[23]Roderic Davison, *Reform in the Ottoman Empire, 1856-1876* (Princeton, 1963).

to that class control of the respective Christian communities. The edict sought the reorganization of the traditional *millets*, which had been the backbone of the Ottoman sociopolitical system since the classical constitutional order was established by Mehmet II in the fifteenth century, so as to give power to the lay leaders of the communities—the merchants, craftsmen, and intellectuals. In pushing these reforms through their respective governments—i.e., England, France, and Austria—the Protestants and especially the Catholics effected the liberation of the Orthodox Christians not only from Ottoman rule but also from the jurisdiction of their own Church. Indeed, conversions to Protestantism and Catholicism accelerated greatly after 1856.

The Orthodox Church was, in fact, the primary target of the European-inspired *millet* reform, for the reforms not only envisaged the transfer of power from the Church officials to laymen but also sought to encourage the establishment of new *millets* for each national religion. While until about the middle of the nineteenth century the term *millet* meant a large, basic religious community, after the edicts of 1839 and, especially of 1856, the term referred to a small ethnoreligious and national congregation. By the end of the century the number of *millets* had been increased from the original three to first nine and then eleven, usually by the separation of one group from the mother *millet*. I should point out that the Ottoman government did not want to become involved in the reform of the non-Muslim *millets* and did so only after the governments of France and England had applied great pressure.[24] Finally, in the period 1862-1867, the government compelled the Orthodox, Armenian, and Jewish *millets* to undertake the reforms desired by the Europeans and their own middle classes. This reform, which enabled laymen to elect and be members of the Synod and ultimately to elect the patriarch, was outwardly democratic, but it led not only to the secularization of the Church but also to its subordination to various private interests. It also destroyed the special position of the Patriarchate and subordinated it to the direct authority of the Ottoman government as a rank-and-file institution. These were inevitable outcomes.

Once the non-Muslims were free to organize themselves as they wished, the Muslims had the right to govern the society under their political control not according to the universal Muslim law but

---

[24]Ibid.

according to the principles borrowed from the West of national and territorial states. Indeed, in response the Ottoman state, or what was left of it, was turned first into a Muslim state and then, in 1923, into a Turkish national state. The reforms inspired by Europe led to a much more centralized government and to the subsequent loss of the autonomy which had been the hallmark of various Muslim and Christian institutions under the old system. For example, the state gradually assumed the power to administer the property of the *vakifs* in a flagrant violation of one of the most basic of Muslim laws.

At this point, instead of pursuing my own analysis of the transformation of the Orthodox Church, I shall let the Orthodox patriarch himself express his views about the reforms and the position of the Orthodox Church towards ethnicity, nationalism, and national languages, employing passages from several memoranda addressed by the patriarch to the European ambassadors. These memoranda are found in the Archives of the French Foreign Ministry.

In the first memorandum the Patriarch protested against the implementation of the edict of 1856, specifically against the decision of the Ottoman government in 1867 to dissolve the Synod so that a new Synod could be elected by the Orthodox community as required by the edict of 1856.[25] It is ironic that the patriarch addressed his complaint to the Catholic ambassador of France, who had been instrumental in writing the edict of 1856 and was forcing the Ottoman government to implement it:

> The Synod was constituted in a permanent manner by the Patriarchal throne since 1764 [said the Patriarch's memo], and the members of the Synod could not go back to their sees without the authorization of the Patriarch, without the Church being previously informed, and without the Sultan's decree. Now, this Synod has been dismissed, in fact dissolved, by a letter of Fuat Paşa [Foreign and Prime Minister] in such a violent fashion, without the Patriarch having provoked this action, without warning the Church, and, what is worse, without a new law which sanctioned the creation of a new Synod.

Continuing, the patriarch complained that many people who were

---

[24]Ibid.

[25]French Foreign Ministry Archives (FFMA) Section *Memoirs et Documents,* Vol. 117, Documents 7-10, pp. 14-103 *passim.*

engaged in personal rivalries and did not "examine the nature of things" might rejoice at the fate of the Synod but that "the entire Orthodox community has realized the gravity of this action directed against the inviolability of the Church . . . the privileges of the Church have been violated not only because of the dissolution of the Synod but especially because this dissolution took place without the proposition of the Patriarchate." The patriarch further complained that some people were rejoicing because they regarded the Elders as an obstacle to their national ambitions and interests; but

the divine master of the religion does not make any difference between nationalities, between races and languages. The Church is a moral entity living in the heart of society. It exerts a very specific kind of influence and activity, and therefore in its outward representation and in its administrative existence the Church cannot have but one homeland and one nationality . . . Greek. But having said this one should not think that these ideas are the basis of a policy of exclusivity within the Greek Church of the East, a policy imposed on the other races sharing the same religion and by forcing the conscience of other co-religionist peoples who have an [ethnic] origin other than Greek. This is not so. The Greek Church has always respected the language and the [ethnic] origin of the nations under its sway. Beginning in the ninth century and until our days the Church has said to the Bulgarians, Serbians, Vlahs, and in general to all the Slavic races under its jurisdiction "you have your own language, your own priests, and your own churches." This right has been respected by the Church even among the peoples of Asia, who were allowed to worship the God of the Christians in their maternal tongues. The Greek Church has reserved for itself only one right, namely a supervision from high above exercised by the trusted Bishops in whose selection Greekness could not be and is not a matter of importance.

Finally, referring to the entire question of reforms, the Patriarch queried the European powers as follows:

Nobody is opposed to wise and prudent reforms . . . But do you want to see at Constantinople a weakened Church, and a Synod which meets [only periodically]? Do you want to give to the might, the right to convene as it wishes, to an assembly [Synod] which could change at once the order of things? Do they wish to abolish the national character of the Patriarch, do you want to deprive him of all privilege and lower him from the rank of a chief of nation to be just the Bishop of Constantinople? Europe must become aware of the importance of these events and come to [our] help by protecting the present state of things in order to conserve intact in the Christian East the most sacred [heritage] left to us by past centuries.

The establishment of a Bulgarian Exarchate, that is, of a national Bulgarian Church, in open defiance of the universality of the Orthodox Church brought out the patriarch's views on nationality. The Patriarch Anthimos VI excommunicated the exarch, the Metropolitan Anthimos of Vidin, and refused to receive him. The patriarch of Istanbul found the root cause of the Bulgarian rebellion—as he called the establishment of a national Exarchate—in the principle of nationality. He described the idea of secular nationality as being

anti-canonic and anti-religious and subversive to the principle of Christian charity, since the idea (of nationality) led to the creation of 'national churches,' that is, to a system contradictory to the teaching of Jesus Christ who wanted to destroy all distinctions of race and tribe and wanted to give to all people one single mother Church and one single land, the celestial Jerusalem.[26]

To another letter about the Bulgarian Exarchate, the patriarch found the principle of

nationality (based) on race as stemming from an anti-evangelical and deadly principle. There is not a single faithful Christian who does not understand without doubt that this execrable principle stands in manifest contradiction to the doctrine of our Lord Jesus Christ, that this principle destroys the basic foundations on which the sacred Bible stands and thus it attacks the very foundations of the Christian religion. The doctrine of our Lord has abolished all distinctions of race and nationality and has gathered all the nations together by giving them . . . a common mother in the sacred Church.[27]

---

[26]FFMA, *Correspondence Politique* 392 (May-August 1872), p. 27.
[27]Ibid., annex to dispatch of 2 July 1872, p. 185.

Meanwhile the Bulgarian Exarch was delivering before the sultan the following speech:

Today, thanks to the high justice and equity of Your Majesty who in his paternal solicitude decided to re-establish this ecclesiastic administration by an imperial *firman,* the Bulgarian nation is full of hope living as such under the benign shadow of your majesty . . . It is impossible for me to express all the gratitude of the nation for such a great work, but I affirm that the Bulgarian people will always remain faithful to your glorious majesty as it has been until this day.[28]

Yet, only six years after this declaration, in 1878, the Bulgarians led by the Russian army, killed hundreds of thousands of Muslims and expelled a million Muslims, Greeks, and Jews in order to establish their independent and national state of Bulgaria. For all practical purposes religion had been replaced by a racist, bigoted nationalism.

Finally nationalism destroyed the old spiritual world order created by the Ottoman sultan Mehmet II and Patriarch Gennadios in the fifteenth century. As the Ottoman Empire gradually shrank and came to its end (1918-23), the Patriarchate of Constantinople also became only a shadow of what it was before. The mutual respect and tolerance between the Muslim and the Christian turned into a savage, bloody struggle for national domination. Today we are still in that bloody phase of nationalism. Let us hope that together we Muslims and Christians can overcome the destructive, barbaric nationalistic impulse that has destroyed the essence of our religion, and return to a spiritual understanding of man and society so that we can live in peace as our ancestors did a century and a half ago.

---

[28]Ibid. p. 38.

Islam and Bioethics

OSMAN BAKAR

IN THIS PAPER, our primary aim is to discuss the nature and the main characteristics of the Islamic response to what is today known in the West as bioethics.[1] In compliance with the request made by the organizers of the Symposium, we will focus our discussion on the specific issue of the human body in the light of Islamic teachings. In our view, the choice of this issue is a wise one, for many of the highly controversial aspects of contemporary biomedical practices and the ethical issues which they raise concern the treatment of the human body. The views which a particular people hold concerning the human body are clearly reflected in one way or another in almost every facet of their culture and civilization including the arts and sciences, particularly medicine. A discussion of the fundamental Islamic views of the human body will therefore help to throw an important light on the attitude of Islam toward many of the issues that are debated in contemporary bioethical discussion.

Nature and Characteristics of the Islamic Response
Thanks to the modern means of communication, the worldwide Muslim community is immediately made aware of the latest biomedical innovations in the West. Although from the practical point of view

---

[1] For a bibliography of contempory Muslim writings on this subject and related topics, see M. A. Anees, "A Select Bibliography on Islamic Medicine" in *The Muslim World Book Review,* 5.1 (Autumn 1984).

Muslim society is still spared the intrusion of many of these new, controversial technological inventions in the biomedical field, or is not affected by them to the same degree as is Western society, it cannot escape from having to deal with their ethical and intellectual or philosophical implications. The very nature and character of Islam as a religion demands that a definite stand be made on these issues. This obliges us to make a few remarks about the character of the Islamic religion itself insofar as this has an important bearing on the question under discussion.

The most fundamental teaching in Islam is the doctrine of Unity (*al-tawḥīd*) which is expressed in the most universal manner possible in the first "testimony" of the Islamic faith, *Lā ilāha illa'llāh*, usually translated as "there is no god but God." This doctrine conveys the basic attitude and spirit of Islam which every Muslim seeks to realize in his own being by organizing and integrating all his thoughts and actions into a harmonious whole and a unity. Once this unity is achieved, there is no longer any distinction, be it in the domain of thought or of action, between the spiritual and temporal or between the religious and profane. All thoughts and all actions, including those which are otherwise seen as the most mundane of activities such as carrying on trade or conducting the administrative affairs of the state, then possess a religious character and a spiritual significance. Islam therefore seeks through its principle of Unity to integrate all knowledge and human actions into a single realm of the religious and the sacred so that no true and useful knowledge and no good and beneficial act can possibly be excluded from this realm and be identified instead as secular and profane. By virtue of this fact, no human activity, and that includes the technological, can escape the moral judgment of Islam. Likewise, Islam cannot remain indifferent to any form of science which claims to provide a knowledge of reality or some particular aspect of it. It judges the latter in the light of its own conception of knowledge.

In order to relate in a more concrete manner the character of Islam as the religion of Unity to our discussion of the Islamic response to bioethics, we need to be more precise: how is the principle of Unity specifically applied in Islam, making the integration of knowledge and human actions possible? At the level of thought, integration is achieved through the application of the idea of unity and hierarchy of knowledge as well as of existence, an idea which is not unique to Islam but is common to all traditional civilizations including that of Christianity. However, there is something striking about the Islamic application of this idea that is not found to the same degree in other civilizations. Firstly, the vast synthesis that Islam created out of such diverse and historically alien sciences as those of the Greeks, Chaldeans, Persians, Indians, and the Chinese, with which it came into contact, was unprecedented in the history of human civilization.[2] Islam integrated many elements of these sciences into a new body of knowledge, which it further developed, to the extent that these elements were compatible with its own idea and spirit of Unity.

Secondly, Islam produced a large number of universal figures whose names appear in almost every branch of knowledge known to its civilization. The idea of unity and hierarchy of knowledge was a living reality by virtue of the fact that the different levels of knowledge lived in harmony within the mind and soul of each of these figures. And thirdly, in order to preserve the unity and hierarchy of the sciences, successive generations of Muslim scholars, from al-Kindī in the third/ninth century to Shāh Walīullāh of Delhi in the twelfth/ eighteenth century, have devoted a considerable deal of their intellectual talents and geniuses to the classification of the sciences, for it is through this classification that the scope and position of each science within the total scheme of knowledge is always kept in view. These are some of the striking features of the Islamic concern with the integration of knowledge and ideas.

In Islam, the highest knowledge is that of Unity which refers to knowledge of the divine essence, names, and qualities as well as knowledge of the divine effects and acts embracing God's creation. All other knowledge must be organically related to this knowledge and all ideas, concepts and theories in whatever domain of study are to be judged in the light of it. This supreme knowledge of Unity serves as a compulsory guide in any Muslim attempt to deal with the intellectual and philosophical implications of contemporary biomedical discoveries and their application, which in fact are numerous.[3] It is, however,

---

[2] See S. H. Nasr, *Science and Civilization in Islam* (Cambridge, 1968), pp. 29-40.

[3] Many molecular biologists like J. Monod, G. Stent, and R. Sinsheimer have given philosophical and ethical meanings to modern biomedical discoveries that have the gravest implications for traditional religious worldview and ethics.

beyond the scope of this paper to deal with the above-mentioned implications.

At the level of actions, integration is achieved through the application of the *sharī'a*, the divine law of Islam, which is the concrete embodiment of the divine will. The divine law in Islam is concrete and all-embracing in the sense that it includes not only universal moral principles but also details of the way in which man should conduct every facet of his earthly life, both private and social. It is extremely important for us to know the Islamic conception of law if we are to understand fully the nature and characteristics of the Islamic response to bioethics. The role of the divine law in Islam may be compared to its importance and centrality to that of theology in Christianity. Like the teachings on divine Unity, the *sharī'a* is an integral aspect of the Islamic revelation. It is therefore a religious and sacred law which serves as the guide for a Muslim to conduct his life in harmony with the divine will. It is the source of knowlede of what is right and wrong. In Islam, therefore, its moral injuctions and attitudes are to be found in its law which, because of its all-embracing nature, sanctifies the whole of human life and leaves no domain outside the sphere of divine legislation.

According to the *sharī'a*, there is a hierarchy of values of human acts and objects in the sight of God. Every human act must fall into one of the following five categories: (1) obligatory (*wājib*), (2) meritorious or recommended (*mandūb*), (3) forbidden (*ḥarām*), (4) reprehensible (*makrūh*), and (5) indifferent (*mubāḥ*). It should be remarked here that although in essence all of the *sharī'a* is contained in the Qur'ān the above classifications of human acts into five legal categories did not appear until the third century of the Islamic era when Islamic jurisprudence came into existence as an independent science and the Islamic law became well codified and systematized by men of great genius and religious integrity.[4] Further, there are several schools of Islamic law which, while agreeing upon the fundamental principles of the law and upon many of the obligatory acts such as the five daily prayers and those that are prohibited such as wine-drinking, may differ in their views when it comes to the question of determining the precise technical legal status

---

[4] For a detailed account of this codification and systemization of Islamic law, see for example, A. Hasan, *The Early Development of Islamic Jurisprudence* (Islamabad, 1970).

of many of the other acts, or with reward to the details of those major obligatory acts and prohibitions. Also, since the teachings of the *sharī'a* are meant to be applied in all ages and climes, it is the task of doctors of the law (*fuqahā'*), especially the experts (*mujtahids*) among them, to interpret and apply those teachings to newly arisen problems and situations in whatever sphere of human activity.

Today, we are confronted with a host of new problems and situations in the biomedical field that have never existed before, problems made possible by new discoveries and the application of new techniques. Problems like those relating to organ transplantation, artificial insemination, and genetic and behavior control are entirely new while such age-old problems as contraception, abortion, and the question of the appropriate treatment of the dying have incorporated new issues into them as a result of the introduction of modern biomedical technology. It has come to be widely realized now that all these problems are multi-dimensional in character. They are at once ethical and legal, medical and scientific, social and philosophical, and thus require a multi-dimensional approach in their solutions. In the light of what we have said regarding the centrality of the *sharī'a* in the religious and spiritual life of the Muslims, it is only natural that the first question a Muslim would ask when confronted with these new developments is this: Is such and such an innovative act permissible to not from the point of view of the *sharī'a*? The first and most important Muslim response to contemporary bioethics therefore comes from the deliberations of the jurists (*fuqahā*) whose legal rulings (*fatwās*) on these matters are immediately sought after by the Muslim community to provide it with the right code of conduct, since they are the authoritative interpreters and guardians of the divine law of Islam.

There is, in fact, in Islamic tradition a well-established discipline of biomedical jurisprudence which has dealt with many of the biomedical issues currently debated in the West, especially those relating to contraception and abortion, the question of dissection of the human body, and the meaning and definition of death with all its implications upon the duties and responsibilities of the living toward the dying and the dead. We may also recall here the fact that some of the Muslim physicians like Ibn al-Nafīs (d. 1288), who is now celebrated as the real discoverer of the minor circulation of the blood, were at the same time eminent figures in the field of jurisprudence (*fiqh*).[5] This traditional biomedical jurisprudence provides the necessary background and guidelines for any Muslim attempt to deal with contemporary bioethics.

In our own modern times, many people have spoken of the need for a new value orientation and reappraisal of the traditional system of values in the light of what they term revolutionary scientific and technological progress in the biomedical field. As far as Islam is concerned, although many modernized Muslims have joined this chorus, there can be no question of undertaking a religious reform of the *sharī'ah* for the sake of conforming to this so-called scientific and technological progress which is the fruit of a totally alien and antireligious concept of life. Moreover, for millions of Muslims throughout the Islamic world, especially in the Indian subcontinent, modern Western medicine has never proved itself to be indispensable. They have a more well established medical tradition on which to rely, in the form of the various types of traditional medicine which have survived to this day and which, in contrast to modern medicine, are intimately and harmoniously linked to their religious worldview and ethics.

The traditional Islamic views concerning issues such as contraception, abortion, dissection of the human body, the proper treatment of dying patients, and the meaning and definition of death, are not going to be affected by new developments in biomedical technology. This is because the Islamic attitudes toward these issues are directly shaped and governed by the imutable teachings of Islam on the more fundamental question of the meaning and purpose of human life and death.[6] It is not possible for us in this paper to go into the detailed Islamic views of each of the above-mentioned issues. What we wish to convey here is that in their response to these contemporary issues, present-day Muslim jurists are only reasserting the traditional Islamic views. In other words, new discoveries and new techniques do not provide them with any logical justification to call into question the ethico-legal basis on which their predecessors have

---

[5] Ibn al-Nafīs taught *fiqh* (jurisprudence) at al-Masrūriyyah School in Cairo, and his name was included in the *Ṭabaqāt al-Shāfi'iyyīn al-Kubrā* (Great Classes of Shāfi'ī Scholars) of al-Subkī (d. 1370). See A. Z. Iskander, "Ibn al-Nafīs" in C. Gillespie (ed.), *Dictionary of Scientific Biography* (New York, 1969), p. 603.

[6] For a good account of the various views on death and life after death in Islamic tradition, see J. I. Smith and Y. Y. Haddad, *The Islamic Understanding of Death and Resurrection* (Albany, 1981).

formulated their legal views on the above issues. It must be emphasized, however, that we are only speaking here of those cases which have historical precedents in Islam.

Let us illustrate the above point with an example. In traditional sources which contain references to biomedical jurisprudence, we find detailed discussions of specific conditions and circumstances under which contraception and abortion are permissible in Islam.[7] While Islam generally prohibits abortion at all stages of pregnancy, Muslim jurists, guided by the principle of the *sharī'a* that allows necessity to remove restriction and says that in having to choose between two evils the lesser one is recommended, have also agreed on the exceptional situation in which it is necessary to perform abortion even when the fetus has been completely formed. This exceptional situation arises when it is reliably established that continued pregnancy would greatly endanger the life of the mother. As to why the saving of the mother's life is to be given priority over that of the child, a jurist explains: "For the mother is the origin of the fetus; moreover, she is established in life with duties and responsibilities, and she is also a pillar of the family. It would not be possible to sacrifice her life for the life of a fetus which has not acquired a personality and which has no responsibilities or obligations to fulfill."[8]

Now, modern biomedical knowledge and technology have certainly made available new methods of contraception and abortion and introduced new variables into modern man's encounter with these two problems, such as the possibility of having prenatal knowledge of some aspects of the fetus, but in no way do these new scientific and technological developments affect and alter the basic Islamic ethico-legal equations of the problems since the legitimate factors for contraception and abortion in Islam are valid at all times. Prenatal knowledge of some kinds of defects in the child-to-be may have provided many people of our times with a justifiable basis for carrying out abortion because they only want to have a perfectly normal and healthy child. But Islamic law cannot make these known defects a legitimate basis for abortion unless they are deemed to endanger the very life of the mother. In the light of clearly spelled out views in Islam as to what are

---

[7] For a modern discussion of these issues but based on traditional sources, see Y. al-Qaradawi, *The Lawful and the Prohibited in Islam* (Indianapolis), pp. 198-202.

[8] Ibid. p. 202.

legitimate and illegitimate conditions for contraception and abortion, the question of whether or not to use modern methods and techniques of these two acts, once their necessary ethico-legal conditions are ful- illed, becomes essentially a medical issue rather than an ethical one.

Not all the bioethical issues which arise from modern biomedical discoveries and techniques and which are currently debated in the West have been taken up by Muslim religious scholars or, if they have been taken up, they have been resolved in a conclusive manner. As far as those issues which have been posed in the Muslim community are concerned, we would say that in most cases Muslim jurists have achieved quite a remarkable degree of consensus in their legal views, enough so as to put those issues to rest. Such was the case, for example, with the issue of artificial insemination. When the insemination is re- stricted to the semen of legally maried couples, it is permissible from the point of view of the *shari'a*. The question of organ transplanta- tion, however, generated lengthy and controversial debates in many parts of the Islamic world. Whatever the technical legal status of each of the still disputed issues finally turns out to be, it is now clear to us that in the encounter between Islam and contemporary bioethics the nature and pattern of its responses is essentially determined by the teachings contained in its sacred law which is at once ethical and legal.

As we have remarked in the introduction to this paper, many of the controversial bioethical issues in the contemporary debate con- cern directly or are related in one way or another to the treatment of the human body. It is in the light of this awareness that we now turn to a discussion of the human body according to the teachings of Islam. Through this discussion, we hope to throw further light on the attitude of Islam toward contempory bioethics. In traditional Islamic literature, there is an extensive treatment of the subject by different intellectual schools. In this paper, we can only bring out those elements that are considered central to the Islamic teachings.

The Human Body

According to Islam, man is God's most noble creation and this fact is symbolized in the Qur'ān by the prostration of the angels be- fore Adam upon the divine command.[9] There are numerous verses in the Qur'ān and also sayings of the Prophet which praise the perfect mould and proportions in which man has been created as well as the

---

[9] Al-Qur'ān (2.34).

beauty of the human form.[10] The Prophet, while gazing at his own reflection in a mirror, prayed to God for his soul to be adorned with perfect moral and spiritual beauty just as his body had been made beautiful.

Man is a creature of many levels and facets. He is body, soul, and spirit. But Islam, faithful to its fundamental doctrine of Unity, views man as a unified whole in which all the parts are interdependent. Islam shares with Judaism and Christianity the view that man is created in the image of God. A consequence of this view is that the human body must also participate in certain respects in this dignity of man as the "image of God." Ali, the cousin and son-in-law of the Prophet and the fourth caliph of Islam, refers in one of his poems to man as the microcosm (*'ālam ṣaghīr*). This idea of man as the microcosm, as we shall see, constitutes one of the most fundamental principles of many of the sciences cultivated by Islam, particularly the biomedical sciences. And all of the above Islamic views of man have important consequences upon the spirit with which Islam carries out the study of the human body and also upon the way in which Islam enjoins its followers to treat the human body.

At the level of the law, Islam conceives of the human body mainly in terms of its rights and duties. Islam attaches great importance to the overall health, welfare, and well-being of the body, not for its own sake, but for the sake of the spiritual soul which constitutes the real essence of man. A body that is normal and healthy may serve as a perfect instrument for either virtues or vices. Islam insists that all activities of the body must be for the sake of the health and felicity of the soul. In other words, in Islam, and this is true of all religions, the idea of having a perfectly healthy body is so that it may act as a perfect instrument of the soul to realize the very purpose for which it has been created. The relationship between the body and the soul has been described by Muslim scholars by means of various analogies depending on the point of view from which a particular relationship is envisaged. But in all these relationships the body is subordinated to the soul. Al-Ghazālī, for example, describes the body as the vehicle or riding-animal of the soul and the latter as a traveler who visits a foreign country, which is this world, for the sake of merchandise and will soon return to his native land.[11] The vehicle should be taken care of and well looked after but not to the point of forgetting or neglecting

---

[10]"We have indeed created man in the best of moulds," al-Qur'ān (95.4).

[11]Al-Ghazzālī, *The Alchemy of Happiness* (Lahore, 1979), pp. 21 and 49.

the final goal for which the traveler has set out on his journey.

Islam enjoins the fulfillment of all the legitimate needs of the body. What constitutes the body's legitimate needs are defined and determined by the divine law of Islam. In legislating its laws for the human collectivity as a whole Islam takes into full account both the strengths and weaknesses inherent in human nature. It is also aware of human tendencies either toward the excessive pursuits of the needs of the body or toward the neglect of its legitimate needs. Both tendencies can have detrimental effects on man's total health. The general aim of Islamic legislation on such basic needs of the body as food, sex, and dress as well as its other needs is to ensure not only man's physical health but also his psychological and spiritual health insofar as these seemingly purely physical needs of man also possess aspects which affect his psyche and spirit. For Muslims, it is by faithfully observing the law that man's physical, psychological, and spiritual needs are harmoniously met.

In a number of his sayings, the Prophet speaks of the rights of the body which every Muslim is required to respect and safeguard. The Prophet was unhappy when he learned that several of his Companions had vowed to fast every day,[12] to pray all night, and to abstain from sexual relations. He reminded them that his own life and practices provide the best examples for Muslims to follow and those who deviate from his ways are not of his community. Thus Islam is against the denial to the body of its basic rights or needs even in the name of the spirit. We have so far spoken of the basic rights or legitimate needs of the body in rather general terms. Let us now refer to them in a more concrete manner.

The teachings of Islam greatly emphasize the question of personal hygiene and cleanliness. This assertion is likely to be viewed with scepticism by many Westerners, especially those who have traveled to different parts of the Islamic world where they see before their own eyes numerous evidences for unhealthy conditions and unsanitary practices. Whatever the reasons or causes are for the present-day conditions of hygiene and state of cleanliness among the Muslim peoples, the fact remains that the *shari'a* contains numerous injunctions concerning hygiene and cleanliness.[13] The teachings of the

---

[12]The best practice in fasting, according to one hadīth, is that of Prophet David who fasted on alternate days.

[13]On the importance of the religious element in hygiene in Islam, see S. H. Nasr, *Islamic Science: An Illustrated Study* (London, 1976), pp. 164-66.

sharīʿa in this domain became incorporated into the general body of Islamic medicine. In its theory and practice, Islamic medicine views these religious injunctions on matters of hygiene and cleanliness as the best means of preventing illnesses. It also sees certain medical merits in many of the rituals and religious practices of Islam. Ritual cleanliness requires Muslims to wash themselves regularly. In order to perform their five daily prayers, they must be in a state of ritual purity. To be in this state, they have to perform an act of ablution in which they are required to wash specific parts of the body as prescribed by the law. Further, Islamic law requires that after every sexual union both husband and wife take a ritual bath or the major ablution[14] without which the minor ablutions, as the former ones are called, are deemed invalid before the law. We may also mention here the traditional Islamic practice of circumcision which is also to be found in Jewish religious tradition and which is not unrelated to the question of hygiene and cleanliness. This practice has come to be widely accepted and recommended by the medical profession of our times.

Another factor of health upon which Islam places great emphasis is diet. The dietary habits of the Muslims, as regulated by the *sharīʿa*, have an important effect upon their overall state of health.[15] On the importance of diet from the point of view of Islamic medicine, Nasr writes:

> It plays a much more important role than does diet in modern medicine. The Muslims considered the kind of food and the manner in which it is consumed to be so directly connected to health that the effect of diet was considered by them as being perhaps more powerful than that even of drugs on both health and illness. It is not accidental that the Andalusian physician Abū Marwān ibn Zuhr in the sixth/twelfth century wrote the first scientific work on diet ever composed, the *Kitāb al-Aghdhiya* (The Book of Diet), and that food plays such an important therapeutic role to this day in the Islamic world.[16]

---

[14]In Arabic, major ablution is called *ghusl*. It necessitates the washing of the whole body. The term for minor ablutions is *wuḍūʾ*.

[15]On the principles of the *sharīʿa* governing the dietary habits of the Muslims, see al-Qaradawi, *The Lawful*, pp. 39-78.

[16]S. H. Nasr, *Science*, p. 166.

From the point of view of the *sharīʿa*, food in general also falls
into the various legal categories previously mentioned. The most important of these, as far as Muslim dietary habits are concerned, is
the prohibited category. Included in this category are alcoholic drinks,
pork, and meats of certain species of birds and animals. There were
no lack of attempts in Islam to provide a kind of philosophical and
scientific justification for these dietary prohibitions, some of which
also exist in various other religions such as Judaism. For example,
the *Ikhwān al-Ṣafā'* (The Brethren of Purity), a group of fourth/tenth
and fifth/eleventh century scholars, maintained that plants and flesh
of animals that man takes as food have an effect upon both his body
and his soul.[17] This is because beautiful and good qualities as well
as evil qualities are inherent in each of the three kingdoms of mineral,
plant, and animal. It is well to remember that for the *Ikhwān* the
three kingdoms come into being as a result of the mixing of the four
elements to various degrees by the Universal Soul. The beautiful and
good qualities are manifestations of the good souls, while the evil
qualities are due to the evil souls. Different sets of qualities are inherent in different plants and in different animals. It is these qualities
which affect both the physical body and the soul of man, either in
a positive or a negative sense, depending upon the particular plants
and animals which he consumes as food. In the context of Islamic
spirituality, some religious scholars have also offered spiritual justifica-
tions for the dietary prohibitions. According to them, one of the factors which influence one's degree of concentration in prayer, and
hence the spiritual efficacy of one's prayer, is the kind of food one eats.

Apart from dietary prohibitions, Islamic religious injunctions like
fasting, eating less than one's full appetite, and eating slowly constitute important elements in Muslim dietary habits. The medical value
of these injunctions to the human body is duly recognized and appre-
ciated. But for Muslims the supreme motive in doing all these acts
is religious and spiritual, namely obedience to the divine will and
the salvation of the soul.

While Muslims are enjoined by their religion to strive and pray
to God for good health, they are also taught to have the correct attitudes and responsibilities toward illness. Both health and sickness
of the body are ordained by God. As for the believer, he derives

---

[17]S. H. Nasr, *An Introduction to Islamic Cosmological Doctrines*, (Boulder, 1978), p. 70.

benefits from both of them. If he is sick, he views that sickness as a trial from God and bears it with patience, resignation and thankfulness. When a believer succeeds in responding to his illness in this particular manner, he is then able to derive spiritual benefits from his physical suffering. Diseases, in the traditional Islamic perspective, therefore possess a spiritual dimension and a spiritual significance. In one sacred *ḥadīth* God speaks through the Prophet: "O my worshipper! Good health forms a link between you and yourself but sickness makes a link between you and me."

Islamic law does not permit inflictions of bodily pain for the attainment of spiritual well-being. But in sickness or physical afflictions which it is his fate to receive, a believer finds an excellent occasion to derive spiritual benefits from them and to strenthen his relation with God. The following collection of prophetic *ḥadīths* as given by Sūyūṭī, a famous Egyptian scholar of the late fifteenth! early sixteenth century, in his work *Medicine of the Prophet*,[18] further demonstrates the positive value and spiritual significance of illnesses or physical afflictions in Islamic teachings:

> Verily a believer should not fear sickness; for if he knew what he derives from sickness, he would desire to be sick even to death.

> The people who meet with severe pain are the prophets of God, the devout and the very best of men. A man is afflicted in proportion to his love of the Faith. Affliction does not cease for the devout as long as they walk this earth and until they are free from sin.

> If God loves a people, he will give them affliction.

> There is no sickness or pain which a believer receives that is not a penance for his sins whether it be a thorn which pricks him or a disaster that overwhelms him.

> No Muslim receives any injury without God shedding from him his sins, as a tree sheds its leaves.

As we have said, these sayings of the Prophet seek to stress the positive value of diseases and physical afflictions and to define the correct spiritual attitudes toward themn if and when they occur. They

---

[18]See C. Elgood's English translation of this work as well as that of Chaghmīnī, known by the same title, in *Osiris*, 14 (1962) 33-192.

do not at all mean that Muslims ought to prefer sickness to health. Abū Dardā, a Companion of the Prophet once asked him: "O Prophet of God, if I am cured of my sickness and am thankful for it, is it better than if I were sick and bore it patiently?" The Prophet replied to Abū Dardā: "Verily, the Prophet of God loves sound health just as you do." There are numerous other *hadīths* which call on the sick to find medical treatment for their sickness, and on the believers in general to visit the sick and to offer them both physical and spiritual comfort.[19] The Prophet, however, has also advised against excessive use of medicine because "sometimes medicines do leave behind diseases."[20] To appreciate the significance of this prophetic advice, it is perhaps pertinent to refer to the fact that the so-called iatrogenic diseases, namely diseases caused by medical treatment, are today ranked third in importance among all the recognized ailments of contemporary man.[21]

Thus, in both his states of health and of sickness, a Muslim is enjoined by his religion to provide a proper treatment of his body. And when he dies, his body deserves all the respects it should get in accordance with the Islamic divine law. Islamic law requires that burial should take place at the earliest possible time and that there should be no unnecessary delays. It is not possible here for us to go into the details of the whole set of rites associated with Muslim burial.[22] What we wish to emphasize, however, is that it is the religious duty of the community to make sure that the dead be given their proper and immediate burials. The Islamic respect for the dead also manifests itself in its attitude toward the dissection of the body. Islamic law does not permit this act although there have been jurists over the ages who question its strict prohibition. Thus, Ibn al-Nafīs, whom we have mentioned earlier, tells us that what prevented him from practicing anatomy was his religion.

---

[19]For the various *hadīths* pertaining to this question see the *Ṣaḥīḥ* of Imām Bukhārī in the two major chapters dealing with sickness and healing, or Elgood's translation mentioned above.

[20]See Ibn Qutayba, *'Uyūn al-akhbar,* 3, p. 273, quoted by A. Ali in his "Contribution of Islam to the Development of Medical Science," *Studies in History of Medicine,* 4 (1980) 49.

[21]J. Needleman, *Consciousness and Tradition* (New York, 1982), p. 99.

[22]For a description of the various processes connected with the preparation of bodies for final burial, see A. A. Tritton, "Muslim Funeral Customs," *Bulletin of the School of Oriental and African Studies,* 9 (1937-39) 653-61.

In speaking of the total health of the individual, and not just his physical health, it is necessary also to say something, however briefly, about the Islamic view of dres since clothes directly pertain not only to the body but also to the soul. Indeed, a man's clothes are among the nearest of all things to his soul, exercising upon it a perpetual and immensely powerful influence, although they belong to the outer aspects of his life. The clothes one wears, apart from reflecting the state of one's inner beauty, are also closely related to one's views of the human body.

What are fundamentally aimed at in the Muslim dress habits, which are again regulated by the *sharī'a*, are decency, spiritual dignity, and beauty.[23] Decency demands that Muslims wear clothes which cover their bodies. In particular, the dress of the Muslim woman should not be transparent or be too tight as delienate and display the parts of her body. The idea of spiritual dignity includes the question of the preservation of masculinity for men and femininity for women so that the dress of men must clearly be distinct from that of women. The spiritual dignity that one normally associates with the robe and turban of the traditional Muslim male dress and with the veil (*ḥijāb*) of the traditional female dress has the effect of reminding man of his spiritual function and responsibilities. Moreover, dress is in conformity with those responsibilities. The spirit of Islamic dress is beautifully summed up by a contemporary scholar:

> His (i.e. a Muslim's) clothes were in keeping with the dignity of man's funciton as representative of God on earth, and at the same time they made it easy for him to perform the ablution, and they in perfect conformity with the movements of the prayer. Moreover they were an ornament to the prayer, unlike modern European clothers which rob the movements of the prayer of all their beauty and impede them, just as they act as a barrier between the body and the ablution.[24]

In Islam, the beauty of the human form is veiled. From the point of view of the law, the main reason for this veiling, apart from those already cited, is to govern human passions so as to create a healthy

---

[23]See al-Qaradawi, *The Lawful*, pp. 79-94.

[24]See Abū Bakr Sirāj al-Dīn, "The Spiritual Function of Civilization," J. Needleman (ed.), *The Sword of Gnosis* (Baltimore, 1974), p. 107.

religious and spiritual climate in which man is constantly reminded of his duties to God. This veiling is the more necessary in the case of the female body. The esoteric teachings of Islam as embodied in the Ṣūfī tradition would explain this by saying that the female body symbolizes certain esoteric truths concerning the divinity and, in Islam, the inner mysteries are likewise veiled.[25] Therefore, there is also a metaphysical significance in the traditional Islamic dress. In Islam the beauty of the human form becomes interiorized and spiritualized and not exteriorized and profanized. Because of the presence of these inner teachings in Islam which see in the human body a message of the highest spiritual truths, coupled with the strict injunctions of the *sharī'a* concerning the display of the human form, including in art, the Islamic appreciation of the beauty of the human form did not lead to its profane glorification or the cult of the "body beautiful" as a purely physical and sexual object.

While the beauty of the human form is to be veiled, the dress that veils it should present itself as something beautiful. Once the Prophet said: "Anyone who has an atom of pride in his heart will not enter the Garden." A man then asked him, "What about the one who likes to wear a handsome robe and good shoes?" The Prophet replied: "Surely Allah is beautiful and loves beauty."[26] More important than the beauty of clothes, however, is the beauty of one's outward behavior and bodily movements since it is the latter which constitutes the real essence of one's overall external beauty. This brings us to the question of the duties of the human body and its various parts.

Beauty of man's general appearance and outward behavior results when movements of the different parts of his body become balanced and harmonized. According to al-Ghazālī, there is an appropriate

---

[25]"Woman even in a certain manner incarnates esotericism by reason of certain aspects of her nature and function; "esoteric truth," the *ḥaqīqa*, is "felt" as a "feminine" reality, and the same is true of *baraka*. Moreover the veil and the seclusion of woman are connected with the final cyclic phase in which we live—and they present a certain analogy with the forbidding of wine and the veiling of the mysteries." See F. Schuon, *Understanding Islam* (London, 1972), p. 37.

[26]In another version of this *ḥadīth*, a handsome man came to the Prophet saying: "I love beauty and have been given some of it, as you can see, to the extent that I dislike anyone's having a better pair of sandals than I. Is this pride, O Messenger of Allah?" The Prophet replied: "No. Pride is to reject the truth and to view other people with contempt."

pattern of movement for each bodily member based on a general law of balance and harmony willed by God.[27] If man is to achieve a balanced and harmonized relationship between his physical body and his spiritual soul or spiritual heart, which is the center or "nucleus" of his whole being, then his bodily movements must conform to that appropriate pattern. For Muslims, it is in the bodily movements of the Prophet himself that the perfect pattern is to be found. Thus, al-Ghazālī maintains that Muslims, as far as possible, should follow the example of the Prophet even in his bodily movements which, in fact, have been recorded in a detailed manner and preserved to this day as an integral part of the *Sunnah* or prophetic tradition. Millions of Muslims throughout the ages have sought to emulate his manner of walking, eating, sleeping, putting on his sandals, and so on.

Balanced and harmonized movements of the body are realized by one's acting in harmony with the divine law itself. One must abstain from doing those acts which are forbidden and discouraged by the law since each sinful act, says the Prophet, produces a veil of rust over the heart. At the same time, one must perform acts that are made obligatory and recommended by the law. This is what we mean by the duties of the human body. In his magnum opus *The Revivification of the Religious Sciences (Iḥyā' 'Ulūm al-Dīn)*, a book dealing with the mysteries of fasting, al-Ghazālī speaks of the necessary conditions for a fasting that is perfect and acceptable to God. Not only must one who is fasting abstain from food and sexual pleasures but he must also restrain all of his bodily members, especially the eyes, tongue, ears, hands and feet, from acts that are sinful before the law. The effect of this abstinence is profound, not only on the soul but even on the whole pattern of one's bodily movements. The basic idea of fasting is so that this abstinence becomes a lasting habit and so that this habitual abstinence results from a conscious awareness of its harmony with the divine will as embodied in the law. Moreover, says al-Ghazālī, by way of this abstinence we remove obstacles, in the form of unchecked carnal desires, to the remembrance of God that is directed toward the heart. Indeed, according to the Qur'ān, fasting has been prescribed so that men might attain a state of God-consciousness.[28]

Abstinence goes hand in hand with the performance of affirmative

---

[27]Gai Eaton, "Perfecting the Mirror," *Parabola*, 10.3 (August, 1985) 45.
[28]Al-Qur'ān (2.183).

or positive acts, the most important of which, from the point of view of the *sharī'a* is the five daily prayers. It has been said in Islam that in the ritual prayer the spiritual, intellectual, psychological and physical elements of man are all in perfect harmony and equilibrium. At the physical level itself, the whole pattern of bodily movements acted out in prayer is said to be in perfect balance and harmony and to signify the various possible relationships between Creator and creation. As one scholar has summarized it:

> In the ritual prayer itself the spiritual and intellectual element is represented by the recitation from the Qur'ān and the emotional element by the feelings of fear and of hope with which he is commanded to call upon God, but what might be called the existential element is acted out in physical movements which utilize the body as a vehicle for the spirit. In the first part of each unit of prayer the worshipper stands upright while he recites certain passages from the Qur'ān, and this uprightness, this verticality, is an image of the "straight" (or "vertical") path upon which he asks God to lead him. The body has itself become a symbol of the ray which connects heaven and earth, the divine and the human.

But the Muslim prays not only on his own behalf and on behalf of his fellow men and women but also in the name of creation as a whole; this is an aspect of his function as the "vicegerent of God on earth." The standing is followed by a bowing in which the worshipper is instructed to keep the upper part of his body, from head to hips, parallel with the ground, and it is sometimes said that all the creatures which move upon four legs, their bodies horizontal, are represented by this posture. This bowing is followed by the prostration in which the worshipper places his forehead on the ground, his body folded up as though in the fetal position, and although this is primarily an acknowledgement of the power and glory of the Transcendent it is also, according to certain sages, a representation of the inanimate realm, the mineral order in particular. While bowing he had glorified God as the infinite, the all-embracing on the horizontal level. Now—in the prostration— he is, as it were, reduced to the dimensions of his own innermost "nucleus." In this way the worshipper's physical body has acted out the variety of relationships between Creator and creation.[29]

---

[29]Eaton, "Perfecting the Mirror," pp. 47-48.

In Sufism, moreover, there is the "prayer of the heart," the *dhikr* or invocation of the divine name, which is the most universal form of prayer. The Ṣūfī technique of *dhikr* is of various forms. This is, however, not the place to go into its detailed discussion. Here, we only wish to mention its connection with the body's natural activity of breathing and with the rhythm of the beating of the heart, in order to emphasize further the role of the body in the spiritual life of Islam. The Prophet is reported to have said: "He who does not vibrate at remembrance of The Friend has no friend."[30] In *dhikr* there is the making use of rhythmical breathing and movements of the body. Such rhythm is the basic characteristic of the Ṣūfī sacred dance which has its basis, among others, in the above *ḥadīth*. Whether the *dhikr* is done silently or in the form of a chant, its aim is to enable man to remember God by invoking his name at all times so that it becomes ultimately integrated into the very rhythm of the beating of the heart.[31]

It is clear from our whole discussion of the human body so far that Islam attaches great importance to the health of the body, not viewed independently of the rest of the constituents of man, but as an integral element of that state of total health in which the spiritual, intellectual, emotional, and physical elements of man are all in perfect harmony and equilibrium.

The Human Body as Microcosm

We have earlier asserted that the idea of man as the microcosm constitutes a fundamental principle of many of the Islamic sciences. The meaning of this idea is that the whole universe is essentially contained in man. In other words, man is a universe in miniature. Here, we will limit our consideration of this idea to its important consequence on the spirit with which Muslim scholars throughout the ages have approached and carried out the study of the human body. There is no doubt that Muslim scholars have viewed its study as a very important one. The body is studied not only for biomedical benefits but also for man's intellectual and spiritual benefits. The significance of the anatomy and physiology of the human body, for them, is not limited to the biomedical sciences but extends to the spiritual domain as well. The spirit of its study is described by al-Ghazālī in these terms:

The science of the structure of the body is called anatomy: it is a great science, but most men are heedless of it. If any study it, it is only for the purpose of acquiring skill in medicine, and not for the sake of becoming acquainted with the perfection of the power of God. The knowledge of anatomy is the means by which we become acquainted with the animal life; by means of knowledge of animal life, we may acquire a knowledge of the heart and the knowledge of the heart is a key to the knowledge of God.[32]

Since man, being a microcosm, recapitulates within himself the whole of existence, there exists a correspondence between man and the universe. Islamic medicine adopts this correspondence as one of its fundamental principles. The human body, like those of the other animals, is comprised of the four humors (i.e. blood, phlegm, yellow bile, and black bile) mixed according to certain principles[33] just as the world of nature is formed from the mixture of the four elements (fire, air, water, and earth). The humors themselves are composed of the elements and the four natures (heat, moisture, cold, and dryness). To be more precise, each humor is related to two elements and two natures so that it possesses qualities at once similar to and different from the other humors. It is this humoral constitution of the human body which provides the basis for the definitions of health and illness in Islamic medicine. What is called health refers to the state of balance and harmony of the humors while the disruption of this state of equilibrium is what is called illness. The task of the physician is to restore the balance of the humors.

The correspondence between the microcosm and the universe has important consequences upon diagnosis and treatment of illnesses in the Islamic medical system. The balance of the humoral constitution may be disrupted by both internal and external causes. Muslim physicians pay much attention to the external factors also because, in consequence of the above correspondence, there exists a constant action and reaction between the total external environment of man and the humors.[34] If Muslim physicians see much medical wisdom in the various injunctions of the *sharī'a* that we have previously

---

[33]For a more detailed discussion of the humoral constitution of the human body, see S. H. Nasr, *Islamic Science*, pp. 159-62; also his *Science and Civilization in Islam*, pp. 219-25.

[34]According to Muslim physicians, there are six fundamental external factors of health of the individual: breathing, eating, bodily rest and movement, sleep, emotional rest, and excretion and retention (including the effects of sexual intercourse).

discussed, it is because they see them as the means which enable man to live in harmony within himself and with his external environment.

It is significant that in our own times a number of individual physicians in the Indian subcontinent have sought to verify the truth of the above correspondence by making use of modern scientific discoveries. They argued, for example, that if the human body is really a microcosm then it should possess all the elements that are present in the macrocosm. According to the latest study conducted by one of these scholars, eighty-one elements, out of a total of ninety-two that are known to occur naturally, are found to be present in the human body.[35]

As we have said, in Islam the human body is not only studied from biomedical and scientific points of view. The body is far from being only of interest to the physicians since its meanings are not exhausted by man's physical and biomedical understanding of it no matter how far that understanding may reach. Even when the body is studied by Muslim physicians from the biomedical point of view, it is never viewed as a kind of machine which is functioning autonomously. Rather, they see the body of man as an extension of his soul and as being related to both the spirit and the soul. That is why many of them were masters of psychosomatic medicine and psychology. For example, al-Rāzī, the Latin Rhazes, wrote a work entitled *Spiritual Physick*[36] in which he discussed the various moral and psychological illnesses which ruin the mind and the body and ways in which these ailments might be overcome.

If the human body is also of great interest to the philosophers, theologians, and Ṣūfīs, that is because it is a great treasure of wisdom and of symbols which point to other levels of reality. Those biomedical facts about the body which are of great utility to the physicians, especially anatomy and physiology, also include numerous symbolisms which demonstrate to us that the wisdom of the Creator pervades the whole creation. The Qur'ān speaks of the human body as one of the "signs of God." In other words, knowledge of the body necessarily leads man to the knowledge of God. We have already quoted al-Ghazālī's assertion of this view. According to the Ikhwān

---

[35]See S. B. Vohora, "Is the Human Body a Microcosm?: A Critical Study," *Studies in History of Medicine*, 5.1 (March, 1981).

[36]See Rhazes, *The Spiritual Physick of Rhazes*, trans. A. J. Arberry (London, 1950).

al-Ṣafā', man cannot know within his own lifetime the whole universe by going around and studying it, but God, in his Wisdom, has placed everything in the universe in man himself. Thus, by studying himself man can come to the knowledge of all things.[37] The Ikhwān maintained that the study of the anatomy and physiology of the human body is a key to the knowledge of the power and wisdom of the Creator. By making use of numerical symbolism they established a correspondence between the anatomy of the human body and that of the heavens. But they also saw a striking analogy between the body and the terrestrial world. In those physical features of man which distinguish him from the other animals, the Ikhwān see a spiritual significance. For example, man's vertical position is described as symbolizing an ontological and metaphysical ascent and the yearning of man to reach toward the spiritual world.

Al-Fārābī, generally regarded as the founder of political philosophy in Islam, made use of the symbolism of human anatomy to explain his theory of human society. There is an analogy between the interrelation of the bodily organs and that of the components of the traditional human society. In this context, Muslim scholars generally refer to the body as the kingdom of the heart and speak of it as being analogous to a great city. Famous Ṣufis like Ibn 'Arabī, al-Jīlī, and Nasafī have dealt with the idea of the body as the "temple" of the spirit. And Rūmī, the great mystical poet of Islam, making such references to the human body as the "whale of Jonah" and as the "shadow of the shadow of the shadow of the heart," and while maintaining that both body and spirit are necessary and good, sees in the contrasting nature and qualities of the body effective examples of illustrating the true nature of the spirit.[38]

We wish to conclude our discussion of the human body in the Islamic perspective with a few remarks about the symbolism of the male and female bodies. When earlier touching on the question of the traditional female dress, we have made the remark that the female body symbolizes certain aspects of the divine reality. Now, the profoundest spiritual message of the human body is a consequence of the fact that the human being is a theomorphic being who reflects God's names and qualities. Insofar as the male and female are both

---

[37]S. H. Nasr, *An Introduction to Islamic Cosmological Doctrines*, p. 98.
[38]See W. C. Chittick, *The Sufi Path of Love: The Spiritual Teachings of Rumi*, (Albany, 1983), pp. 28-31.

human, they symbolize the same truths concerning the divine.[39] But insofar as there is a polarization of the human form into the male and the female, they symbolize different aspects of the divinity. The female is said to symbolize the uncreated aspect of God and indeed it is of much significance that the Arabid word for divine essence (*dhāt*) is in the feminine form. The male, on the other hand, is said to symbolize God as Lord and Creator. According to Ibn 'Arabī, the contemplation of God in woman constitutes the highest form of contemplation possible. In Islamic spirituality, sexuality is mainly seen in its positive aspect although its negative aspect is certainly not ignored as made very clear by the strict injunctions of the *sharī'a* concerning the relationship between the sexes. Sexual union, which is a sacred act when kept within the bounds of the *sharī'a*, becomes for the contemplative a symbol of that beatific union originally possessed by the androgynic ancestor of humanity in the paradisal state. These few remarks are intended to highlight the fact that there were great representatives of Islamic spirituality who attach the profoundest spiritual significance to the sexual aspects of the human body.

Not all the views concerning the human body found in Islam have been mentioned. Those we have mentioned are only treated in a rather scanty manner. It is, however, hoped that the above discussion will contribute to a better appreciation of the Islamic views of man in general and of the human body in particular. This will in turn lead to a better appreciation of the nature and characteristics of the Islamic response to contemporary bioethics insofar as that response is going to be, and has been, determined by Islam's views of man and of the human body.

---

[39] On the spiritual message of the male and female bodies in Islam, see S. H. Nasr, "The Male and Female in the Islamic Perspective," *Studies in Comparative Religion*, pp. 67-75. For a treatment of this subject from the points of view of the various religious traditions, including that of Islam, see F. Schuon, *From the Divine to the Human* (Bloomington, 1982), the chapter entitled "The Message of the Human Body."

Orthodox Christianity and Bioethics

STANLEY S. HARAKAS

THE TOPIC OF Orthodox Christianity and bioethics is quite broad and could only be handled in a most cursory and general manner in the time allotted for this presentation. On the other hand, it is clear that immediate immersion in a particular bioethical problem from an Eastern Orthodox perspective would not permit this particular audience to deal coherently with the general approach of Eastern Christianity to ethical questions broadly conceived, and bioethical issues in particular. I have therefore decided to try to bridge the gap between these two approaches by beginning with a quite cursory introduction to the approach of Eastern Orthodoxy to ethics. In the second part of this presentation I will attempt to sketch out the application of the principles and approaches of Orthodox ethics to one issue, the body. The third part will seek to sketch — again, briefly yet concretely—"approaches to the body in the contemporary bioethical discussion."

Ethics in Eastern Orthodox Christian Teaching

Quite briefly, what needs to be affirmed under this rubric is the conviction and practical approach within Eastern Orthodoxy that ethics is a derivative discipline which studies the practical living of the Orthodox Christian faith. The source of both the ethical life and disciplined reflection upon it in Eastern Orthodox Christianity is the faith, i.e. the fundamental belief system which is understood to be primarily doctrinal in nature. The corrolaries to this approach are fairly obvious. It means that in a larger and inclusive sense the ethical

life and the reflection on it reject the concept of an adequate autonomous ethic, without moorings in a belief system. Specifically, this
means that Orthodox draw their ethical norms and "do ethics" out
of the doctrinal, spiritual, and ecclesial teachings of the Church, and
not vice versa.

While it is true that this dependency of the ethical life and
disciplined reflection on it (i.e. the theological discipline of Eastern
Orthodox ethics) emerge from the faith commitment and teaching
of Eastern Orthodoxy, and that in one sense or another, all parts of
the revelatory experience are seen as sources for "doing ethics," some
aspects are more important than others. Practically speaking, ethics
draws its teaching from Scripture, patristic writings, the liturgical
treasure of the Church, some elements of ecclesiastical and cultural
history, and canon law as expressions of the Church's normative mind
set. Doctrinally, the fundamental Christian understanding of God's
economy of salvation is the background for the ethical life and ethical
reflection.

Central, then, to ethics and the moral life are the teachings of
the Orthodox Church regarding: the one triune God as creator, as
a community of persons, and as love; the creation of humanity in
the image and likeness of God; the human condition as fallen and
in need of redemption; the incarnation of the second person of the
Holy Trinity in human nature for the salvation of humanity in the
person of Jesus Christ; his teaching, direction, and guidance; his ontological victory over the enemies of humankind, death, sin, and evil
through his crucifixion and resurrection; the pentecostal presence of
the Holy Spirit in the Church; the sacramental approach to life as a
whole; the transfiguring and transforming direction of growth toward
God-likeness (theosis) as the goal of human life; the synergy of human
self-determination and divine grace in the process of growth; and the
eschatological perspective that places all of human life within a concurrently this-worldly Kingdom of God understood as being always
in the process of becoming in this existence.[1] On the basis of these
theological presuppositions Orthodox Christian ethics approaches the
traditional themes of ethics such as the good, evil, sin, human moral
capacities, freedom, conscience, moral law, the evangelical ethic,

---

[1]For a more full treatment of the doctrinal foundations of Orthodox
ethics, see Stanley S. Harakas, *Toward Transfigured Life: The Theoria of
Eastern Orthodox Ethics* (Minneapolis, 1983), ch. 2.

character, virtue, vice, duties, rights, moral formation, ethical decision-making, and the personal and social praxis of the ethical life. Even the most particular moral directives will be rooted in the faith foundations which stand at the heart of the Eastern Orthodox ethic.

Therefore, one should not be surprised that the Orthodox approach to any ethical topic will be built upon the inherited doctrinal and ecclesial tradition and can only be considered compelling when it is in harmony with it and is preceived as a natural outgrowth and application of it. Such is the case as one approaches the question of the ethical evaluation of the body, and the endeavor to address the ethical issues now so prominently attached to it.

The Body in Eastern Orthodox Theology and Ethics
The place of the body in Eastern Orthodox Christian teaching is determined in large part by the Christian doctrine of creation. Its moral evaluation, not unexpectedly, comes out of the theological perception of its source and its place in the whole economy of salvation. The doctrinal and ecclesial sources of the doctrine of the body are many and varied, however the chief of these are the evaluation of creation, the creation of humanity in the image and likeness of God, the incarnation, the strong sacramental approach of Eastern Christianity, and the doctrine of the resurrection.

The Old Testament Genesis account, as understood within the Eastern Orthodox tradition, distinguishes sharply between the Creator who is God and the world which he has brought out of nothing and into existence through his creative divine energies.[2] Since, however, God is goodness itself, the product of his work of creation is good. Thus, the hebraic affirmation of the goodness of creation stands immediately in contrast to some strands of thought in the Greek environment into which Christianity was thrust in its early and formative years. These strands of thought saw the created world as evil.

Dualistic philosophical systems which preceived the material world as evil, in contrast to the spiritual world which was seen as good, very quickly were perceived by Christians as contradictory to basic Old and New Testament revelatory truths. While one side of the ancient Greco-Roman culture honored the body as a thing of goodness and beauty to be represented in art as an object of admiration, much of the philosophical tradition identified it with evil. Thus, Plato identified

---

[2]Gen 1 and 2.

it in the *Gorgias* as "our tomb,"[3] affirming rather in his work *Alkibiades* that the "soul *is* the human being."[4] The Stoic philosopher-king, Marcus Aurelius, thus informed the reader of his *Meditationes* that "You are a poor soul, which carries about a dead body."[5] The understanding of the Old Testament of the creation of humanity in the image and the likeness of God clearly focused on the spiritual aspect of human nature, but refused to allow this approach to split the psychosomatic unity of human nature. For Christians, this was made theologically necessary not only because of the Old Testament assumption of this unity, but also because of the central affirmation of the doctrine of the incarnation of the second person of the Holy Trinity, the Son, into a fully human nature consisting of both body and spirit or soul. God was "enanthropized," to use the Greek term in anglicized form: he took on the full nature of humanity, both body and soul. Thus could only mean that the human body was in itself good, for God could not himself assume that which was fundamentally evil. Saint Ephraim the Syrian in his writing on the transfiguration of Jesus Christ, dramatically affirms the physical side of the "enanthropized" Lord with a series of biblically based rhetorical questions, culminating in a restatement of the doctrinal affirmations of the Church's ecumenical teaching on the incarnation. Here are four of Saint Ephraim's thirty three affirmations of the divinity and the humanity of Christ:

> . . . if he were not flesh, for what reason did Mary bring him forth? And if he were not God, who then did Gabriel call Lord?

> If he were not flesh, who then lay in the manger? If he were not God, to whom did the angels coming on earth give glory?

> If he were not man, who fasted and hungered in the desert? And if he were not God, to whom did the descending angels minister?

> If he were not flesh, who wore the garments of a man? And if he were not God, who then was it that wrought signs and wonders?

Ephraim then restates the Orthodox Christology:

---

[3]3g, 3a.
[4]1, 130.
[5]4.41.

He is Christ the Son of God: the only-begotten of the Father, the only-begotten of his mother. And I confess that the same is perfect God and perfect man, who in his two natures is acknowledged to be indivisibly, unchangeably, and without confusion, united in the one *hypostasis* or person; clothed in living flesh, and having a soul that is endowed with reason and understanding, subject in all things to the same afflictions as ourselves, sin alone excepted.[6]

I have dwelt on this incarnational dimension, because it is the primary source of the subsequent vast liturgical development which in practically every phase is a sacramental reality which brings the whole of human life, including its most physical aspects, into the kingdom of God and reciprocally brings the divine presence to the created reality. Thus, in the sacramental system of the Orthodox faith, all kinds of material things are both vehicles of divine grace and objects of blessing and sanctification. Water, oil, bread, wine, metal, wood, incense, and paint are perceived as carriers of grace, and the humblest of concerns dealing with human life become objects of blessings.

The sacramental approach includes the human body as well. In its prayers the Church repeatedly includes petitions "for the health of body and soul." Moreover, from New Testament times the Christian Church has an ongoing concern for the healing of body and soul through the sacrament of holy Unction.[7] This emphasis on "soul and body" is important for underscoring the incarnational emphasis on the distinction, but not the division, between the physical and the spiritual, the somatic and the spiritual dimensions of the single reality of the created world in general and human life in particular. The phychosomatic unity of human life is a permanent prolegomenon to the discussion of the human body in Orthodox thought and practice.

Perhaps the culmination of all of this doctrinal focus is to be seen in the heavy emphasis of the Orthodox Church on the twin beliefs of the bodily resurrection of Jesus Christ and the eschatologically anticipated resurrection of all persons at the second coming of Christ and the general judgment. This teaching is succinctly articulated in

---

[6]Vossio, *Sanctio Ephraem Syri Opera Omnia* (Cologne, 1616), p. 686; Jn 17.19.

[7]Jas 5.14-15.

the articles of the Nicene-Constantinopolitan Creed: "... and he shall come again with glory to judge the quick and the dead. ... I look for the resurrection of the dead, and the life of the world to come."[8] Such a view sees the body, then, in an ultimate sense, as an inseparable and permanent part of what it means to be a human being, and it rejects, again, in an ultimate sense a dualism of body and spirit.

Thus, in the patristic tradition the body finds its due appreciation, honor, and place. That there are some tendencies within the ethos of Eastern Orthodoxy in the opposite direction, that is, toward a dualism denigrating the body, especially in some streams of monastic thought, cannot be denied. Yet this excessive "spiritualization" of human life is repeatedly countered by an affirmation of the importance of the bodily dimension in the patristic tradition. Thus, an early voice in the life of the Church put this truth in a salvation perspective. The early Tertullian cautioned: "I would call your attention to this in order that you may know that all God's purpose and promises to man are for the benefit not of the soul alone, but of the soul and the flesh ... "[9] In his fourth century *Lenten Lectures,* Saint Cyril of Jerusalem in a section entitled "On the Ten Doctrines" says:

> Let no one tell you that this body of ours is a stranger to God ... What is it that they complain of in this wonderful body? For what does it lack in comeliness? What is there in its structure that is not wrought skillfully?

And with this he begins a litany of rhetorical questions culminating in an appreciation of the sexual, procreative function of the body: "Who, when the human race was likely to fail, made it perpetual by a simple conjunction, "thus indicating that sex, as well, is a gift of God?"[10]

Examples of this same struggle to maintain the importance and dignity of the body in Christian thinking are to be found in the canon law of the Church. The treatment of marriage is a case in point. Not only are married men ordained to the priesthood, but if the motive on the one hand for avoiding marriage by candidates for the clergy

---

[8] Some New Testament passages affirming the ressurection of the body are: Mt 22.23ff., Jn 5.25-29; Acts 26.8; 1 Cor 6.14, 15.35-44; 2 Cor 4.14.

[9] *The Resurrection of the Body* 5, 6.

[10] *Catechesis* 4.22.

as seen in the thirteenth canon of the Sixth Ecumenical Synod, or on the other the breaking up of an already existing marriage of a clergyman, is "scornfulness of marriage," as it is described in the fifth Apostolic Canon—which, of course, is a dualistic position—it is condemned. This is true as well of laypersons as seen in the fourteenth canon of the Synod of Gangra.

The Church's treatment of the body, in addition to this basic respect, is seen also in two other dimensions. First, there is a small corpus of writings in which theological writers examine the body in what today we would call an "objective, scientific" manner. In another place, I have presented these writings in some detail.[11] One can mention in this connection the strong appreciation of Clement of Alexandria for the human body and his concrete and specific treatment of its parts in his writing, the *Stromata*. The work of the fourth-century bishop of Emesa, Nemesios, entitled *On the Nature of Man* is another example of this approach to the body. In chapter four, Nemesios deals with the physiological body and in chapter five with the materials from which it is formed. In subsequent chapters he treats of perception, sight, feeling, taste, hearing, and smell. His primary sources, it appears, are the medical writings of the physician Galen, yet he places these "scientific" observations within a Christian world view.[12] More familiar, though not widely studied, are the physiological portions of Saint John of Damascus' *Fount of Knowledge*, found even within the portion dealing with the Orthodox faith, known as "An Exact Exposition of the Orthodox Faith."

Similar to Nemesios' treatment but much more detailed and objective, is the work of Meletios the Monk titled "Concerning the Construction of Man," which is a ninth- or tenth-century study by a physician-monk with obvious first-hand knowledge of human physiology but who also concurrently reflects the tradition of Aristotle, Galen, and Nemesios.[13] In all these cases, however, the authors integrate their physiological descriptions into a larger view which sees the human being—body and spirit—as a microcosm of the universe with

---

[11]"Christian Faith Concerning Creation and Biology," *La Théologie dans l'Église et dans le Monde. Études Théologiques 4* (Chambesy, 1984), pp. 226-47.

[12]William Telfer, trans. *Cyril of Jerusalem and Nemesius of Emesa*, vol. 4 of *The Library of Christian Classics* (Philadelphia, 1955).

[13]PG 64.1075-1310.

a special calling to relate the body to nature, self, others, and God. Meletios ends his study with a beautiful paen to the dignity of the human being who is described as "sharing in the temporal and the eternal" and for whom the study of human anatomy is undertaken ". . . so that you might reverence the Lord's provident care for you, and that you may stand in awe of the work."[14]

Even from the perspective of Orthodox theology, the spiritual and physical unity of human life was a recurrent theme. Typical is Gregory of Nyssa's fourth-century work entitled *On the Making of Man*, which on the one hand distinguished the bodily, spiritual, and rational dimensions of human nature, but kept them closely together in a single unity, even though in his perspective, he tended to emphasize the rational nature of human life.

As important as this reverent attitude is, the ethical evaluation of the body and the care due to it is equally necessary to note. The sins associated with the body are clearly condemned by scripture and tradition, but the distinction is consistently made in tradition between the sins of the body and the body itself. The body, as a creature of God, is good, as we have already noted. It is a Pauline teaching that the body is properly characterized as the "temple of the Holy Spirit," a remarkable phrase which is uttered in the context of a discussion on the impropriety of sexual misconduct by Christians.[15] Thus, the ethical teaching on the body can be distinguished, classically, into two general categories. The first deals with the distinction between the goodness of the body and inappropriate submission of it to sinful purposes. The second deals with the obligation and concern which the Christian has for the physical well-being of the body, that is, health and sickness. We will briefly examine the first of these to close this section, and begin the following section with the second.

The distinction between the body as the good creation of God and the body as a vehicle for a host of sins is not always clearly delineated, however, in Scripture. Often the impression of a confusion between the two takes place for the casual reader. Generally speaking, the New Testament Greek word "soma," usually, though not always translated "body" in English translations, refers in a more or less neutral way to the physical body, implying its moral goodness. Not so the word "sarx." This word is used in a number of different

---

[14]Ibid. 1277D
[15]1 Cor 6.15-19.

ways in the New Testament. One use is to designate human or bodily existence in general. Translated usually as "flesh," it can refer, for example to the incarnation of Christ, e.g. "σὰρξ ἐγένετο" (Jn 1.14). Or, it may be used to refer to human life in general. Thus, in Luke's phrase, the Holy Spirit is poured out "on all flesh," "ἐκχέω ἀπὸ τοῦ πνεύματός μου ἐπὶ πᾶσαν σάρκα." (Acts 2.17). Sometimes it can also mean "body" as opposed to "spirit" or "soul." Thus, Saint Paul writes in second Corinthians: "let us cleanse ourselves from every defilement of body (σαρκός) and soul (πνεύματος)" (7.1). But very frequently, "sarx" means sin, or the sinful use of the body, or the mind-set which is opposed to the spiritual things of life. Thus in Ephesians Saint Paul says: "We all once lived in the passions of the flesh (σάρκα), following the desires of body and mind, so we were by nature children of wrath . . . " (2.3). Submitting one's self to the "desires of the flesh" creates a certain kind of mentality, a "fleshly mentality," which leads one away from God. This teaching is clearly articulated in the eighth chapter of Romans. Persons who are "fleshly," are not able to please God. Thus, the perspective of Saint Paul: "those who live according to the flesh set their minds on the things of the flesh, but those who live according to the spirit set their minds on the things of the spirit. To set the mind on the flesh is death, but to set the mind on the spirit is life and peace. For the mind that is set on the flesh is hostile to God; it does not submit to God's law, indeed, it cannot; and those who are in the flesh cannot please God" (Rom 8.5-8). It obviously, however, became easy to confuse the body itself with the "desires of the flesh." The hidden, yet always incipient moral dualism of the Greek tradition was frequently to appear in the spiritual literature of the Church and particularly the monastic tradition.

The patristic tradition, however, consistently found a place in the whole Christian lifestyle for the body, sometimes very sensitive to the body's susceptibility to sin, while at others, to its sacramental potential. A case for the more pessimistic view is Clement of Alexandria, whose perception of the body patrologist Margaret Miles has aptly and succinctly described as "either temple or tomb."[16] On the side emphasizing the supreme sacramental and even mystical potentialities of the body is Gregory Palamas and the spiritual tradition

---

[16]Margaret R. Miles, *Fullness of Life: Historical Foundations for a New Asceticism* (Philadelphia, 1981), p. 43.

of Hesychasm. The latter, in spite of its empasis on the Jesus Prayer and the imageless vision of God, always related its spiritual practices to the body. It was Saint Gregory Palamas' teaching that the incarnation of Christ is a pattern for the spiritual life of human beings. Palamas taught: "In the same way as the divinity of the Word Incarnate is common to soul and body . . . so in spiritual men, is the grace of the Spirit transmitted to the body."[17] The middle of the road position, which is the most widely accepted in the patristic tradition can be represented by Saint Cyril of Jerusalem, who in the treatment of the body mentioned above, says:

> Tell me not that the body is the cause of sin; . . . The body is the soul's instrument, its cloak and garment. If then it is given up to fornification by the soul, it becomes unclean; but if it dwells with a holy soul, it becomes a temple of the Holy Spirit . . . Defile not, then, your flesh in fornification; stain not your fairest garment. But if you have stained it, now cleanse it by repentance; for it is the time for purification.[18]

These commands then lead us to the third part of this presentation, to a brief assessment of the body as regards its place in the area of bioethics.

Approaches to the Body in the Contemporary Bioethical Discussion
This respect for the body in mainline patristic teaching led effortlessly to the ethical sense which proclaimed a moral responsibility for the care of the body, the concern for its health, and the responsibility to seek the cure of disease. Thus, representatively, Saint Basil could write the following:

> Acquire an exact understanding of yourself, that you may know how to make a suitable allotment to each of the two sides of your nature; food and clothing to the body; and to the soul, the doctrines of piety, training in refined behavior, the practice of virtue, and the correction of vice.[19]

---

[17]Quoted in John Meyendorff, *A Study of Gregory Palamas* (Crestwood, 1964), p. 143.

[18]Lenten Lectures, pp. 130-31.

[19]"Give Heed to Thyself," *St. Basil: Ascetical Works.* trans. M. Monica Wagner (Washington, D.C., 1950), p. 435.

This consistent ethico-spiritual tradition of Eastern Christianity is abundantly witnessed to in the teachings of the great figures of spiritual discernment. An example is the nineteenth century Russian mystic and spiritual father, "Staretz" Saint Seraphim of Sarov. Some of his sayings on this issue which reflect the ongoing tradition are the following:

> The body should be the soul's friend and help in the work of perfection . . .

> We must take the greatest care of the soul, as for the body, we must look after it proportionately as it serves the soul well. If we exhaust our bodies to the point of also exhausting our spirits, we are like madmen . . .

> Since man possesses both body and soul, his life is of necessity both corporeal and spiritual, action and contemplation.[20]

The proceedings of the 1984 conference on "Byzantine Medicine" will be published in the forthcoming volume of the *Dumbarton Oaks Papers*. This remarkable collection of papers provides a mass of historical detail, building upon Demetrios Constantelos' research[21] on the importance of the practice of healing in the Orthodox Christian tradition. Insurmountable evidence is presented to show that by and large, though with some exceptions, spiritual healing and rational medicinal healing were understood to be complementary to each other and not contradictory or opposed to each other in Byzantium. Frequently, the healing shrine and the hospital were within close proximity to each other. Strong evidence indicates that each referred patients to the other.

Significant also is the fact that until the eleventh century the hospitals were almost exclusively built, supported, and administered by the Church. Physicians were the employees of the Church in their hospital work. Concurrently, the Church's sacrament of unction, which promised to the sick healing of body and

---

[20]Quoted in Valentine Zander, *St. Seraphim of Sarov*, trans. Sr. Gabriel Anne (Crestwood, 1975), pp. 8, 104, 106.

[21]*Byzantine Philanthropy and Social Welfare* (New Brunswick, 1968).

soul, consisted during these eleven centuries of variations of two prayers whose source was in the fourth-century compilation of earlier liturgical materials, known as the *Sacramentary of Serapion*. The one prayer was for the consecration of the healing oil, and the other was used at its administration. In the eleventh century, physicians wrested control of the hospitals away from the Church. It seems significant that concurrently, in the eleventh century, the rubrics for the sacrament of unction were radically enriched to its present form with seven epistle readings, seven Gospel readings, seven prayers, and seven sets of petitions. Clearly, the Church did not want to abandon its healing ministry, which included concern for both the health of the body and the soul, when it lost control of the hospitals. I have described in detail these observations in a chapter in a forthcoming volume on *Health and Medicine in the Religious Traditions*.

The integrative approach to the body which has been described above provides the basis for my next set of comments. In a book of bioethics widely used in seminary classrooms, *Human Medicine*, by James B. Nelson, another approach to the body is adopted.[22] The volume's main strength is the excellent presentation of the rationales used by conflicting schools of thought on the issues of concern for human health, abortion, artificial insemination, human experimentation, genetics, dying, organ transplants, and the distribution of medical care resources. As much as I appreciate Nelson's clear, balanced and fair presentation of the alternative approaches to these issues, I find myself disagreeing with him on nearly every conclusion to which he comes on these topics. In the inside front cover of this volume I have written my judgment on the reason for this persistent difference between us: "Nelson's basic error in ethical reasoning: the spiritual-psychological- soul-personhood dimension in practice *supplants* the biological-physical. Theologically this book tends toward a gnostic or dualist rejection of the bodily claim."

The February, 1985 issue of *The Hastings Center Report*, a major bioethics journal, was largely dedicated to issues in bioethics relating to the body, including the "Baby Fae" issue, the treatment of dead bodies, artificial hearts and the donation of body parts. A reflective article in a philosophical mode by Leon R. Kass, Henry R. Luce Professor of the Liberal Arts of Human Biology at the

---

[22]James B. Nelson, *Human Medicine: Ethical Perspectives on New Medical Issues* (Minneapolis, 1973).

University of Chicago, is worth noting here. Kass shows that in to-day's intellectual climate both out and out physicalist approaches, and those claiming to focus on human personhood, essentially deny what we have here described as the integrative approach, and which is espoused by Eastern Orthodox Christian theology and ethics. Kass' description, I believe, shows why I as an Orthodox Christian ethic-ist found Nelson's approaches and conclusions to be inadequate. He says:

> On one side are the corporealists, for whom there is nothing but body and who aspire to explain all activities of life, including thought and feeling, in terms of the motions of inorganic parti-cles. On the other side, say especially in ethics, are the theorists of personhood, consciousness, and autonomy, who treat the essen-tial human being as pure will and reason, as if bodily life counted for nothing, or did not even exist.

Kass proceeds to make what I feel is a foundational point which is essential to the direction of the bioethical effort especially as it relates to the presuppositions with which we approach bioethical decision-making. He continues:

> The former seeks to capture man for dumb and mindless nature; the latter treats man in isolation, even from his own nature. At the bottom of the trouble, I suspect, is the hegemony of modern natural science, to whose view of nature even the partisans of personhood and subjectivity adhere, given that their attempt to locate human dignity in consciousness and mind presupposes that the subconscious living body, not to speak of nature in general, is utterly without dignity or meaning of its own.[23]

Kass concludes his article with a negative judgment on the domi-nant mind-set in current bioethical thinking, a judgment which in many ways reflects Eastern Orthodox Christian thinking on the wide range of bioethical questions we face today. I quote this remarkable article once again:

---

[23]Leon R. Kass, "Thinking About the Body," *The Hastings Center Re-port*, 15, No. 1 (Feb., 1985) 20.

[W]ith our dissection of cadavers, organ transplantation, cosmetic surgery, body shops, laboratory fertilization, surrogate wombs, gender-change surgery, "wanted" children, "rights over our bodies," sexual liberation, and other practices and beliefs that insist on our independence and autonomy, we live more and more wholly for the here and now, subjugating everything we can to the exercise of our wills, with little respect for the nature and meaning of bodily life. We expend enormous energy and vast sums of money to preserve and prolong bodily life, but ironically, in the process bodily life is stripped of its gravity and much of its dignity. (We have become) rational but without wonder, willful but without reverence . . . [24]

This is not to take a wholesale negative approach to the new developments of modern medicine. It is however, a way of showing that the traditional Eastern Orthodox Christian intergrative approach to the body will of necessity influence bioethical thinking in a direction very often different from those perspectives which are informed by fundamentally contrary perceptions of the body. In the effort to develop a coherent Eastern Orthodox approach to the ethical challenges presented to us by the feats of modern medical science, there will be a distinct and coherent Eastern Orthodox perspective, built solidly on a view of human life which neither absolutizes the body, nor trivializes it to the point where its impact on ethical decision-making is negated. In remaining committed to its wholistic approach to human life, as it struggles to work out its bioethical teaching,[25] Eastern Orthodox ethics must keep before it continually its vision of the body and its significant place in the total meaning of human life. This vision cannot otherwise but contribute, together with many other Orthodox Christian foundational affirmations, toward the development of a distinctive bioethical teaching.

It would not surprise me at all, that traditions which have come to a similar intergrative and wholistic perception of the human body, may find themselves much in agreement on the various issues of bioethics, which perhaps justifies the treatment of this topic as Eastern Orthodox Christians and Muslims meet to dialogue.

---

[24]Ibid. p. 30.

[25]See, for example, two of my own first efforts in this direction, *For the Health of Body and Soul*, (Brookline, 1980) and *Contemporary Moral Issues Facing the Orthodox Christian* (Minneapolis, 1982).

The Prayer of the Heart in Hesychasm and Sufism

SEYYED HOSSEIN NASR

The goblet revealing the universe is the heart of the perfect man;
The mirror that reveals the Truth is in reality this heart.
The heart is the depository of the treasures of the Divine Mysteries;
Whatever you seek in the two worlds, ask the heart and you shall attain it.

Shams al-Dīn Lāhījī, *Sharḥ-i gulshan-i rāz*

IT IS A STRANGE FACT of modern scholarship in the field of religion that despite such great interest in dialogue between Christianity and Islam today and the appearance of so much literature on the subject during the past few decades, relatively little attention has been paid to the inner dimensions of these religions as means of access to each other.[1] Even less has been written about the remarkable similarities between the Hesychast tradition and Sufism, each of which lies at the heart of the religion upon whose soil it has flowered.[2] Perhaps, however, this dearth of material on such a crucial subject should not be the cause of surprise. It should be seen as the natural consequence of that type of ecumenism which is willing to sacrifice heaven for an

---

[1] A notable exception is F. Schuon, *Christianity/Islam—Essays on Esoteric Ecumenism* (Bloomington, 1985).

[2] On comparison between these traditions as concerns the prayer of the heart, see F. Schuon, the *Transcendent Unity of Religions*, trans. P. Townsend (Wheaton, IL, 1984).

illusory earthly peace and which glides over the surface of creeds
and doctrines in search of common factors rather than delving into
the depth or inner core of religious beliefs, symbols, language and actions where alone commonly shared principles and truths can be found.
Hesychasm is the science of prayer or more specifically the prayer
of the heart cultivated within the Orthodox Church. The practices
of Hesychasm go back to Christ and this tradition possesses an unin-
terrupted oral teaching which became gradually formulated and for-
malized from the eleventh to the fourteenth century by such masters
as Symeon the New Theologian, Nikephoros the Monk, and Gregory
the Sinaite who established Hesychasm on Mount Athos.[3] As for
Sufism, it too is based on an oral tradition going back to the Prophet
of Islam, a tradition whose tenets began to become more explicitly
formulated some two or three centuries after the birth of Islam by
such early masters as Bāyazīd al-Basṭāmī and Junayd and which had,
by the fifth Islamic century, crystallized into the Ṣūfī orders.[4] The
remarkable resemblance between Sufism and Hesychasm, especially
as far as the prayer of the heart is concerned, is due not to historical
borrowings but to the nature of Christian and Islamic spirituality on
the one hand and the constitution of the human microcosm on the
other. The prayer which revives the heart does so not as a result of
historical influences but because of the grace that emanates from
a revelation. Likewise, the heart is quickened and brought to life by
this grace because it is the locus of the divine Presence and the center of the microcosm which relates it to higher levels of reality.

There is a striking resemblance between Hesychast and Ṣūfī
teachings concerning the nature and meaning of the prayer of the
heart itself. In his *Ladder of Divine Ascent* John Klimakos asserts,
"Let the remembrance of Jesus be present with you every breath,"

---

[3]On Hesychasm, see the classical work of V. Lossky, *Théologie mystique
de l'église d'Orient,* Paris, 1965. The most important work of this tradition
and one of the most precious books of Christian spirituality is the *Philokalia,*
trans. E. Kadloubovsky, G. E. H. Palmer, and K. Ware, 3 vols. (London,
1951-84), which has finally been made available to the English-speaking audience. Other classical works of the Hesychast tradition include *The Way
of a Pilgrim* and *The Pilgrim Continues His Way,* trans. R. M. French (Minneapolis, 1952).

[4]On the Ṣūfī tradition, see A. M. Schimmel, *Mystical Dimensions of Islam*
(Chapel Hill, 1983); M. Lings, *What is Sufism?* (Los Angeles, 1975);
and S. H. Nasr, *Sufi Essays* (Albany, 1985).

while Saint Diadochos of Photike writes, "The experience of true grace come to us when the body is awake or else on the point of falling asleep, while in fervent remembrance of God we are welded to his love."[5] As for the continuity of prayer, he writes, "He who wishes to cleanse his heart should keep it continually aflame through practicing the remembrance of the Lord Jesus, making this his only study and ceaseless task. Those who desire to free themselves from their corruption ought to pray not merely from time to time but at all times; they should give themselves always to prayer, keeping watch over their intellect even when outside places of prayer. When someone is trying to purify gold, and allows the fire of the furnace to die down even for a moment, the material which he is purifying will harden again. So, too, a man who merely practices the remembrance of God from time to time, loses through lack of continuity what he hopes to gain through his prayer. It is a mark of one who truly loves holiness that he continually burns up what is worldly in his heart through practicing the remembrance of God, so that little by little evil is consumed in the fire of this remembrance and his soul completely recovers its natural brilliance with still greater glory."[6]

In Sufism the remembrance of the name of God (*dhikr Allāh*) which is also the invocation of his Name, since *dhikr* means at once invocation, calling upon and remembrance, is the central method of spiritual realization based on the Qur'ān and the *Ḥadīth*.[7] The Qur'ān states, "Remember (invoke) thy Lord over and over; exalt him at daybreak and in the dark of the night" (3.40). Also, "O ye who believe, remember (invoke) God again and again" (33.41); and "Remember (invoke) thy Lord's Name and devote thyself to him wholeheartedly" (73.8). As for the relation of invocation to the heart, the Qur'ān states, "The hearts of those who believe are set at rest in the remembrance (invocation) of God; verily in the remembrance of Allah do hearts find rest" (13.28).

---

[5]The quotations from the masters of the Hesychast tradition are taken from the *Philokalia*.

[6]Ibid. 3, pp. 293-94.

[7]On the doctrine and practice of *dhikr* in Sufism, see L. Gardet, "Le mention du nom divin, *dhikr*, dans la mystique musulmane," *Revue Thomiste* 3, no. 3 (1952) 542-676 and 53, no. 1 (1953) 197-216; and J. L. Michon, "Spiritual Practices" in the *World Spirituality—An Encyclopedic History of the Religious Quest*, vol. 19 (in press); J. Nurbakhsh, *In the Paradise of the Sufis* (New York, 1979), pp. 31-48; and Ibn 'Aṭā' Allāh al-Iskandarī, *Traité sur le nom Allāh*, trans. M. Gloton (Paris, 1981).

As for the sayings of the Prophet, there are numerous references to the significance of *dhikr* in its relation to the heart, as for example, "There is a means of polishing all things whereby rust may be removed; that which polishes the heart is the invocation of Allah, and there is no act that removes the punishment of Allah further from you than this invocation. The Companion said: 'Is not the battle against unbelievers equal to it?' The Prophet replied: 'No, not even if you fight on until your sword is shattered.' "[8]

Ṣūfī writings are also replete with such references usually in the form of allusion and in a manner that is less direct than what one finds in the *Philokalia* although there are some Ṣūfī texts such as the *Miftāḥ al-falāḥ* of Ibn 'Aṭā' Allāh al-Iskandarī[9] which deal directly with the subject of invocation and the prayer of the heart. The Hesychast tradition and Sufism share the belief that one should remember God constantly and with every breath,[10] that this remembrance is none other than the invocation of a divine Name revealed as a sacrament, that this prayer is related to the heart understood spiritually and that the practice of the incantory method must be based upon the guidance of a teacher and master and is accompanied by appropriate instruction concerning meditation, the practice of virtue and other elements of the spiritual life. Although in the case of Hesychasm the name of Jesus is employed while in Sufism one of the names of Allah is invoked, the teaching of the two traditions concerning the saving power of the divine Name and methods for invoking it display a striking resemblance to each other, bearing witness both to the universality of the method of invocation and profound morphological resemblances between certain aspects of Christian and Islamic spirituality.

---

[8]On references in both Islamic and Christian sources concerning the way of invocation, see Schuon, *The Transcendent Unity of Religions*, pp. 159-66. Concerning the spiritual significance of the heart, Schuon writes, "The organ of the spirit, or the principal center of spiritual life, is the heart. But what is more important from the standpoint of spiritual realization is the teaching of Hesychasm on the means of perfecting the natural participation of the human microcosm in the divine Microcosm by transmuting it into supernatural participation and finally union and identity: this means consists of the 'inward prayer' or 'Prayer of Jesus.' " Ibid. p. 144.

[9]Translated for the first time into English by M. Khoury (in press).

[10]The Ṣūfīs consider the goal of the person upon the spiritual path to be not only to interiorize the invocation but also to make it perpetual. Such a person is called *dā'im al-dhikr,* that is in constant invocation.

An example of this remarkable resemblance in the two traditions can be found in the doctrine of the heart itself. In Hesychasm the heart (ἡ καρδία) is the center of the human being, the seat of both intelligence and will within which converge all the forces of human life. Also grace passes from the heart to all the other parts and elements of the human microcosm. This same doctrine is to be found in Sufism which, following the teachings of the Qur'ān, identifies the heart (al-qalb in Arabic, dil in Persian) with knowledge as well as the will and love, and which like Hesychasm considers the heart to be the seat of the divine from which the grace of his presence issues to the whole being of man.[11] If one can speak of the locus of the intellect (νοῦς, πνεῦμα, al-'aql), it is the heart, for it is with the heart that man can know the Spirit and "intellect" the supernal realities. It is when the spirit enters the heart that man becomes spiritualized (πνευματικός, rūḥānī) and it is with the heart that man is able to "see" reality as it is. That is why the Ṣūfīs speak of the "eye of the heart" ('ayn al-qalb or chishm-i dil) as the instrument with which man can "see" what is invisible to the two eyes located in the head.

In both Hesychasm and Sufism the spiritual path begins under the guidance of a master and with a turning away from the world in an act of repentance (ἐπιστροφή, tawbah). To follow the path both contemplation and action are necessary, contemplation (θεωρία, al-nazar) providing the vision and action (πρᾶξις, al-'amal) making actualization or realization of the vision possible. The balance between the two and the necessity of both in the spiritual life are emphasized over and over again by the masters of both Hesychasm and Sufism.[12] The intermediary stages of the path are not, however, necessarily the same and even within Sufism, the stages of the path have been enumerated in different ways by various masters.[13] As for the end, the stillness of Hesychasm can be compared to the annihilation (al-fanā') of Sufism and deification (θεώσις) to union (wiṣāl, tawḥīd). There is, however, a major difference at this stage and that concerns the question of the possibility of the attainment of the state of union

---

[11]On the relation between the heart and knowledge in general, see S. H. Nasr, *Knowledge and the Sacred* (New York, 1981), pp. 151ff.

[12]On this issue in the context of various traditions including Christianity and Islam, see Y. Ibish and P. Wilson (eds.), *Traditional Modes of Contemplation and Action* (Tehran-London, 1977).

[13]See S. H. Nasr, *Sufi Essays*, pp. 68-83.

in this life. Whereas in Hesychasm deification can be expected fully
in the next life and can only be approached in this life through synergy
or cooperation between God and man, in Sufism union is possible
in this life. There are those Ṣūfīs who, while in this world, have already
passed beyond the gate of death or annihilation and who have experienced already the supreme state of union or unity while still living in this body.

Despite this difference, however, both Hesychasm and Sufism emphasize the significance of the spiritualization of the body. In contrast to certain branches of Christianity, Hesychasm, like Islam in
general and Sufism in particular, sees the body as the temple of the
spirit and its techniques like those of Sufism accord a positive role
to the body which is an extension of the heart. The breathing techniques connected with invocation in both traditions is very much related to the role of the breast and the body in general as are certain
forms of meditation used in both Hesychasm and Sufism. In both
traditions it is taught that holiness is connected with "keeping oneself" in the body.[14] The incantory method can in fact be summarized as putting oneself in the Name and putting the Name in the
heart. If only one could keep the mind in the body and prevent it
from wandering away while concentrating upon the Name located
in the heart one would become a saint. Sanctity in both traditions
comes from the coincidence of the heart and the Name with the body
playing the role of the sacred temple wherein this miraculous conjunction takes place.

In contrast to certain forms of passive mysticism the spiritual path
of Sufism as well as Hesychasm is based on man's active participation in the quest of God. This active aspect of the path is depicted
in both traditions as spiritual combat. In Sufism the constant battle
against the passions is called *al-jihād al-akbar,* the greater "holy
war,"[15] which the Prophet of Islam considered to be much more
worthy than any external battle no matter how just its cause. In Hesychasm the aspirant is taught to battle constantly against the evil

---

[14]See K. Almquist, "Temple of the Heart, Temple of the Body," *Tomorrow,* 12, no. 3 (Summer, 1964) 228-33.

[15]Actually *jihād,* usually translated as holy war in English, means exertion
but it certainly also includes the meaning of waging battle against all that
destroys the equilibrium which Islam seeks to establish in human life. See
S. H. Nasr, "The Spiritual Significance of *jihād,*" *Parabola,* 7, no. 4 (Fall,
1982) 14-19.

tendencies within himself and one of the classics of Orthodox spirituality is called *The Unseen Warfare*.[16] In contrast to much of modern religious thought which has a disdain for the positive significance and symbolism of combat understood in its traditional sense,[17] both Sufism and Hesychasm are fully aware that the peace which surpasseth all understanding cannot be attained save through long and strenuous warfare against those forces within us that prevent us from entering the kingdom of God which is none other than the heart itself.

Finally, in comparing Hesychasm and Sufism one is struck by the significance of light in conjunction with the practice of the prayer of the heart in both traditions. The Hesychast masters assert that God is light (φῶς) and the experience of his reality is light. Symeon the New Theologian even calls spiritual experience the "incessant experience of divine light." Divine light is uncreated and identified with God's energies which he communicates to those who through spiritual practice enter into union with him. As Saint Gregory of Palamas writes in his *Homilies on the Presentation of the Holy Virgin to the Temple,* "He who participates in divine energy becomes himself in some way light. He is united with light and with this light he sees with full consciousness all that remains from those who do not possess this grace ... The pure of heart see God ... who being light dwells in them and reveals to those who love him, their Beloved." The Hesychast tradition speaks of grades of light from the uncreated light of the Divinity to the light of the intelligible world and finally sensible light. The practice of the prayer of the heart leads man from this sensible light which surrounds all beings here on earth to the light of the angelic realm and finally the Divine Light itself.

In Islam also God is called in the Qur'ān itself the "Light of the Heavens and the earth" (24.35). On the basis of this famous verse,

---

[16]See *Unseen Warfare: the 'Spiritual Combat' and 'Path to Paradise' of Lorenzo Scupoli,* trans. E. Kadlouborsky and G. E. H. Palmer (London, 1978).

[17]This is due both to the unprecedented horror and devastation brought about by modern warfare, thanks to modern technology, and a certain type of pacifism which identifies the whole of Christian spirituality with the passive acceptance of the world about us in the name of peace.

It needs to be pointed out, however, that liberation theology as currently understood and practiced has nothing to do with the spiritual warfare of which Sufism and Hesychasm speak and represents from the point of these traditions a further surrender to the world and worldliness in the name of justice which is usually envisaged in solely earthly terms.

numerous schools of Islamic philosophy and mysticism have developed in which the symbolism of light, (*al-nūr*), plays a central role, the best known of these schools being that of Illumination (*al-ishrāq*) founded by Shaykh Shihāb al-Dīn Suhrawardī.[18] The divisions of light by Suhrawardī and other masters of this school bear a close resemblance to those found in the Hesychast tradition without there being necessarily a historical borrowing although Suhrawardī's philosophy did have some followers such as Gemistos Plethon in Byzantium. Many Ṣūfī orders also based their teachings on the symbolism of light, especially the schools of Central Asia, such as the Kubrawiyyah order.[19] There is certainly a sense of spiritual affinity between the golden icons of the Byzantine church and certain Persian miniatures where gold, the supreme symbol of the sun and also the Sun, is used profusely. The light that shines in the heart of the practitioner of Hesychasm on the one hand and Sufism on the other is certainly not based on historical borrowing but comes from God and is the fruit of experiences and types of spiritual practice which display remarkable resemblance to each other.

Needless to say, there are also important differences between the prayer of the heart as practiced in Hesychasm and Sufism. One makes use of the name of the message, that is Jesus, and the other the source of the message, that is Allah. One emphasizes love and the other knowledge without either denying the other element. One derives its efficacy from the grace issuing from Christ and the other from the "Muḥammadan grace" (*al-barakat al-muḥammadiyyah*). One is largely practiced within the context of monasticism and the other within society at large.

Yet, the similarity and consonance of the two paths remain as an undeniable reality and constitute a most remarkable aspect of the bonds which relate Christianity and Islam and which can bring about better understanding between them. In this age of facile ecumenism, when so much is said on the surface and so little effort is devoted to the depth where the heart resides, the Hesychast tradition within Orthodoxy offers a most precious channel through which what is most inward and central to the Islamic tradition can be better understood.

---

[18]See H. Corbin, *En Islam iranien*, vol. 2 (Paris, 1971); and S. H. Nasr, *Three Muslim Sages* (Delmar, NY, 1975), chapter 2.

[19]See H. Corbin, *The Man of Light in Iranian Sufism*, trans. N. Pearson (Boulder, 1978).